U. S. NAVAL LOGISTICS

IN THE SECOND WORLD WAR

U. S. Naval Logistics
in the
Second World War

By Duncan S. Ballantine

PRINCETON, NEW JERSEY

PRINCETON UNIVERSITY PRESS

1949

Printed in the United States of America

TO MY WIFE

PREFACE

THE distinguishing feature of modern warfare is its inclusiveness. Two experiences of so-called total war within the first half of the present century have demonstrated conclusively that the military decision is not made upon the field of battle alone. Into that decision there enter now as major factors elements of political, economic, psychological, and scientific character which in an earlier age were of relatively minor importance. The capacity of a nation to wage war is the sum of many factors, among which its raw material resources, manufactures, transportation network, merchant marine, laboratories, schools, and working population are but a few outstanding examples. Therefore, if we would understand the warfare of modern times, not simply as a phase in the social, political, or economic life of the nation but in the more precise sense of its military history, we must recognize that the interplay between civilian and military effort is more active and pervasive than ever before.

These various resources of a nation do not in themselves represent military force. For all these constituent elements of military power organization is the catalytic agent. It is through organization that the potential resources of a nation are transmuted into instruments of force at the disposal of our military and naval leadership. It is organization in the last analysis that transforms a market economy into a war economy and through which the strategically desirable and the economically possible are brought into consonance with each other.

In its civilian aspects the problem of wartime economic organization is immeasurably better understood than it was thirty years ago. But there are two serious dangers inherent in the great attention which has been justifiably focused upon that panoply of agencies for war production, manpower, prices, finance, and the mobilization of material

resources which makes up the civil side of wartime administration. The first danger is that in the study of this area of
organization by civilian economists and historians it may
come to be regarded as the whole or at least the only
significant portion of our economic life during war. The
peculiar atmosphere of urgency, shortage, and haste which
results from the dominance of military imperatives, and
which conditions most of our judgments at the time, begins
to evaporate as soon as the danger is past. It can be kept in
mind only by referring constantly from the area of civil
administration to the arena of military conflict in which all
problems of wartime organization have their origin.

The second danger is that military and naval officers may
fall back once again into that comforting assumption that
the economic aspects of war are not really part of their
professional concern. No assumption could be more dangerous to the future of our military security, for while the
greater portion of our economic organization for war is undoubtedly the responsibility of civilians, there is, nevertheless, a significant area of economic activity that falls within
the province of military administration and is distinct from
what is normally regarded as economic organization for
war. The tools of war are fabricated under civilian auspices, it
is true, but to specifications and schedules, and in quantities
fixed by military planners in response to the needs of a given
military situation. Before these tools reach the point where
they are consumed or utilized in fighting, they must pass,
moreover, into the military support system for allocation and
distribution.

The subject matter of this book deals therefore with that
limbo between the factory and the beachhead in which
economic and military considerations are inextricably woven
together. It is this link function between purely economic
and purely military effort which in the past has been the
greatest blindspot of both the civilian and the professional
naval officer. If this book can shed some light on the nature

and significance of the function, it will have served its purpose.

The catalogue of my indebtedness is indeed a long one. I must first acknowledge my debt to all of my associates in the historical section of the Chief of Naval Operations. Their preliminary studies, listed in the bibliography, form the basis of this overall study of naval logistics. In particular I should like to mention Elting E. Morison who brought to our group effort a wide acquaintance with naval affairs and an enlightened direction. To the open-mindedness of Admiral F. J. Horne this book owes more than can be told. His conviction that the Navy might be served by informed criticism opened to his historical section many doors that would otherwise have remained closed and provided an atmosphere for objective investigation as favorable as might be desired. Countless other officers in both the regular Navy and the Reserve have offered insight into the problems of naval logistics. In particular I am indebted to Rear Admiral V. J. Murphy, Director of Naval History, and his successor Captain J. B. Heffernan for many helpful suggestions. I must also thank Richard Leopold and David Owen of Harvard University who have read the manuscript and given me the benefit of their criticism. Similarly Robert G. Albion of Princeton University, Director of Naval Administrative History, has lent assistance in countless ways. If this book owes more than is customary, however, to the assistance of other people, its deficiencies are no less my own contribution.

TABLE OF CONTENTS

CHAPTER I

LOGISTICS IN MODERN NAVAL WARFARE

The Meaning of Logistics

I**N** its broadest definition the term logistics signifies the total process by which the resources of a nation—material and human—are mobilized and directed toward the accomplishment of military ends. Officially naval logistics has been defined as "the supply of material and personnel, including the procurement, storage, distribution and transportation of material, and the procurement, housing, training, distribution and transportation of personnel, together with the rendering of services to Naval operating forces." Comprehensive and suggestive though that definition is, it tells little of the real factors and forces which determine the nature of the logistic process during war. For logistic support is an integral part of the function of making war. It can be understood only in its relation on the one hand to the end it serves and on the other to the sources from which it springs.

Naval logistics during the Second World War embraced all the activities essential to build, support and maintain naval fighting forces. It comprised, therefore, a single, broad effort, rooted in the productive economy of the nation and extending through successive phases of planning, procurement and distribution of men and material to the theater of military operations. There the elements of naval power, fashioned, selected and distributed by the logistic process, were consumed or utilized in the direct act of making war.

Broadly conceived, the logistic process is thus the means whereby the raw warmaking capacity of the nation is translated into instruments of force ready to be employed in pursuit of strategical or tactical objectives. As such it is both an economic and a military undertaking. It is also both a military and a civilian task. At their sources the elements of logistic support are produced and procured through means which are economic, commercial and civilian in character. Progressively, as elements move through the logistic system from factory to beachhead or battleline, the process by which they are made available for consumption becomes more military.

The whole of the process, it is obvious, is conditioned by a military end and takes its form, therefore, from the nature of the military task to be performed. In no sense is any phase of it a normal economic or commercial undertaking. It is carried on in the wholly unnatural environment of war which in modern times at least has tended to infiltrate the total life of the nation. Yet with respect to the problems encountered and the assumptions, techniques and forms of organization required there is a wide gulf between the business of procuring and producing at one end of the process and planning and distributing for consumption at the other.

Production, even for total war, must be carried on within the framework of the nation's whole economy, and under such conditions as Lend-Lease it may perhaps have to be governed by considerations even broader than the nation's own requirements. In any case it is the province of the government economist and the skilled producer, for despite its subservience to military ends, it is by nature a civil function. On the other hand, logistic planning, which is the determination of what is required to achieve strategic objectives, and the allocation and distribution of munitions and supplies once they are procured are equally the responsibility of the professional naval or military officer, into whose hands is entrusted the conduct of the military campaign.

On the basis of this distinction logistics may be divided into two main parts, the first being the logistics of production and the second the logistics of consumption. The former is that phase of logistic effort which is carried on under civilian auspices as a predominantly economic function and within a set of conditions imposed by the nature of the nation's economy. The latter is the phase of logistics more intimately involved in military operations in which the determining conditions are those of the military situation. It is with this latter phase of the logistic process that the present study is concerned.

Yet it is important before passing to this more limited field to note that the division thus made is in many ways artificial. Useful though it has been as a basis for administrative organization and as a scheme of definition and discussion, it does some violence to the integral character of the logistics function itself. However far apart they may be in the nature of their activities, there is between the theater of operations and the productive economy an intimate and reciprocal relation. What happens in one sphere has its effect upon the other, sometimes with startling impact and rapidity. The British munitions crisis of 1915 is an instance of what happens when production is not geared to meet military requirements. The near success of German U-boat warfare in April 1917 illustrates in turn the impact of military reverses upon a nation's war economy.

It is, therefore, the function of logistics to bridge the gap between two normally alien spheres of activity, to make intelligible to the producer, for example, the needs of the military commander and conversely to infuse into the calculations of the strategist an appreciation of the limits of the materially possible. As the link between the war front and the home front the logistic process is at once the military element in the nation's economy and the economic element in its military operations. And upon the coherence that exists within the process itself depends the successful articulation of the productive and military efforts of a nation at war.

The character of all logistic effort in war may be said to

be determined by three primary factors. It depends first upon the campaign to be waged—the situation of the enemy, the geography of the theater, the objectives for which the war is being fought, in short, upon all those factors which enter into high-level strategy. Logistics depends secondly upon the character of the forces and weapons engaged. The logistics of land and sea forces contain certain fundamental differences which were of considerable importance during the recent war. Air logistics is in many respects a specialty in itself. The third primary factor is the limitations imposed by the national economy. Mahan in the famous first chapter of his *The Influence of Sea Power upon History* dwelt at length upon the underlying natural conditions of maritime power. The First World War brought forth a wealth of commentary on the significance of industrial factors in modern war. German archives, particularly, should some day reveal the true significance in total war of the factor of economic limitation. The United States has felt only mildly in two great wars the effects of limited economic resources, but it is a factor which must be taken into account in the study of logistics.

In its strictly military applications logistics has long played an important part in warfare, but historically students of the art of war have tended either to ignore it or to regard it as a subordinate and extraneous element. Clausewitz, who generalized so successfully upon the career of Napoleon, preferred to follow that commander's dictum that the moral is to the material as two to one, and built his study of the "Conduct of War" around the predominant role of moral factors. Allowing that certain "activities" stood in a reciprocal relation to strategy and tactics and admitting that provision of the means of warfare might be admitted into the "Art of War" loosely defined, he still excluded logistics from the "Conduct of War," which he defined as "the art of making use of the given means in fighting." Lumping together as "subservient services" everything that remained after strategy and tactics, Clausewitz asked, "Who would include in the real 'conduct of war' the whole litany of subsistence and administration, because it is admitted to stand in constant reciprocal action with the use of troops, but is something essentially different from it?

"If we have clearly understood the results of our reflections, then the activities belonging to War divide themselves into two principal classes, into such as are only 'preparations for war' and into the 'war itself.' This division must therefore also be made in theory."

Clausewitz's distinction between "preparations for war" and "war itself" has been carried over into naval theory in the assumption that a naval force is first prepared and then goes forth to do a battle with little to think about but the "use of the given means." It is an assumption which, as we shall see, has long colored naval thinking. It is apparent in the war plans and also in the line officer's traditional inclination to leave matters of "housekeeping" to the paymasters unless, as in wartime, they are matters of critical importance. The persistence of this neglect of logistics bears witness to the long dominance exercised over naval minds by a too narrow definition of strategy and tactics. One speaks often of the strategic aspects of war as distinguished from the logistic, but in point of fact no strategist can estimate the probable success or failure of a given course of action without weighing carefully the logistic factors involved. In modern times it is a poorly qualified strategist or naval commander who is not equipped by training and experience to evaluate logistic factors or to superintend logistic operations.

Indifference on the part of the line officer does not wholly explain, however, the small part that has been played by logistics in the study of and preparation for war. Against this charge of indifference the line officer might well contend that through the peculiar workings of the Navy's bureau system he has often been excluded by the staff corps and entrenched bureau interests from a voice in the design, maintenance and readiness of ships, guns, aircraft and other tools of war. The familiar charges of Admiral W. S. Sims, that naval ships and guns were designed in the bureaus with too little attention to the views of the officers who must use them, had a sound basis in fact. And the condition to which he pointed has persisted. Thus, if at times the line officer has appeared all too willing to "leave logistics to the paymasters," it is perhaps equally true that paymasters and other bureau and staff officers have doggedly guarded the frontiers of their particular logistic provinces with appeals to the principle of decentralization and legal division of responsibility within the Department of the Navy.

Clausewitz's distinction may be accepted in theory, but it is no longer applicable in practice. So much of the preparation for war runs concurrently with the progress of the war that the two can not be dissociated. The strategic plan must be determined in the light of the combatant nation's state of preparedness. In modern times, moreover, the great emphasis placed upon the mechanization of forces has tremendously increased the task of their maintenance in the field or at sea as distinguished from their initial recruiting or creation. The sounder theory, which accords more closely with the facts of modern warfare, is that logistics is not something distinct from strategy and tactics, but rather an integral part of both; that an understanding of the problems inherent in creating and, even more important, in maintaining naval forces in fighting condition in the theater of operations is essential to high naval command.

There can be no quarrel with the theory that logistics is a "subservient" service, for the raison d'être of logistics is to subserve or make possible the attainment of strategic ends. That logistics takes its form, however, from what is strategically desirable does not alter the fact that in their turn logistic conditions determine in large measure what is strategically possible. Whether or not logistics is a part of or reciprocally related to strategy is in reality of little consequence as long as the dominance of logistic factors in modern warfare is taken into account by professional naval and military officers. For, like any indispensable servant, it is frequently the master.

The administration of logistics is not the least important aspect of naval organization and command. When it is considered that an estimated one-quarter of the total industrial output of the nation went into the building and support of the wartime navy, the immensity of the task can be appreciated. In order that that tremendous effort of producing, assembling, shipping and distributing one million and a half separate items of material support might truly serve the needs of our naval operations, administration was necessary. Effective logistic support is not solely a matter of volume. It is even more a problem of efficiently planning, producing and regulating the flow of materials and services so as to ensure that the right kind of support is available in the right quantity at the right place and at the right time. To meet all of these requirements for the support of highly mobile forces is a most demanding task. Complicated as it is by the uncertainties inherent in war and by the difficulty of drawing a clear line between civilian and military responsibilities, it offers one of the most complex problems in administration to be encountered.

The development of effective logistics administration is further hampered by the fact that logistics is essentially a function of war, quite distinct from what might pass as logistics in peace. No constructive exercise in peace can quite duplicate the urgency and stringency of logistic conditions in war. In peacetime, for example, fleet exercises may be accommodated to the fuel budget allowed by the Congress. Sea transport can generally be provided by existing commercial services. Storage is not a problem, nor is rail transport. Repairs and fleet maintenance can generally be carried on in established continental yards. Above all, the requirements for logistic support are specific and calculable.

In war, however, there are no budgetary limitations. The fleet must operate wherever the military situation requires. If it is to maintain command of the sea, it must remain as an effective force within the area of operations, and the elements of support must be brought to it. The pattern of naval operations is then no longer determined in the committee rooms on Capitol Hill but in the strategic outlines of the emerging campaign. The logistic process in total war must operate in an economy saturated by demand, in which the ordinary laws of the marketplace are in suspension, in which the factor of time supersedes price and the greatest evil is to have "too little, too late."

From the strategic outlines of the campaign and from the constantly changing weapons and forces with which the campaign is pursued must be determined the character of logistic support required and the procedures and forms of administration necessary to ensure its delivery. If logistic support is to be provided effectively, logistics must be regarded, therefore, first as an inseparable part of the making of war and second as a function which can be understood only within the environment of war.

Logistics Old and New

THE distinguishing quality of the environment in which naval warfare is carried on is its lack of any of the resources required to sustain a naval force. Navies are the arms with which the blows of maritime strategy are struck, but the weight and force of the blow depends upon the solid footing which is maintained upon the nourishing earth. The warships of the eighteenth century and earlier, it is true, were more capable of casting off the shackles that bound them to land than are the warships of today. But the qualities of mobility and self-reliance they enjoyed were the result mainly of technical factors in their construction and operation. Only the wind was provided them by the environment of the sea. For the rest they were capable of endurance at sea because they could carry with them a relatively higher ratio of essential subsistence than can the ships of modern times. Provisions could be stocked for a six-month voyage. Fresh water for three months could be taken aboard, and was easy to replenish. Ammunition was more slowly expended. The needs of the ship, in short, were simple; its logistics was therefore of the simple and primary sort—namely the building into the ship itself of a maximum cruising range.

Even so it would be incorrect to assume that logistics played no part in the naval warfare of the eighteenth century. Mahan comments upon the ill effects of St. Vincent's administration of the Admiralty and finds Nelson off Toulon complaining of the condition of his ships. Nelson's genius was founded upon the quality of "the great administrator who never lost sight or forethought for the belly on which his fleet moved." In all his pursuit of Villeneuve, across the Atlantic and back in 1805, Nelson maintained his forces in fighting condition, "never embarrassed about stores because always forehanded." "Compared to these its antecedents," says Mahan, "Trafalgar is relatively a small matter."

The plight of the French admiral, Suffren, and of his predecessor, D'Aché, in the contest for supremacy in India is another noteworthy example. After two indecisive engagements with the British commander, Pocock, D'Aché had exhausted the supply of naval stores at Pondichéry and had to withdraw to Mauritius. Even that remote base offered him little support. He was forced to cannibalize some of his ships in order to refit others and to send several good vessels on a voyage of two or three months to the Cape of Good Hope for provisions. As a result he did not return to the coast of India until the summer of 1759, almost a year after he had withdrawn.

Suffren's situation was not much better. He carried some reserves of powder and ammunition in the troopships which accompanied him, and he received some help from his Dutch allies in Ceylon. But despite his superior forces and skill as a commander, he was at a constant disadvantage. Thus although the French originally had positions in India situated as advantageously as those of the British, they were not able to draw from them the resources required to support their forces. What counted was not simply the possession of bases strategically situated about the globe, but also the ability of the bases to render real support.

The significance of logistic factors in the wars of the eighteenth century has perhaps been obscured by the great increase in their importance which followed the introduction of the ironclad, steam-propelled warship in the nineteenth century. For the United States that technical revolution, which got under way in the 1880's, was doubly significant, for it was accompanied by a revolution in strategic doctrine which intensified the problem of naval logistics. The warship of the "New Navy" had lost even the few qualities of self-reliance of its predecessor. And since the United States had then no foreign establishments either colonial or military, its new warships were, as Mahan remarked, "like land birds, unable to fly far from their own shores." Without coal they were helpless; and in turn the necessity of providing space for bunkers cut down the space available for stores and ammunition. Wooden hulls could go several years without cleaning; iron hulls fouled rapidly and must be scraped and painted at least once a year. Larger crews increased the requirement for subsistence and reduced available storage space. Water for the boilers was as essential as coal. The greater firepower of modern guns raised the problem of replenishment of ammunition. Spare parts and machinery repairs beyond the power of the ship to perform for itself were now necessary.

The increasing dependence of the warship upon external sources of support was accompanied by that revolution in strategic doctrine generally associated with the name of Mahan. Paradoxically, "command of the sea" by modern warships demanded just that ability to keep the sea which the technical revolution was taking from them. The significance of the change was not lost upon Mahan. Speaking to the War College in 1888 he listed with strategy and tactics among the neglected subjects of naval science "the secondary matters connected with the maintenance of warlike operations at sea." "It would be amusing, were it not painful," he said, "to see our eagerness to have fast ships, and our indifference to supplying them with coal." In 1890, "looking outward" Mahan found our Atlantic shores and the Caribbean dotted with British bases, while we had not on the Gulf of Mexico "even the beginning of a navy yard which could serve as the base of our operations." In the Pacific it should be the "inviolable resolution of our national policy" that no European state should acquire a coaling station within three thousand miles of San Francisco. "For fuel is the life of modern naval war; it is the food of the ship; without it the modern monsters of the deep die of inanition. Around it, therefore, cluster some of the most important considerations of naval strategy." In 1890 *The Influence of Sea Power upon History* set forth the rounded philosophy of Mahan, in which he emphasized the importance of naval bases as the link between the now dependent warship and the strategic doctrine of command of the sea.

The world of practice moved somewhat more slowly than the mind of the philosopher. Yet in the Navy Department the significance of the new developments could not be missed. A quarter century before, during the Civil War, the Navy had experienced a foretaste of the problems of modern logistics. Maintenance of the blockade of the southern coast had required new bases such as at Port Royal, Beaufort, and Key West. Between the blockading squadrons and the northern ports colliers and refrigerated supply ships had shuttled in regular service. The repair load of the northern yards had increased greatly. Storage and wharf accommodations in the navy yards proved insufficient for the increased flow of supplies. The delivery of coal and supplies to the naval forces at the mouth of the Mississippi had been a constant source of vexation to the Navy Department. The increased load of administrative work in the Navy Department had made necessary the temporary creation of an Assistant Secretary of the Navy and a reorganization of the bureaus.

The post-war decline of the Navy, particularly its lack of funds to build new ships incorporating the technical advances which had been made during the war, left logistic considerations also in abeyance. But when the work of naval construction was begun in 1881, interest in continental and overseas naval stations was also revived. In 1883 the United States had coaling stations at Honolulu, Samoa, and Pichalinqui in Lower California. In his report of that year Secretary Chandler recommended that Congress make provision for an extensive development of overseas naval and coaling stations, among which he included Haiti, Curaçao, Brazil, the Straits of Magellan, Liberia, Korea and both sides of the Isthmus of Panama. But the response was negative. In 1889, Congress did appropriate $100,000 for a permanent naval station at Pago Pago in the Samoan Islands. In 1892, a survey was made by the Navy Department of the "Coaling, Docking and Repairing Facilities of the World." Both the Navy and State Departments were constantly appealed to by various persons in the naval service and out of it with projects for coaling sites and stations. But the number of overseas naval stations was not increased, and until after the Spanish-American War our naval positions beyond the continental limits were of little significance.

Continental yards and stations fared somewhat better. Under the administration of Secretary Robeson the naval yards had been more than ever the pawn of politics. Beginning in 1883, Secretary Chandler and his successors instituted a vigorous reform which did away with many of the abuses of the preceding years and partly modernized the equipment of the yards. Upon the recommendation of the Luce Commission Secretary Chandler had begun his reforms by closing some of the superfluous yards. Under Secretaries Tracy and Herbert, several new stations were opened of which the most notable was the Puget Sound Naval Station begun in 1891. The result was a somewhat better distribution of yard facilities throughout the United States. Still the progress of navy yard development did not keep pace with the construction of ships. It is significant that in 1897, when the New York dock was out of commission the *Indiana* had to put into Halifax to have her bottom scraped.

Until the Spanish-American War neither the technical revolution in naval construction nor the acceptance of the new strategic doctrine was complete. As a result the derivative problem of maintaining the Navy both at home and overseas could scarcely claim serious attention. Secretary Long in 1897 renewed the appeal of Chandler for overseas naval stations, but the war intervened before any action could be taken. Until that time, although the United States was building a seagoing, fighting fleet, the accepted function of the Navy was the defense of our coasts. Even the tradition of commerce raiding died hard. Through the 'eighties Admiral Porter, mindful like Mahan of the futility of steam cruisers without coal, but unlike Mahan no blue-water strategist, had cried repeatedly to the Secretary for more canvas. Not until the war itself had vindicated the doctrines of Mahan and made the United States a recognized naval and colonial power was there a reason to ponder the problem of maintaining our naval forces overseas.

Logistically the Spanish-American War created more problems that it had to solve. Of the two major campaigns carried on during that brief conflict, Dewey's capture of Manila and the blockade of Cuba culminating in the engagement off Santiago, the latter offered by far the greater problems of logistics. Despite the remoteness of the Philippines from the United States, Dewey's logistics were relatively simple.

Logistic planning may be said to have consisted of the few dispatches to Dewey at Hong Kong to fill his bunkers with coal, purchase a supply steamer, and hold himself in readiness for any eventuality. With these simple preparations completed Dewey was ready to proceed when instructions came.

The dispatch and finality of Dewey's victory at Manila solved his most serious logistic problems. Had his victory been less complete or had the Spanish forces been able to withdraw from Manila and avoid contact for some time, Dewey's situation would have been precarious. The British had already denied him further use of Hong Kong. Facilities for repair in the Philippines were inadequate. His nearest source of coal outside Manila itself was the few thousand tons at Pago Pago and at Hawaii. It was some time before he could expect shipments of coal, and, even more important, of ammunition from the United States. Anything less than the resounding victory he achieved might have raised serious logistic complications.

The support of the blockade of Cuba was a more difficult task because, as in the case of the blockade during the Civil War, it required the maintenance of a naval force constantly at sea. The pattern of logistic support developed during the Spanish-American War resembled in many ways that earlier experience. Coal was first supplied to the blockading ships by deliveries from colliers on the stations or else by withdrawing the ships to Key West for coaling and provisioning. Rotation of vessels between Key West and the coast of Cuba, however, raised the requirement from one-third to one-half over the number of ships considered necessary to maintain a complete blockade, and as a result the blockade was frequently not complete. In coaling at sea the colliers had to be brought alongside, with constant damage to both colliers and warships. Once a coaling station had been established at Guantanamo these difficulties were considerably lessened. It is significant that plans were going forward for another coaling and water station on the nearby Isle of Pines when the war ended.

The lack of fresh water was another serious handicap. During the war two distilling ships, the *Iris* and the *Rainbow* were fitted out and sent to the West Indies, but they were not enough to meet the demands of the many vessels constantly under steam. Machinery breakdowns, particularly of the electrical machinery in torpedo boats, were common. Early in July, the repair ship, *Vulcan*, plans for which had long been in existence in the Bureau of Steam Engineering, was fitted out and reported to the blockading force off Santiago. There it proved of great assistance and demonstrated clearly that repair vessels were essential adjuncts of fighting ships.

Logistics does not loom large among the many "naval lessons" deduced by commentators on the Spanish-American War. Yet it was generally agreed that repair ships, distilling ships, colliers, and coaling stations were essential elements of the naval force. During the years immediately following the war there was considerable activity in the development of yards, docks, coaling stations, and other logistic facilities. In 1900, for example, the proportion of the naval appropriation allocated to the Bureau of Yards and Docks, which since 1893 had run about 5 per cent, jumped suddenly to 12.7 per cent. In the 1903 budget it was 22.6 per cent. Much of this activity may be explained by the fact that navy yard development had lagged about ten years behind naval construction during the preceding two decades, and it was now necessary to renovate continental yards and stations in order to accommodate the expanded fleet. But a considerable portion of the increased budgets for maintenance facilities was earmarked for the logistic development of our newly won positions overseas.

In the Philippines the immediate aftermath of the war was an extensive investigation of possible sites for naval bases and coaling stations. In 1901, following the report of the Remey

Commission, President Roosevelt set aside an extensive tract of land in the area of Subig Bay. The intention was to develop a new naval station at Olangapo and to continue the old one at Cavite. Shortly after the annexation of the Hawaiian Islands lands had also been set aside around Pearl Harbor for naval purposes. Similar steps were taken at San Juan. By 1904, the United States had made a good beginning, having established coaling stations of varying capacity at Pearl Harbor, Sitka, Cavite, and San Juan and having plans afoot for large installations at Olangapo, Guantanamo, and Guam. In 1905, a sectionalized floating dry dock was completed at the cost of one and a quarter million dollars and towed from Baltimore to Cavite, a distance of 13,000 miles. In 1908, a large floating dry dock for Pearl Harbor was authorized by Congress.

The subject of logistics appears also to have awakened some interest among articulate naval officers. In 1904, Lt. H. C. Dinger gave a new, three-dimensional character to the discussion of bases by pointing out in the *U.S. Naval Institute Proceedings* that the United States would be better off with a few, well-developed bases than a flock of barren sites. "The facilities," he declared, "are of more value than the position." Dinger desired that the Navy set up in peacetime a nuclear base establishment capable of expansion in war. "This," he pointed out, would require that "the manner and the means . . . be planned beforehand."

Perhaps the most interesting suggestion of this time was the concept advanced by Civil Engineer A. C. Cunningham of a movable base. Made up of sectionalized floating dry docks, colliers, ammunition, repair, supply and hospital ships, it would move with or behind the fleet, and would offer all the essential services required of a base. Its mobility would make it useful for either defense or offense. The range of its services and its organization as a definite unit of supply and service would make it more than the simple train hitherto attached to the fleet. In Cunningham's idea of a movable

base can be seen the germ of Service Squadron Ten, so successfully developed in the Pacific during the recent war. But
in 1904 it was too much to expect either of the resources
available to the Navy or of the then nascent interest in matters of support that such a plan could be brought to fruition.

The cruise of the fleet around the world from 1907 to
1909 illustrates how much logistic progress had been made
during the first decade of the twentieth century. This fleet,
composed of sixteen battleships, the Atlantic torpedo flotilla
of six ships, two stores ships, a repair ship, a tender, and the
torpedo flotilla parent ship, began its cruise from Hampton
Roads on December 16, 1907. Dropping the torpedo flotilla
and substituting two battleships at San Fransisco, it continued around the world via the Pacific and the Suez Canal,
arriving again at Hampton Roads on February 22, 1909.

The purposes of the cruise have been variously described.
Ostensibly it was a peaceful mission, and at its conclusion
it proved not only to have fostered our good relations, but
also to have enhanced the prestige of the United States as a
naval power. Rear Admiral Robley D. Evans, the original
commander, was instructed by the President on his departure to regard his mission as one of good will, but he was
also advised to be prepared for whatever might come. Considering the recent background of Japanese-American relations and the initial agitation of the Japanese over the mere
prospect of an American fleet in Western Pacific waters, the
possibility of some untoward development could not be entirely dismissed.

Whatever the political issues involved, the professional
naval interest in the cruise was probably well described by
Mahan, who professed to see in it merely a practice cruise in
what would now be called "fleet logistics." To Mahan experience of "the huge administrative difficulties connected
with so distant an expedition by a large body of vessels dependent upon their own resources," should prove of in-
estimable value. By "own resources" he hastened to add, he

meant, "not that which each vessel carries in itself, but self dependence as distinguished from dependence on near navy yards . . . the great snare of peace times. The renewal of stores and coal on the voyage is a big problem . . . a problem of combination, and of subsistence; a distinctly military problem. To grapple with such a question is as really practical as is Fleet tactics or target practice."

The event fully justified the expectations. The constant exercise in fleet operations had welded the various units of the fleet together into a working team. The mere fact of staying at sea had made of the Navy a seagoing force. From deck officer to engineer the organization of each ship had gained what constructive exercises and drills could never give. Yet as Mahan pointed out when the fleet had completed the first leg of its voyage, the conditions under which it cruised were not those of war, for certainly in wartime no fleet of sixteen battleships could ever have passed from the Atlantic to the Pacific and thence around the world without a far greater force of auxiliary vessels. Our own naval colliers delivered coal to the fleet only at two ports, Trinidad, and Rio de Janeiro, early in the voyage. Thereafter the fleet was dependent upon chartered colliers, its own coaling stations and other foreign sources. Of the total of 434,906 tons of coal delivered to the cruising units 9 per cent was on board when the fleet left Hampton Roads, 8 per cent was furnished by naval colliers and 10 per cent by United States coaling stations at Cavite and Honolulu. Seventy-three per cent, or 318,334 tons were delivered from foreign sources. Even in San Francisco the fleet received its coal from British and Norwegian ships and contractors.

The cruise had been a valuable preliminary step toward the creation of a seagoing naval force, but it did little to develop those essential links of transport and supply between ship and shore by which alone the fleet could be maintained overseas as an effective force. The need for colliers and bases was obvious. What was equally essential, if not so obvious, was experience in arranging collier and transport schedules, replenishment tables and methods of estimating, allocating and distributing supplies. It was no longer sufficient, as it had been for Dewey, to destroy the enemy and then cable back to Washington for more ammunition. The manner and the means, as Lieutenant Dinger had pointed out, must be planned beforehand. Without this kind of planning and preparation for administration, as well as the physical facilities like colliers and dry docks, we had still for all practical purposes, in 1909, the fleet of "sea-going coastline battleships" stipulated by Congress in 1890.

In 1909 the Joint Board, after taking into consideration the strategic factors involved, advised against any extensive outlays for insular fortifications in the Philippines. Finding that "no location presented had the necessary natural advantages; that while a few could be made into suitable Naval bases at great expense, the changed conditions in the Pacific made such expense unnecessary and undesirable," the Joint Board suggested that facilities at Olangapo be limited to the floating dock and small repair shops. Under such a policy "its defense would not become one of serious moment." On the other hand, the board did recommend that Pearl Harbor be developed as the principal American naval base in the Pacific.

The recommendation of the Joint Board marks out in rough outline the policy toward Pacific bases which was to be pursued for three decades. Pearl Harbor profited considerably from the policy of concentration, for during the succeeding years much larger sums than heretofore were appropriated and spent on its development as a naval base. The development may be regarded as an attempt to widen the perimeter of America's defense. In theory at least it would support that kind of strategic operation that Mahan had long advocated by which an enemy fleet could be met and defeated before it ever reached our shores. But the base at Pearl Harbor could hardly be construed as offering the means for naval domination of the Western Pacific. On the contrary, the decision not to make installations in the Philippines which would commit us to their defense and the gradual abandonment of plans to develop and fortify Guam imply very clearly that American policy was shaking down once again into one of continental defense.

The lack of bases in the Pacific provided a constant theme for lament by the professional naval officer. And indeed the policy of retrenchment that it implied was hardly consistent with our stated policy in the Philippines and the Far East. But it was obvious that Congress would not appropriate funds for the fortification of distant outposts in the Pacific. The development of Pearl Harbor was at least the first sential step for defense in the Pacific.

The First World War

THE First World War gave to the development of naval gistics the stimulus that only war can give. Even befo America's involvement a renewed interest in the practi problems of fleet maintenance may be observed. In part was the result of the material effort involved in putting in effect the naval building program of 1916; in part it was t natural concomitant of the war in Europe and the prepare ness drive in America. But there was also an increasing ten ency to assess the logistic implications of America's strategi position in the world.

Beginning in 1911, a series of lectures on logistics was de livered at the summer conference of the War College, whic occasionally, as in the case of Captain J. S. McKean's di cussion of naval logistics in 1913, revealed a remarkably cor prehensive grasp of the factors involved in building, mobili ing and maintaining naval forces. In the professional journ as well, the subject of logistics received increasing attentic

The most significant manifestation, however, of the ne importance logistics was assuming in naval affairs was th establishment in 1915 of the Office of Chief of Naval Operations. The creation in the Navy Department of some form of general staff organization had been urged for many years even prior to the time when a modern fleet created a problem of modern logistics. It should be observed as well that the cause of a general staff had been advocated by many line officers who were not primarily concerned with logistics. The problem was essentially one of reaching the proper balance between civilian and military influence in the administration of the Navy. To what extent, in short, should some agency of military direction intervene between the ultimate authority embodied in the Secretary and the working establishment of the bureaus?

The growing importance of material matters in the administration of the Navy had crystallized the issue. As early as 1900, Admiral H. C. Taylor, Chief of the Bureau of Navigation, had made this point the basis of his proposal for a general staff. The creation of a General Board and reliance upon the War College for advice upon military policy had not solved the situation. Through succeeding years the issue of a general staff had been brought to the fore on one occasion after another until in 1910, Secretary Meyer introduced his system of "aides." The system of aides was but a stopgap, however, and Rear Admiral Bradley Fiske, then aide for Operations, continued his advocacy of a general staff organization until, by his own confession, Secretary Daniels was "weary and bored with Fiske." Finally in 1915, a bill creating a Chief of Naval Operations was introduced into Congress and passed.

The bill as enacted was not all that its military advocates had desired. Instead of being charged with the readiness and general direction of the Navy, as originally proposed, the Chief of Naval Operations was charged only with the operations of the fleet and with the preparation and readiness of plans for its use in war. Even so the new system was a notable advance over that which had prevailed before, for, in theory at least, it created an agency which would concern itself not only with the operations of the fleet but also with material and logistic affairs. Weak though the new office was, it was to prove essential for the conduct of naval affairs during the First World War.

That war was the first great example of "total war" as it is understood today. Behind masses of men in motion on the various fronts, the factories, farms, mines and railroads of the contending nations were no less engaged. Despite America's late entrance into the war, this experience of the "nation in arms" belonged to this country as well as to the various European powers. But while the war involved for the United States an unprecedented mobilization of her material and human resources, it was not primarily a naval war, and it did not, therefore, involve a commensurate effort in naval logistics. The Navy's experience in providing for the support of its forces was limited and on a relatively small scale as compared with that of the Army.

In order to maintain its forces overseas during the war the Navy established all told fifteen naval bases and twenty-seven aviation bases and operating stations. Port organizations were set up in twenty European ports. Supplementing these facilities ashore logistic support was provided to the operating forces by repair vessels and tenders at Queenstown, Brest, Gibraltar, Corfu and other strategic positions. The Cruiser and Transport Force carried over 900,000 troops to France and returned over 1,600,000, while in addition the Navy manned and operated a fleet of 378 cargo vessels totalling 2,900,000 deadweight tons. These vessels, operated primarily for the account of the Army and the United States Shipping Board, delivered approximately 6,000,000 tons of cargo of all kinds to Europe during the war.

Within the United States the naval building program begun in 1916, and the support of operating forces after our entrance into the war, presented logistic tasks of considerable magnitude. The Navy increased from a force of 58,000 personnel in 1916, to almost half a million before the end of the war. The naval appropriation of 1919 was over two billion dollars, thirteen times the sum required in 1916 and almost equal to the total amount expended between 1883 and 1916. The Navy was unquestionably a big business.

Apart from shipping and the establishment of non-continental bases, however, its overseas logistic effort was limited. The Navy had begun the war under the assumption that except for aviation purposes no shore facilities would be established overseas. What support was required for operating forces would be rendered by repair vessels and tenders such as the *Dixie* and *Melville* at Queenstown. But before the war was over the Navy discovered that mobile support was insufficient; more and more it depended upon shore-based facilities.

In constructing naval bases overseas the United States received considerable assistance from its allies. At Queenstown, Plymouth and at the two Scottish bases at Inverness and Invergordon used for the North Sea Mine Barrage the labor and materials were almost wholly provided by the Admiralty. At Brest in addition to the facilities of the *Bridgeport* and *Prometheus* repairs were carried on at the French navy yard on the Penfeld River and by private contractors. In April 1918, when all these facilities began to be inadequate, arrangements were made to fabricate and ship from the United States the buildings and tools required to erect and operate machine shops for Brest, Lorient and Pauillac. The first shipments did not arrive, however, until mid-September, and the whole project was canceled after the armistice before it was fairly under way. Materials for the tank farm constructed at Brest were prefabricated in America and shipped to France in knockdown condition by the Bureau of Yards and Docks. But apart from consumable supplies the greater portion of the materials going into American bases overseas were of foreign origin.

It should be noted as well that American bases were established in British and French harbors which were already well developed. Piers, docks, buildings and warehouses were already available. In many cases they required alteration or renovation, but the labor and effort involved were by no means comparable to that of starting from the ground up.

Another fact of supreme importance is that with few exceptions only light naval forces were involved. The American battleship division at Scapa Flow, which was the principal exception, enjoyed all the comforts of a well established British base. Admiral Sims described the idea of moving the whole North Atlantic Fleet to European waters as strategically poor and logistically impossible. "What Naval experts call 'logistics' of the situation," he said, "immediately ruled this idea out of consideration. The one fact that made it impossible to base the Fleet in European waters at that time was that we could not have kept it supplied, particularly with oil." Even for the lighter forces many heavy repairs were done in the United States. When destroyer boilers needed replacement or retubing, the vessels returned to the United States despite the protests of the naval commanders in Europe who desired to keep them in operational waters.

The Navy's shipping effort during the war was an accomplishment of the first magnitude. Manning, husbanding and operating the large fleet of cargo vessels of the Naval Overseas Transportation Service, to say nothing of the forty-two transports of the Cruiser and Transport Force, was a huge task. But without belittling this achievement it is necessary to draw a distinction between the role of carrier which the Navy played and the broader logistic task of shipper and supplier. As a carrier its responsibility for the movement of materials was limited to picking up the cargo at one terminal port and delivering it at another. Responsibility for loading and unloading cargo, for warehousing, for scheduling shipments and for the orderly flow of materials to tidewater ports belonged to the shipper, which in this case was predominantly the Army. During the twenty months of our active participation in the war the total of naval dry cargo shipments (excluding liquid and bulk fuels) was roughly 400,000 tons. This represented about one-fifteenth of the total carried by the Naval Overseas Transportation Service and only two-thirds of the amount of naval dry cargo shipped overseas during a single month of 1944. The result was that the Navy was not faced with that problem, which is the essence of logistics, of integrating all the many factors involved in the mass movement of material support.

Despite the tremendous increase in the fleet and in the naval establishment the First World War did little to shake loose the Navy as a whole from its continental dependency. Its participation in the war, though highly successful, was limited. As far as facilities for support are concerned, the Atlantic Ocean might be regarded as a friendly lake whose shores were lined with suitable havens. The true logistics test of the Navy was yet to come.

Between Two Wars

THE United States emerged from the First World War with a navy already of unprecedented size. From a force of about 350 vessels of all types fit for service prior to our entrance the Navy had increased to 795 vessels. The total tonnage built or building had doubled over that of 1910. Nor was this all. With the approval of the President, the Navy Department pushed forward with the authorizations of 1916 and 1918, determined to capitalize upon the moment for creating a "Navy second to none." Between 1919 and 1922, the United States laid keels for 9 battleships, 4 battle cruisers, 8 light cruisers, 2 aircraft carriers and 81 destroyers. The result was intended to be a navy capable of maintaining the freedom of the seas against any foreign naval power, if not the combined navies of the world.

Even more significant from our point of view than the projected increase in the size of the Navy was the new fleet organization announced by the Secretary in 1919. For years the western coast of the United States had lain relatively exposed to Japan's growing naval might in the Pacific. The visit of the Atlantic Fleet in 1908 had been received with great satisfaction by the people of the Pacific states, and they hoped that with completion of the Panama Canal United States naval forces might be distributed more equitably about our coast. But the war in Europe had necessitated a postponement in the shift of forces to the Pacific. With the completion of the war and the destruction of German naval forces at Scapa Flow the moment had arrived, however, and in the summer of 1919 half of the battleship force, including many newer and heavier units, was moved to the Pacific and constituted as the United States Pacific Fleet.

Instructed by the experience of the war, the Navy Department meanwhile was pressing not only for the naval building program, but also for the development of the naval shore establishment. Taking as its starting point the recommendations of the Helm Commission of 1916, a new board in 1919, headed by Rear Admiral J. S. McKean, the acting Chief of Naval Operations, made an exhaustive survey of the West Coast shore establishment and of facilities at Pearl Harbor and in Alaska. The board recommended an expenditure of $157,000,000, of which $27,000,000 was earmarked for facilities at Pearl Harbor. Secretary Daniels in his report of 1920, asserted that shore establishment development would be carried "to the nth degree."

These events of 1919 marked the beginning of a new era in our naval history. American naval forces were now facing westward; from our shores they could survey the vast reaches of the Pacific sparsely dotted with sites for naval bases which were as yet only potential. With the creation of the Pacific Fleet a new mission was marked out for the Navy. This included not only the defense of our Pacific shores but implied as well a closer union between our foreign policy in the Far East and our naval policy in the Pacific. The problems of naval logistics thus posed were entirely different from anything we had before experienced. Unlike the case of the

First World War, where American naval forces had operated along lines of communication and support anchored securely on both sides of the Atlantic, the measure of our effective operating range was now our ability to project supporting elements outward into an area which offered no resources but widely scattered fleet anchorages and unprepared positions.

The Washington Treaties of 1922 brought to an end the immediate prospect of United States naval domination of the Pacific. The agreed ratio of 5:5:3 left our fleet to all outward appearances far superior to the Japanese. But in return for Japanese assurances that henceforth its continental policy would be conducted along lines acceptable to the United States the latter had assented to Article XIX of the Five-Power Treaty under which both powers agreed not to make any further fortification of certain specified islands in the Pacific. For the United States these included Guam, Midway, Wake, Samoa and the Philippines. For Japan the prohibition applied to the Kurile, Bonin, and Loochow Islands, Amami-Oshima, Formosa, the Pescadores and "any insular territories or possessions in the Pacific Ocean which Japan may hereafter acquire."

In effect Article XIX marked out a neutral or intermediate zone in the Pacific which might contribute to the stability of relations between the two principal Pacific powers. Each power would henceforth be secure in its own home waters. For Japan to concede this security to the United States was no sacrifice, since in the Eastern Pacific she had no possessions which might have been fortified, and she had no announced interests which would require to be defended. For the United States, however, still committed to the defense of the Philippines and possessing in Guam, the "Gibraltar of the Pacific," the agreement represented a major concession. More even than the scrapping of the American fleet this limitation upon the development of Pacific bases rankled in the minds of American naval officers. Indeed they could point with some justification to the fact that American policy in the Far East made commitments which we were unable to carry out and that the various agreements which paralleled the naval treaty offered no sure guarantees of enforcement. On the other hand, it could also be argued that to expect Congress to appropriate the sums necessary to develop America's overseas positions was equally unrealistic. The Washington settlement was an attempt on the part of our government to reach a comprehensive settlement in the Pacific. It is possibly true, as Captain Dudley Knox maintained, that naval interests were not properly represented, and it is certainly true that most of the concessions made by the United States were at the expense of our naval power, actual or potential. Of these by far the most important, as astute officers then recognized, were the limitations imposed on the development of Pacific naval bases.

The Navy Department did not abandon its plans completely. Early in 1923 a board headed by Admiral Rodman reported to the Secretary on the shore establishment of the Navy, recommending in particular that Pearl Harbor and the Canal Zone should have priority of development over our major continental yards. In June 1923 a second board headed by Captain A. L. Willard laid out in great detail a twenty-year program for the development of Pearl Harbor and other Pacific positions allowed by the treaty. But by now the initial impetus behind the naval program was fast dwindling. In subsequent years, just as our naval building programs fell below the parity allowed by treaty, so the development of our positions in the Pacific and the acquisition of other logistic facilities fell short of both the necessary and the allowable. The Washington Treaties, therefore, marked not only the end of America's greatest bid for naval supremacy in tonnage and capital ships; it marked also the beginning of that situation in the Pacific, which lasted legally until 1936 and in fact until the outbreak of the Second World War, in which our foreign policy and our military

policy in the Pacific were almost divorced from each other.
Whatever the actual strength in combatant ships of the
American Navy, it was debarred by lack of prepared positions from any serious bid for control of the Western
Pacific. From that time forward naval planning for war in
the Pacific had to be premised upon the assumption that
both the Philippines and Guam would fall at once to the
Japanese and that bases for support of our forces in the
Western Pacific would have to be rewon against enemy
opposition. Only with this essential preliminary could we
hope to engage the Japanese anywhere west of the 180th
meridian.

The period from the Washington Treaty down almost to
the outbreak of war was one of increasing torpor and
frustration within the Navy. Caught between the United
States' avowed policy of disarmament on the one hand
and an economy-minded Congress on the other, the Navy
was first reduced by treaty to what was in fact only a hemisphere force and then allowed by successive Congresses to
fall even below treaty strength. Some of America's newest
vessels had been scrapped, even before they were completed.
In 1924 AlNav No. 25 set up an effective bar to modernization by providing that since funds would seldom be available for all purposes, the repair and maintenance of vessels
in their existing condition should have priority over altera-
tions. What was perhaps worst, niggardly appropriations for
the operation and maintenance of the Navy put naval operations into a veritable straitjacket. Limited fuel for cruising,
the lack of auxiliary vessels and of suitably prepared advance
positions from which a major force might operate continuously all served to constrict the range of fleet exercises and
war games. Too frequently the criterion determining the
Navy's annual operating plan was not our military or
strategic situation but rather the fact of having to live
within its meager budget.

When a nation maintains only a nuclear military or naval

force in time of peace, plans for the mobilization, expansion, and employment of wartime forces become doubly important. It is equally important that its professional military and naval personnel be kept attuned to the conditions which will be confronted in wartime. During the years of peace the Navy could plan and study for the contingencies which might be expected to arise, but it seldom had the opportunity to test by such a practical exercise as the cruise of 1907 the adequacy of its plans and preparations. For practical lessons it could go back only to the limited experience of the First World War, an experience which could hardly be useful for a full-fledged war in the Pacific. The result was that plans were conceived and underlying concepts were rooted in a world of hypothesis diverging farther and farther from reality.

In such an atmosphere the science of providing the means of warfare must inevitably suffer more than the study of "the use of the given means." It was possible to assume in the famous "war games" played upon the checkered board at the War College that the means were available. It was possible there to concentrate upon the enduring "principles of war" with little reference to the actualities with which our Navy might be confronted in real conflict. It was even possible in one admittedly extreme instance for a commander of the Orange Fleet to execute a smashing attack upon the flank of the Blue Fleet with four cruisers which had been accidentally obscured from the view of the Blue commander beneath a wooden table, and for that fortuitous circumstance to be ruled by the referee a legitimate hazard of war.

Of greater moment was the failure to make a more serious study of logistics at the War College. In 1926, Captain R. E. Bakenhus succeeded in setting up a logistics section at the War College, and instituted a system of committee projects in which the logistic requirements of various naval situations and campaigns were analyzed. This excellent effort was short-lived, however. Captain Bakenhus's successor as head of the logistics section was unsympathetic to the study of logistics at the War College, believing as he said that such matters as "shovelling coal and combat loading" did not belong with the study of the principles of war. The result was the abolition of the logistics section and the abandonment of logistic studies.

Logistic planning—or, more properly, war planning—in the Navy Department suffered also from that hypothetical quality which belonged to all naval activity during the interlude of peace. The problem of the war planner is admittedly difficult. He must project his estimate of the military situation sufficiently far in advance to allow for the implementation of his plans in the construction and readiness of military or naval forces. He must deduce from assumed situations the strategic implications and the logistic requirements of the operating forces. He is therefore compelled to plan broadly and in general terms in the hope that the detailed implementation of his plan will bring it into accord with current and actual conditions. Secondly, the planner becomes aware as he compares the strategically desirable and the logistically possible that in peacetime the latter must always fall short of the former. He tends, therefore, to concentrate upon the strategic aspects of his plan, assuming for the purposes of planning that the logistic resources will be available when they are required. The list of his logistic assumptions grows longer, and the tendency is always toward assuming that all things strategically desirable are logistically possible. Only the stern realist of the naval profession can remain unaffected by this *maladie de paix*.

The necessity of planning in general terms and leaving the detailed development and application of the plan to the subordinate working agencies is also productive of many complications. The ideal in planning is to separate the planning function itself from responsibility for the administration or implementation of the plan. But since no plan of broad scope can comprehend all the minutiae of conditions to which it must be applied, such an ideal is seldom realizable in practice. The most that can be hoped for is that subordinate agencies, in working out the detail, will conform to the broad outlines of policy laid out in the overall plan and that the sum of their efforts will conform to the general ends in view.

This problem of planning and administration had long beset the Navy and had been accentuated by the lack of proper departmental organization. The creation of the General Board in 1900 with planning and advisory functions, "to ensure the efficient preparation of the Fleet in case of war," had provided a planning agency, but the General Board had been so divorced from the administrative and executive functions in the Navy Department that its plans were largely vitiated in implementation. The need to establish a planning agency somewhere near the seat of executive authority had underlain much of the agitation for a general staff organization in the Navy. It had been the intention of Admiral Fiske that the assistants requested in his original bill for a Chief of Naval Operations should devote their time to planning, unencumbered by administrative responsibilities. The bill of 1915 had struck out the provision for assistants; and when, in the revised bill of 1916, fifteen assistants were provided, they were soon so involved in the administrative work of the office that they had little time for planning.

The first step toward a genuine planning staff was taken in London during the First World War when a planning section was set up by Admiral Sims. This section was relieved of all other responsibilities and directed to carry on planning studies to be submitted to the Force Commander via the Chief of Staff. The studies ranged over a variety of subjects —strategical, tactical, and logistic—but by the conclusion of the war they had demonstrated the utility of a planning body properly situated in the command organization. When in

1919 a War Plans Division was created under the Chief of Naval Operations, the experience of this London planning section was drawn upon. The War Plans Division was divided into specialized sections dealing with policy, strategy, tactics, logistics and education. Thus by the conclusion of the First World War an organized planning unit which included a section for logistics had been established under the Chief of Naval Operations.

Since planning occupies an important place in peacetime preparation for war, the plans developed during succeeding years offer an excellent index to the Navy's logistic thinking. Beginning with the first War Portfolio of 1919, logistics appears to have occupied at least nominally an important place in the war plans. In the Basic Readiness Plan of 1924, for example, the "mobile base" idea first suggested in 1904 by Civil Engineer Cunningham was accepted as the principal means of fleet support at sea. In 1929 the concept of the mobile base was supplanted by that of a "western base," a major shore base which would presumably be established in Manila six months after the opening of hostilities. In this connection it is interesting to observe that plans were already being laid for Naval Base Construction Battalions similar to the Sea Bees. Provisions were also made for the mobilization of personnel and merchant shipping, for the organization of rail transport, for securing piers, warehouses and other terminal facilities, for critical materials and for industrial mobilization. These were to be carried into greater detail in the contributory logistic and material plans and in the war plans of the District Commandants.

The War Plans and their various logistic and material annexes grew more elaborate as the years progressed. Yet in many ways as the actual logistic readiness of the Navy declined, they grew less and less realistic. One of the major premises of the strategic planning for an Orange (Japanese) war, for example, was an early offensive into the Marshall and Caroline Islands. Successive plans therefore called for the concentration at Hawaii of a force capable of seizing objectives in the Marshalls only 60 days after the declaration of war. In 1929, the Joint Plan called for an Army expeditionary force of 55,000 troops ready to embark from Hawaii only 45 days after the declaration of war. Most certainly the Army could not have mounted such a force, and the Navy could not have transported it.

Another feature of the War Plans to which hindsight calls attention was the absence of any provision for reporting or communicating logistic requirements from fleet commander to the continental shore establishment beyond the normal process of requisition by individual unit. Throughout the War Plans there appears a strong tendency to assume that fleet and force requirements were calculable, that they could be reduced to specific and unvarying tables of allowances, and that war usage tables would conform fairly closely to those which had been calculated in peacetime. This failure to weigh carefully the problem of replenishment planning and administration was to prove one of the most serious defects in logistic administration after the war had begun.

Even more serious than the omissions and false assumptions of the War Plans was the lack of follow-through in carrying out the policies and concepts outlined in the plans themselves. In the administration of the peacetime Navy there were many established procedures which could obviously not be employed by an overseas force cut off from reliance upon the continental shore establishment. Yet the habits of peacetime support persisted. The entire continental shore establishment of the Navy was geared to the process of rendering support to a home-based fleet. As Admiral Coontz pointed out to the War College in 1926, "The volume of daily business with the shore establishment during the fiscal year 1925 averaged 1,000 items per day requisitioned. To provide means for meeting this volume of requirements under circumstances in which the Fleet is separated from the continental United States is the major problem now confronting the Commander-in-Chief." Yet as the Navy expanded during the years before the war until its volume of business was many times more than 1,000 items requisitioned per day, the lack of more suitable means of communicating requirements and delivering supplies remained.

Another very clear example of lack of follow-through was the case of the Naval Transportation Service. The Navy had assumed for many years, and the War Plans had provided, that in war the merchant marine would be mobilized and manned by the Navy. Yet as late as September 1939 no arrangement had been made with the Maritime Commission, the sole agency empowered during war to requisition merchant vessels, for the transfer of vessels to the Navy. Until that time, moreover, the Naval Transportation Service existed as an administrative unit only on paper. In February 1939 the whole task of planning and preparing for the mobilization, manning, and operation of the merchant marine in war was the collateral duty of a single officer in the Navy Department.

In many other ways this lack of follow-through is evident. Essentially it derived from the fact that, despite pious references to its importance, the subject of logistics offered little of interest to the average naval officer. The more obvious and tangible deficiencies in the Navy's logistic readiness were frequently remarked. The annual report of the Secretary continually called attention, for example, to the need for auxiliary vessels. After 1936, when the Washington and London Treaties had expired, the Navy resumed its advocacy of advance base development. Yet as long as the fleet itself could continue to rely upon home bases, the problems of wartime logistics remained fictitious. The established procedures were adequate for the support of the Navy, and the lack of system and organization, as well as material facilities, for accomplishing the logistic tasks required by strategic war planning did not become apparent.

In October 1939, when the Hawaiian Detachment of eight cruisers, one aircraft carrier, and sixteen destroyers was based on Pearl Harbor, the lack of provision for overseas support suddenly became apparent. Admiral H. R. Stark, then Chief of Naval Operations, stated at the time that he was "hopeful [this move] will show up the weakness in the habitability of that yard to support even a moderate sized force," and in this his hope was realized. Unfortunately, little time remained to take the remedial measures Admiral Stark hoped would follow the demonstration. In the spring of 1940, upon the completion of the spring maneuvers, the entire United States Fleet was ordered to Pearl Harbor, and from this time forward the Navy was compelled to grapple with a genuine logistic task. In March 1940, Admiral Richardson, Commander-in-Chief of the U.S. Fleet, wrote to Admiral Stark asking how long the fleet would remain at Pearl Harbor and stating that he did not consider the basing there of the United States Fleet or even a substantial portion of it "a remote possibility." To Admiral Richardson's protestations Admiral Stark replied, explaining the political reasons behind the decision to keep the fleet at Pearl Harbor and suggesting that among other incidental benefits which might result would be the solving of logistic problems.

Subsequent events were to demonstrate that despite the inconvenience and the serious hindrance to fleet training involved, basing the fleet at Pearl Harbor was a logistic blessing in disguise. In July 1940, Admiral Richardson reported that "the prolonged stay of the majority of the U.S. Fleet in Hawaiian waters has disclosed the many deficiencies of this area as a major outlying and training base." In June 1941, his successor, Admiral Kimmel, was able to state that "Many of the deficiencies of this base disclosed by the prolonged stay of the U.S. Pacific Fleet . . . either have been or are now in the process of correction." Certain deficiencies remained in the facilities of the base itself, and in addition the Base Force, which was responsible for the delivery of supplies from the mainland to the fleet, was hard pressed with the available vessels to keep the stocks of stores, refrigerated provisions, ammunition and other expendables at the minimum required level.

With all its failings, Pearl Harbor was immeasurably better prepared in 1941 to support our naval operations in the Pacific than it had been in the early months of 1940. What is most important is that for the first time in its history our Navy had been able to assume and maintain a position two thousand miles distant from our shores. In the sense of logistics it had already begun that "Fleet Advance across the Pacific" which had long been the subject of study at the War College and in the War Plans. It had taken the first of the many steps by which we ultimately projected across the entire reaches of the Pacific a naval force capable of taking and holding the command of the sea.

CHAPTER II

THE FIRST PHASE

Outbreak of the War

THE military situation confronting the United States on the morning of December 8, 1941, was the result less of the Japanese attack on Pearl Harbor than of the failure of the United States during the years preceding that attack to prepare adequately its defenses in the Pacific. Pearl Harbor stands out in the minds of most Americans, not only as a date which will live in infamy, but as the most severe defeat ever suffered by an American fleet. It is true that the blow suffered was severe and crippling. Our naval forces in the Pacific had been materially depleted. We were left with but a remnant of the striking force with which we had expected to carry on war with Japan. But the extent of our losses did not modify, except in a small degree, the strategy we had intended to pursue in the Pacific during the opening phases of a war with the Axis powers.

Nor did the success of the attack at Pearl Harbor seriously alter the immediate strategic situation in the Western Pacific as it affected the Japanese. The road to Manila and thence on at least as far as the Netherlands East Indies would have been open, whatever the condition of our forces in Pearl Harbor. The situation of Guam and Wake was not materially altered. There is no reason to believe that the original Japanese impetus could have been stopped much short of the important positions they assumed in New Guinea and New Britain during January 1942. The United States did not then have sufficient ready resources to halt such a campaign or to offer to it a serious counterthrust which might have drawn off the forces and attention of the enemy.

Material and technical modernization of the United States Fleet was admittedly incomplete when war broke out. The antiaircraft defenses of our battleships and other surface craft were inadequate. We lacked sufficient modern aircraft, carriers, and escort vessels. Above all, we lacked adequately trained personnel in the fleet itself. Expansion of the naval establishment, both ashore and afloat, had resulted in the dispersion of seasoned ratings into key positions in the growing Navy and the consequent dilution with green personnel of highly trained tactical units. So conscious was the Navy itself of its own unreadiness that some naval officers have since hazarded the informal opinion that our Navy was fortunate to have fought its first engagement in the shallow waters of Pearl Harbor where losses could be redeemed. Such calculations are purely speculative, however, and in any event have little bearing upon the case. An engagement between our Pacific Fleet and the Japanese forces in the waters adjacent to Pearl Harbor would not seriously have changed the strategic course of the early phases of the war in the Pacific.

The strength and weakness of the United States Navy to resist the Japanese offensive in the Western Pacific lay not in the condition of our combatant forces themselves. The true index of our power to repulse the Japanese lay in our logistic readiness or unreadiness to conduct continued operations in the areas threatened. Pearl Harbor was then our only important naval base west of the Pacific Coast. A few air stations, still improperly developed, formed its outer ring of defense. Guam offered nothing. Cavite and Olangapo, if not inaccessible, were already under attack and must be presumed to be untenable. Our naval resources in the Pacific, exclusive of the fighting force, as a British observer had remarked some years before, resembled a clearly marked highway which gradually lost its way in the mid-reaches of the Pacific. And such is the character of modern naval power that it can move only on broad, clearly marked highways.

It was the great good fortune of the United States and the cardinal error of the Japanese that the attack at Pearl

Harbor was directed almost exclusively against ships, and not to a greater extent against the supporting installations. Had a comparable blow been dealt to the piers, repair shops, fuel tanks, warehouses, ammunition dumps, and dry docks, our own ability to operate in the Central and Western Pacific would have been still further reduced. Japanese freedom of action to penetrate into the South and Southwest Pacific would have been that much more enhanced. The major portion of the United States Fleet would have had to fall back two thousand miles to our Pacific Coast for a base of operations. Given our current shortage of tankers and oilers, supply vessels, repair ships, tenders, and other supporting craft, its effective operating range would have been severely curtailed. What the consequences would have been for our advance outposts at Midway, Johnston, Palmyra, Canton, and Samoa during this temporary period can only be surmised. But in a war of advanced island positions, such as the Pacific campaign was to become, the importance of a major base at Pearl Harbor in operable condition is manifest.

Nothing could illustrate more dramatically the complex of elements which make up modern naval power and which enter into naval strategy than the inability of our Navy in 1941 to wrest from the Japanese Navy the control of the Western Pacific. Harassing operations against commerce or island positions were feasible as we soon demonstrated, even with the limited forces still operating. But the control of the Western Pacific in sufficient strength to bar the Japanese from their objectives to the south was impossible without other resources than a striking force. Without prepared positions from which it might draw continued support, without adequate auxiliary vessels, repair facilities, skilled craftsmen, garrison forces, supply ships, tankers, and transports—to mention only the more obvious resources—our fleet was as unable to operate continuously in this area as a naked man to cross the Sahara. Without these essential elements of support, our naval power could be brought to bear within only a limited radius of the islands of Hawaii. It was by these limitations, therefore, by the whole complex of conditions of geography, time, combat strength, and the elements of support, encompassing but far outweighing the immediate damage to our fleet, that the strategic pattern of the Pacific war was first determined. And it was determined long before the fateful morning of December 7.

The military situation at the outbreak of the Pacific war and, in fact, the outline of our subsequent campaign had been so clearly described by a prescient British naval writer more than twelve years before, that it would be useful to quote at some length from his analysis. Expounding a thesis which he had put forward repeatedly, Hector Bywater wrote in *Navies and Nations* in 1929:

"Problem (4), viz, the defence of outlying territories, particularly the Philippines, Guam, and Samoa, opens up the whole question of Pacific strategy. . . . Here it suffices to repeat that the American Navy would be powerless to prevent the conquest of the Philippines and Guam in the event of war with Japan. Once lost, they might possibly be recovered by an almost superhuman effort. This would involve an amphibious campaign exceeding in magnitude and difficulty anything of the kind that has previously been attempted. It would necessitate the building of an entirely new fleet of warships and auxiliary craft; the conveyance of an army and its impedimenta across the Pacific, the greater part of the route lying within the sphere of enemy naval action; the seizure of intermediate and terminal bases, which would probably be found in a state of defence; the holding of such bases against determined counter-attack; the guarding of communications thousands of miles in length; and finally the development of offensive operations in the advanced war zone on a scale sufficient to force a decision. By no other form of military action could the lost islands be recovered." This was exactly what we were to accomplish; it was the prospect, dimly foreshadowed, which faced us at the end of 1941.

More immediately, however, the United States was faced
with the necessity of restoring its own defense around the
North American continent and of setting limits to the progress of the Japanese in the South and Southwest Pacific.
Both of these undertakings were purely defensive. The former task involved the immediate reinforcement of the three
key points in our Pacific defense system—Alaska, Hawaii,
and the Panama Canal. The latter task, upon which depended the subsequent development of our campaign, required
also immediate steps, but had to be carried out with an eye
to the long-range prospect as well.

The principal point of our long-range strategy was to hold
the island positions necessary to maintaining a line of communications with Australia and containing the Japanese offensive within the Pacific theater. The positions we already
had such as Palmyra, Midway, Johnston, and Samoa had to
be strengthened and developed. Others, which would complete the link with the Southwest Pacific and which would
serve as points of mutual support, must be established. The
pattern of the Japanese advance into the Philippines, the
Dutch East Indies, New Guinea, and New Britain had demonstrated a keen appreciation of the interplay between land
positions and sea and air forces. It was well adapted to the
island character of the area and could be successfully com-
bated with our present forces only by a defense developed
along the same basic lines.

Apart from the need for rapid construction, our bases in
the Pacific were required to possess a high degree of flexibility and adaptability. Initially, they must be garrisoned, developed as operating bases for air patrol and search, and
equipped with harbor defense installations. These were the
defensive and wholly operational qualities with which they
must first be endowed. To support an offensive, however,
and to make possible the operation of our forces in the areas
to the north, the bases had also to assume logistic properties
in ever increasing proportions as our operations and forces

expanded. They were to be fueling stations, protected anchorages, staging points for airplanes and subsequently for troops, and repair and supply points. It was to these purposes ultimately that the great weight of advance base development was directed.

In these early months the ultimate size of the effort involved could only be dimly appreciated. Nor was it possible, then, if ever, to draw a clear line between the military or defensive features and the logistic properties of any single base. The ratio between logistic and military factors entering into each base might vary with reference to its proximity to the zone of active operations, its peculiar topography, and its particular role in the broad scheme of our defense. The essential features, therefore, were imprecise—flexibility and versatility. What was apparent almost at once was that the campaign would center in the South Pacific, that it would be primarily defensive in its initial phases, and that it must be waged in terms of advance base positions possessing both defensive and offensive potentialities. The major decision of strategy was, therefore, to direct all our available resources to the establishment of advance base positions around which the campaign in the South Pacific would be carried on.

As one studies the map of the South Pacific and notes the positions we originally assumed there, certain factors in our immediate situation can be discerned. The first condition we faced was that the initiative was almost entirely in the hands of the Japanese. Such slender resources as we might mobilize must be distributed in the Pacific with a view to their not being wasted in a vain effort to hold a position which was in fact untenable. Most of the advantages of geography lay with the enemy. Possessing interior lines, he might proceed in any one of various directions with concentrated force against our thinly guarded lines. The Japanese possessed also the immense advantage of prior preparation in the region of the Central Pacific. We knew little of what Japanese forces were actually concentrated in the Carolines and Marshalls, but it was necessary to regard them, nevertheless, as a powerful salient. Around these factors, therefore, using such positions as we already had, the pattern of defense must be woven. Forces must be deployed far enough to the north to bear upon the probable zone of operations; far enough south to give reasonable security against invasion.

The line of bases developed consisted essentially of a wide arc stretching from Hawaii southwest through Palmyra, Canton, Samoa, the Fiji Islands, and New Caledonia to the coast of Australia, with an important salient thrusting north into the New Hebrides. It proved to be on the whole a sound estimate of what we might conceivably defend and develop for future use in staging and supporting offensive operations.

The naval situation in the Atlantic at the outbreak of war, while wholly different in character, was no less acute. The mission of our Atlantic forces was two-fold. It was first to assure the defenses of the Western Hemisphere and second to guard the vital flow of shipping across the Atlantic in order to maintain the war-making capacity of the British Isles, render assistance to Russia, and establish our own forces overseas. Of the two missions the former was more basic to our own security but in actuality involved a much less immediate threat. Upon the struggle with the German submarine, might depend the outcome of the war.

The support of our naval forces in the Atlantic was relatively simpler than the logistic problem of the Pacific. Although the Germans derived immense advantage from the possession of submarine bases in France, our own strategic position reckoned in terms of bases was vastly superior to theirs. We had in the United States and Great Britain well developed naval bases and stations not far removed from the scene of conflict. We had some prepared positions in the Caribbean, to which had been added, in 1940, the British bases leased in "exchange" for our over-age destroyers. Iceland had been occupied by the British in the summer of

1940, and a year later, by United States forces. The war against the submarine, moreover, was not entirely new. We had in the First World War a pattern of experience which made it simpler to assess the tactical problem and to determine therefrom the probable logistic requirements.

The critical need in the Atlantic was not for the means of supporting our forces, but for the forces themselves. Patrol craft, destroyers, aircraft, and small carriers—escort craft of all kinds—were in demand. The task in the Atlantic was thus primarily one of procurement, of building and equipping the necessary ships and aircraft, of training their crews, of developing and supplying the highly technical equipment by which the anti-submarine war was successfully waged. This is not to minimize the importance or the magnitude of the supporting task, to which must be added the deployment of forces required for strengthening our hemisphere defense. But as compared with the situation in the Pacific at the outbreak of the war the physical structure of support in the Atlantic was already well defined.

Organization for War

THE accomplishment of the logistic task imposed by these dictates of our naval strategy involved a multitude of efforts large and small, direct and indirect, stretching from the point where supplies were furnished and services rendered back through many stages and processes to the point where they received their original impetus in the determination of policy and the direction of action on a broad scale. It would be a mistake to concentrate attention entirely upon either end of this process. In theory it may be regarded as a single function performed in many specialized ways and by many different hands, high and low, but all contributing toward the accomplishment of a single end. We assume in theory that all action which conduces in detail to the furtherance of an effort is comprehended at least in general terms in the broad policies at the center. The assumption upon which organization and action are predicated is thus one of centralized determination and decentralized execution of policy.

But in practice the natural pyramid of organization and effort, which springs to mind in explanation of the theory, does not always apply. Many of the most outstanding accomplishments originate without reference to broad policy, sometimes in opposition to it. In some instances the power of decision in smaller matters may be delegated so habitually that the cumulative practical effect is to transfer authority for the determination of large matters. Policies conceived at the center may not always rest upon the best information as to the actual conditions to which they are to apply, or, on the other hand, a policy soundly conceived may be mutilated progressively in transmission through subordinate echelons by the limited outlook of local agencies. Such incoherences are the natural concomitant of all large, organized human effort; they are inevitably multiplied by the atmosphere of urgency and uncertainty in which war is carried on.

Departure from the theoretical pattern of action and responsibility was particularly common during the days succeeding our entrance into the war. The immediate steps required to activate our defenses were problems of local action, either foreseen or not foreseen in the formation of war plans. Such for example were the initial steps taken to repair the damaged ships at Pearl Harbor, the alerting and mobilization of local defense forces within the Naval Districts, the disposition of fleet forces still in operable condition. But decisions of this kind affected only the resources already available on the scene. Most of our war resources, on the other hand, were potential, in process, or undelivered. Decisions affecting these were the business of the central command.

Naval organization at the outbreak of the war was unfortunately ill-suited to the demands which such a war were to impose upon it. In particular, the distribution of authority and responsibility among its principal agencies was poorly adapted to the prosecution of the logistic task presented. The task of logistics breaks down logically into three broad divisions—planning or the determination of requirements, procurement, and distribution. These broad divisions themselves are but a grouping of many subordinate logistic tasks, some of which were, in fact, performed on a peacetime basis by the Navy. But the interrelation of elements within the broad task of logistics had never been clearly defined, and, it is not necessary to add, was not reflected in the form and structure of the naval organization itself. The result, in part deriving from inadequate organization, was that many important functions of logistics were not performed at all, others were performed in part, but with inadequate resources, while almost all tasks of logistic administration were performed without adequate reference to each other or to the larger, ultimate end they served.

The key to the system's inadequacy, insofar as it may be explained in terms of organization, lay primarily in the relation of the Chief of Naval Operations to the technical and material bureaus, under whose auspices the actual work of provision was done and to whom the funds were allotted. A traditional fear that too much authority over material means in the hands of the Chief of Naval Operations would make the Secretary a "figurehead" and would invade the rightful province of the bureaus had militated constantly against the creation of central military direction over material matters in the Navy Department. The result was compromise, a system of checks and balances persisting until the outbreak of war, in which as we have seen the Chief of Naval Operations was "charged with the operations of the Fleet, and with the preparation and readiness of plans for its use in war," but had no power to direct the bureaus toward the accomplishment of any action necessary to carry out plans. In peacetime the condition of bureau autonomy thus created was of no serious consequence. Maintenance of the fleet was

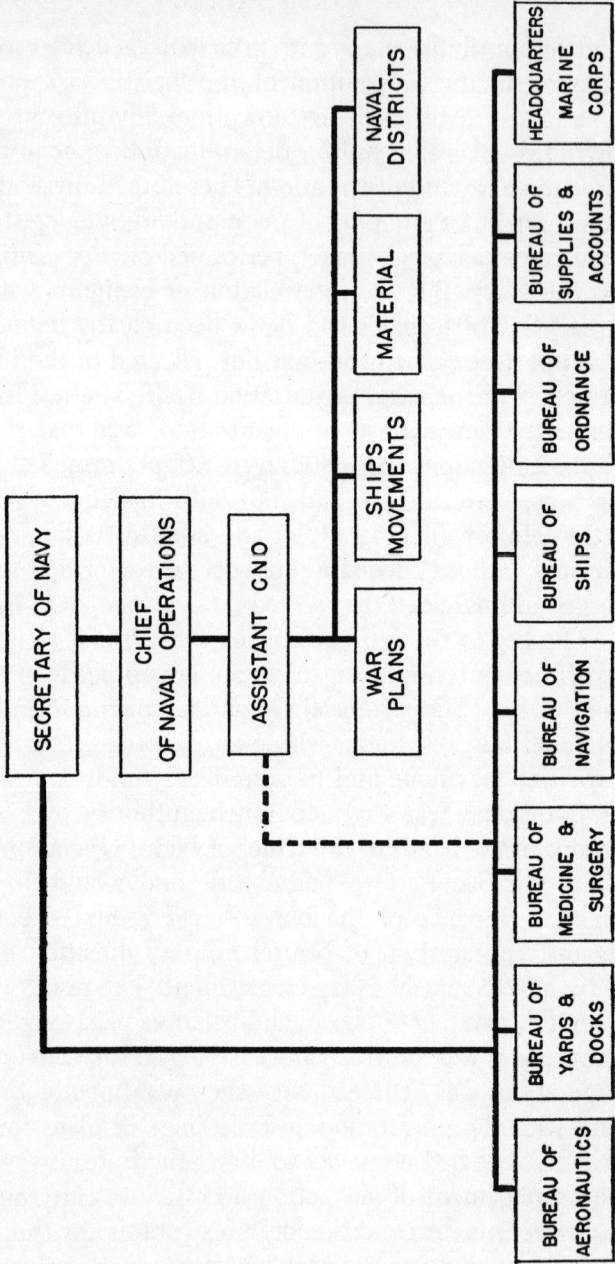

ORGANIZATION OF PRINCIPAL LOGISTICS AGENCIES IN THE NAVY DEPARTMENT AT THE OUTBREAK OF WAR

SECRETARY OF NAVY

CHIEF OF NAVAL OPERATIONS

ASSISTANT CNO

WAR PLANS

SHIPS MOVEMENTS

MATERIAL

NAVAL DISTRICTS

BUREAU OF AERONAUTICS

BUREAU OF YARDS & DOCKS

BUREAU OF MEDICINE & SURGERY

BUREAU OF NAVIGATION

BUREAU OF SHIPS

BUREAU OF ORDNANCE

BUREAU OF SUPPLIES & ACCOUNTS

HEADQUARTERS MARINE CORPS

largely a routine matter; requirements were known, expenditures were carefully estimated well in advance, and supply flowed automatically. In short, the operations of the logistic part of the naval establishment were spelled out in detail in the terms of the naval budget. But then, as the well-worn anecdote goes, "war came and threw everything out of gear."

The outbreak of the war brought to the fore at once the problem of gearing the material efforts of the naval establishment to the military direction of the war. Inevitably this task devolved upon the Chief of Naval Operations, for it was in his hands that the military plan was formed, to whose execution all material efforts were addressed. Lacking personnel, procedures adaptable to the tempo and urgency of the task, and above all, the habit and practice of direction, the Office of Naval Operations was ill-equipped to take up the task.

The Office of Naval Operations was hampered, moreover, by the dual load of operational and administrative work for which it was responsible. The definition of strategic aims and plans and the direction of forces were constantly entangled with matters affecting material support to the detriment of both essential lines of activity.

The first step, therefore, in the necessary reorganization was the creation on December 18, 1941, of the Office of Commander in Chief of the United States Fleet, with headquarters in the Navy Department. To him was given "supreme command of the operating forces of the several fleets of the United States Navy and the operating forces of the naval coastal frontier commands" with responsibility "under the general direction of the Secretary of the Navy, to the President of the United States therefor." To the Commander in Chief was also assigned the preparation and execution of current war plans, while to the Chief of Naval Operations there remained "the preparation of war plans from the long range point of view." The Commander in Chief would keep the Chief of Naval Operations informed of "the logistic and other needs of the operating forces," and the latter would furnish information on the extent to which they could be met.

The obvious intent of the Executive Order creating a Commander in Chief was to set up a supreme agency of military direction free to devote itself exclusively to the formation and execution of strategic plans, while the Chief of Naval Operations would similarly be enabled to concentrate upon matters of material support. But the division as specified in the terms of the order was neither clear nor complete. The retention of war planning "from the long range point of view" suggested that the Chief of Naval Operations would still concern himself with certain aspects of strategy, which by their broader nature must ultimately exercise governance over the current war plans developed by the Commander in Chief. It may also be noted, that with respect to the direction and coordination of material efforts the legal status of the Chief of Naval Operations over the bureaus remained unchanged.

The immediate effect of the separation was to precipitate an extended discussion as to what sections and divisions of the old Office of Naval Operations would be assigned to Admiral King, the new Commander in Chief, and what should remain with Admiral Stark, the Chief of Naval Operations. Unfortunately no clear distinction between the purely operational and the administrative functions of the original office had ever been maintained, with the result that it was not always easy to distinguish exactly under which category a particular section might belong. Strategy and logistics are not in fact separable elements in the conduct of war. Nor are they, apart from importance, coequal. The establishment of two coequal offices in which the functions of one were contributory to the other and in which the Chief of Naval Operations had cognizance of major matters of strategy was bound to encounter serious difficulties.

The result was to throw the supreme command of the

Navy into a state of uncertainty and confusion. Early in February a tentative formula was developed by the General Board, which appeared to the Secretary to have "pretty well defined the whole operation so there will be no twilight zones" and to Admiral King as "entirely satisfactory." But if understanding had been reached upon the proper relation between the two offices, it was short-lived. On March 13, upon the recommendation of the Secretary, the President signed Executive Order 9076, authorizing the combining of the duties of Commander in Chief and Chief of Naval Operations under one officer who should hold the double title, with responsibility to the President for the "conduct of the war." As Chief of Naval Operations he was charged under the direction of the Secretary with the "preparation, readiness, and logistic support of the operating forces . . . of the United States Navy and with the coordination and direction of effort to this end of the bureaus and offices of the Navy Department. . . ."

The most significant part of the order from the point of view of logistic organization was the creation of a Vice Chief of Naval Operations clothed with "all necessary authority" for executing the plans and policies of the Commander in Chief and Chief of Naval Operations so far as pertained to the duties of the latter office. The Commander in Chief was thus in principle left free to concentrate upon the strategic direction of the war. At the same time it was presumed that major plans and policies determined at this highest level would comprehend both strategic and logistic matters as suggested in the dual office. The Vice Chief, whose office would, in fact, be the principal logistic agency, was therefore placed in a subordinate relationship to the organ of military direction, but at the same time he was given the power to direct the bureaus in their own separate and contributory tasks. The basic lines of organization and function were thus in theory brought into correspondence with each other.

One other development in organization affecting responsibility for logistic matters was of paramount importance. The issue of what authority the Chief of Naval Operations should have over the task of procurement had long stood in doubt. Within his office a shadowy cognizance had always been exercised over material programs and procurement, but as the national mobilization expanded in the immediate prewar years and various "super agencies" burgeoned in the government, the small section in Naval Operations responsible for working with these agencies had failed to keep pace. The vast litany of materials allocation, priorities, production facilities, statistics, clearance, legal and other procurement problems grew rapidly beyond the capacity of the few naval officers assigned to master it. Under existing policy expert civilian assistants could not be brought into the military branch with rank commensurate with their abilities. The Materials Section reflected the general weakness of the Office of Naval Operations in its important relation with the bureaus; it lacked information and had itself insufficient administrative status under the Chief of Naval Operations. Since the establishment in June 1940 of an Under Secretary of the Navy specifically charged with the procurement program, moreover, the actual work involved had passed more and more into the Secretary's own office. The Materials Section under the Chief of Naval Operations was little more than a vestigial appendix.

. In October, anticipating the outbreak of war by only a few weeks the section was enlarged into a division, but the real sources of its weakness were not removed. The division continued in existence, performing to the satisfaction of no one either in the Navy or in the Office of Production Management, which was dependent upon it for necessary information and cooperation. At the end of December, Mr. Ferdinand Eberstadt, then Deputy Director of Production Management, recommended to the Secretary a number of changes in the Navy's Materials Division which he believed necessary for the requirements of his own office. He laid particular emphasis upon the need for drawing all the Navy's procurement managing agencies together and urged that they be placed in the Secretary's own office. One month later, on January 30, the Materials Division was abolished, and there was set up immediately under the Under Secretary a new Office of Procurement and Material to coordinate all material procurement activities and supervise programs for the procurement of ships and other materials. The function of procurement itself was thus removed from the Office of Naval Operations and from the sphere of what was to constitute military logistics.

The removal of procurement from the province of military direction was perhaps necessary and inevitable under the conditions then prevailing. Involving as it did a close relation with civilian agencies of government and private industry, concerned with matters of civil economy and business procedure for which few naval officers had either training or inclination, the management of wartime procurement unquestionably belonged under civilian auspices. But under such an arrangement, if actual procurement programs were to remain sensitive and responsive to military requirements, there was need of a strong liaison between the Office of the Secretary by which procurement would be managed and the Office of Naval Operations by which requirements were determined. There would be need also, as long-range programs developed, of an efficient instrument in the military organization by which strategic requirements could be translated into firm and comprehensive logistic plans for the guidance of procuring agencies.

The ultimate result of these various changes in organization was the emergence in light etching of a group of tasks and functions which were to comprise what may be called the logistic support system of the Navy. Of the three major tasks of logistics, procurement was excluded from immediate military cognizance. Sequentially administration of the logistic task would begin and end under military auspices.

A "plan" or requirement would be formulated by the logistic planners and passed to the bureaus for fulfillment. Coordination of that phase of bureau activity would be the responsibility of the Office of Procurement and Material. As goods became available from industrial sources, however, they would pass once more into the logistic system for distribution throughout the structure of naval support.

As the new-found naval organization addressed itself to the actual logistic task in hand—the construction of bases; the movement by land, sea, and air of men and materials; and the selection, assembly, storage and organization of the multitude of elements required to develop the physical structure of support, the organization which must breathe life into the system was only roughly sketched out. The broad concepts under which it must operate were at best only dimly perceived. The high-level reorganization described above was in process, moreover, over a period of several months during which it was necessary that plans be made and put into execution, however ill conceived the planning and however inadequate the means for executing them. Throughout the naval establishment the same process of readjustment to a war footing was going on at every echelon, accompanied by the substantive task of providing support and reinforcement.

Plans and Programs

THE result of this dual process of reorganization and substantive effort was that initial steps in providing logistic support to operating forces were taken with little reference to ordinary lines of procedure and organization, either existing or proposed. Nor could the logical sequence of steps, beginning with a definition of strategic aims and passing through the determination of logistic requirements, procurement, and distribution be followed. The immediate response to the conditions presented by the outbreak of war was a spontaneous "turning to" at every point in the existing system. The centers of interest during this critical period were in most instances the operating agencies, both in the field and in the Navy Department, the points where resources existed or might be mobilized quickly. District organizations, supply depots, port directors, and field agencies of the bureaus shouldered the immediate responsibility. Within the Navy Department the burden fell mainly upon the bureaus, which were functioning entities possessing some experience in the actual procurement, assembly, and movement of supplies. Central direction both in outlining the strategic plan and in defining in rough form its logistic requirements came principally from the new office of the Commander in Chief.

Under existing conditions logistic planning, in the sense of long-range determination of requirements, was impossible. Certain major programs of procurement and production needed, of course, to be set in motion at once. Requirements for combatant ships and to a lesser extent aircraft had largely been fixed before the war in the programs for 20 per cent increase and for a two-ocean Navy authorized by the Congress in 1938 and 1940. Additional vessels, particularly destroyers and other small categories suitable for anti-submarine warfare were required, but insofar as their numbers were not automatically determined by programs for larger vessels, they were dependent upon the immediate strategic situation in the Atlantic, and the initial program goals were set therefore by the Commander in Chief himself. A beginning had also been made on the auxiliary vessel program in the bill of 1941 authorizing an increase of 500,000 tons and 400 smaller craft for local defense purposes. All of these programs were already in the design or production phases. The problem, therefore, was one of expediting delivery on contracts which were in most cases let, rather than of immediately laying on additional programs defined in terms of long range strategic requirements.

In order to secure the most rapid delivery in desired sequence of all classes of vessels it was necessary to survey the construction program as a whole and to assign priorities to various much needed types. On December 17, 1941, the Bureau of Ships presented its first "Master Plan for Maximum Ship Construction." This was developed by the Office of Naval Operations, the General Board, the Commander in Chief, the Maritime Commission, Congress, and the President into the guiding document for the Navy's vessel construction program. The plan as approved by the President in February 1942 was subjected to many modifications during succeeding months and in its original form it neglected many categories such as destroyer escorts and landing craft which had later to be greatly expanded. It was, however, a remarkable instance of rapid assessment of requirements and possibilities, and served as the principal guide to other bureaus in the procurement of necessary components and materials.

The inception of the landing craft program is an excellent illustration of many of the difficulties which beset long-range planning in these early months. On the initiative of the Marine Corps, experiments in landing craft had been begun at least as early as 1936. After 1939, an added impetus was given by the interest of the British government in landing craft types. But at the outbreak of the war, although certain minimum requirements had been fixed for vehicle and personnel landing boats, no agreement upon design had yet been reached. Amphibious craft perhaps more than any other kind of naval vessel must be tailored to the exigencies of combat, and until we had some experience of actual conditions of assault, discussions of design remained highly conjectural and academic. Requirements in terms of numbers and types, moreover, were directly dependent upon the character of operations to be undertaken, a judgment impossible to reach at this time. They were dependent as well upon the types of tanks and vehicles to be developed by the

Army for use in assault operations, and it was impossible to stabilize either in design or in number at an early stage in the war planning, lest the Navy be committed to a program of craft which would soon be wholly obsolete. In larger types these various difficulties were not as serious an impediment, and it was possible almost at once to set up projects for the three larger types of craft (LST or Landing Ship-Tanks, LCI or Landing Craft-Infantry and LCT or Landing Craft-Tanks). These projects began to bear fruit about June 1, 1942. Not until almost the end of 1942, however, was it possible to make any firm plans on landing boats and tank lighters, with the result that programs developed more tardily.

One of the major items of logistic support, construction and other equipment necessary for the establishment of advance bases, fortunately received early attention. The development of the advance base program will be treated in some detail in subsequent pages. Under the head of planning, however, we may note the initial steps taken to map out a long-range program. Picking up from the peacetime program to construct advance bases in the Atlantic and Pacific, the Office of Naval Operations began in mid-January 1942 to provide for base requirements once the initial effort in the Pacific had exhausted the Navy's reserves of equipment. On January 15, the War Plans Division under Rear Admiral Turner laid out a program calling for the procurement and assembly of material for four main advanced bases and twelve secondary bases, the former to be capable of providing logistic support for a major part of the fleet, the latter for a small task group of light forces. Facilities were determined largely in terms of those already provided for repair ships and aircraft and destroyer tenders. On February 12, the program was defined in more specific terms. Materials for one major base and three secondary bases were to be assembled at designated depots by July 1. The remainder were to follow at the rate of one major and three secondary bases per quarter. It was provided as well that certain bases should be for cold zones and others for temperate and tropical zones.

Major and secondary base units were designated as "Lions" and "Cubs" respectively and to them shortly was added a third unit called "Acorn" which included the personnel and materials required to construct and operate an air base. Lions, Cubs, and Acorns became henceforth the standard units upon which the Navy was to develop its advance base system, the goals of procurement, and the origin of subsequent requirements.

Requirements for ordnance and electronic equipment, fuel, aircraft, personnel, training facilities, and the great mass of detailed accessory equipment were fixed in most cases by the cognizant bureaus on the basis of overall plans for the expansion of the fleet. In this respect, however, the Master Plan for ship construction provided only a general and approximate guide. It left considerable leeway in the formulation of detailed plans and requirements for independent judgment by the procuring agencies themselves, and since "lead time"—the time required to produce an item for use in a given project or operation—was an all-important factor, the ability of bureau planning agencies to estimate accurately the long-range requirements for essential components determined the success or failure of major programs. Coordination of various programs for ship components was supplied largely on a personal basis by Rear Admiral W. S. Farber, first as Director of Fleet Maintenance and later as Assistant Chief of Naval Operations for Maintenance.

As Admiral King stated in his first report to the Secretary, it was evident at once that no matter how much material of all types was produced during 1942, it would not be enough. In practice, therefore, few limits were set upon forecast requirements; procurement agencies moved ahead into the actual task of procuring subject only to the limited availability of raw materials and plant capacity. The nearest approximation to logistic planning which could be applied at this time was to determine the specific requirements of each individual base expedition and each continental facility, and in the case of overseas movements to supply some coordination to the assembly, loading, and transportation of the component men and materials.

The lack of suitable personnel also stood in the way of long-range logistic planning at this time. Qualified personnel were in great demand both under the Commander in Chief and the Chief of Naval Operations. Almost all the officers originally assigned to War Planning under the Chief of Naval Operations were transferred to the Office of the Commander in Chief, where they became engaged either in strategic planning or in the day-to-day administration and expediting of current logistic plans. The small remnant of a planning staff which remained in the Office of Operations was entirely inadequate for the task of long-range planning. The alternatives were either to shift long-range logistic planning to the strategic planners under the Commander in Chief, to place it upon other officers under the Chief of Naval Operations primarily responsible for implementing plans, or to suspend the development of comprehensive planning.

One further obstacle may be noted. During this early phase, when most of our resources were still in this country, the detailed task of planning and execution which ordinarily would fall upon the Theater or Expeditionary Force Commander devolved now upon the central command and other continental agencies. Not until some reserves had been built up in the advanced areas could the burden of detailed planning and administration be delegated. Gradually, as reserves of material were accumulated and certain basic procedures in the task of distribution were put in practice, logistic planning became possible. But during the early months the day-to-day task claimed almost the whole attention of the Navy's administration.

Advance Bases

THE establishment of advance bases in the Pacific during the early months of the war was primarily an effort to make up in a brief period for the failures of preparation stretching back over many years. Within a few weeks or months it was necessary to create means of support which informed opinion of only a few years before had considered would require a period of years. Early in 1941, Admiral Stark had stated apropos of a war plan to capture and develop Truk as an American base for operations in the Western Pacific that "As a practical matter, the installation of maintenance facilities, such as shops, wharves, and dry docks, is a laborious process, taking under the best circumstances two to five years." Admiral William D. Leahy in the hearings on the Hepburn report in 1938 had set a figure of five years for the establishment of a major fleet base at Guam. He had not believed it possible "even should we press our efforts, to provide a first-class, fully developed advanced naval base at Guam by 1946," the date set for Philippine Independence. An underlying assumption in much of the prewar agitation for better development of advance base positions had been that bases required time for development and must therefore be begun before the outbreak of war.

Unlike the positions of strategic importance in the Atlantic area and to a lesser extent in the Caribbean and South America, the important outposts of the Pacific were tiny atolls or small tropical islands entirely lacking in industrial resources and in many cases lacking also in such rudimentary elements as potable water, habitation, local labor, fresh food, and roads and docks. Almost everything required to support a working population of any dimensions would have to be brought in and established before work itself could begin. Climate, terrain, unhealthy environment, and distance offered positive obstacles as well to their investiture in any strength.

Fortunately the Navy was not entirely without advantages and experience as it undertook the difficult task in the beginning of 1942. The program of naval expansion begun in 1936 had given impetus to the development of the shore establishment, as may be seen in the rise of appropriations for the Bureau of Yards and Docks from $7,000,000 in 1938 to $454,000,000 in 1941. The major portion of these appropriations was destined, it is true, for the expansion of our continental shore establishment, but a part of it was for advance base construction. All contributed to the expansion and strengthening of the Bureau of Yards and Docks, upon which would rest the responsibility for the provision of construction and base materials.

Some experience in the construction of advance bases undertaken before the war, moreover, was to prove invaluable in suggesting the methods and concepts, and in providing a small backlog of the materials, which would be employed in the wartime task. In 1939 Congress had appropriated $65,000,000 to begin the expansion of those air facilities most urgently recommended by the Hepburn Board, notably at Hawaii, Wake, Midway, Johnston, Palmyra, Kodiak, Sitka, and San Juan, Puerto Rico. Other appropriations were made for public works projects within the United States and its possessions, under which contracts were let in 1940, for example, for two additional dry docks at Pearl Harbor.

Conditions at most of these outlying points approximated those which were later to be encountered in the South and Central Pacific. The Navy received, therefore, a small foretaste of the task ahead. At the same time a beginning was made in securing from industry a few of the non-standard items of equipment necessary for advance base construction. In setting the Hepburn Board's program in motion the Navy had thus gone into production in the construction of advanced bases. Yet the methods of construction and of organization did not differ much, except in scale, from those which had been employed by Pan American Airways, for example, in building commercial aviation facilities on Wake and Midway. Most of the facilities employed were of conventional design. The pace of construction as compared with that of the war was leisurely, and there were, of course, no threats of attack and no large accompanying garrison force.

A second significant development grew out of the need for an adequate defensive screen on the western side of the Panama Canal. Early in 1940, upon his return from a cruise in the Panama area, the President called the attention of the Navy Department to the need for air patrols west of the Canal, and both the General Board of the Navy and the Joint Army-Navy Board began studies of the problem. The solution offered was a constant seaplane patrol based partly on tenders and partly on shore facilities in the Galapagos and in other parts of Central America. Although the possibility of making military installations on foreign soil during peacetime was remote, the Navy Department began preparations for the investment of the Galapagos if and when the necessity arose.

To provide against this contingency the Chief of Naval Operations on June 1, 1940, requested the Bureau of Aeronautics to draw up plans and guide the other bureaus in the procurement of materials to be assembled in the Canal Zone. This the Bureau did, and ultimately the lists of materials drawn up for the Galapagos were utilized by the Chief of Naval Operations for the preparation of other air base units. "Galapagos units" came to represent a standardized set of materials and facilities intended to fit generally the needs of any similar project, but not custom-designed for any particular base. After the lease of British bases in the summer of 1940 a board headed by Rear Admiral J. W. Greenslade, similar in composition and purpose to the Hepburn Board, had drawn up a program for air facilities development in the Caribbean in which the "Galapagos units" proved a useful tool for the rapid planning and assembly of material components.

A second step of importance in the preparation of the Galapagos bases was the establishment at the suggestion of the Bureau of Yards and Docks of an Advance Base Depot in the Canal Zone. The function of the depot was to provide a place where machinery and other equipment could not only be stored, but also kept in operable condition. The depot in the Canal Zone was shortly followed by others situated in strategic assembly areas in the United States.

The greatest impetus in the prewar preparation of advance bases came, however, from the plan to establish four bases in the United Kingdom prior to the outbreak of the war. In January 1941, the United States agreed in staff conversations with the British to assume some of the responsibility for the security of sea lanes in the North Atlantic. The creation of a Support Force in the Atlantic Fleet composed of destroyers and patrol planes to carry out the neutrality patrol posed the problem of their support at the eastern terminus of the sea lanes. In February, a mission headed by Captain Louis E. Denfeld visited England and reported in favor of the establishment of four bases in the British Isles—two for air support and two for destroyers—all to be undertaken with the greatest urgency.

The establishment of these bases and the preparations for them were to be of great significance in our subsequent base-building efforts in the Pacific. The passage of the Lend-Lease Act in March 1941 opened the way to a much greater expenditure than had hitherto been possible. Materials for the bases could be assembled and shipped under Lend-Lease appropriations for British use, and in the event of our actual involvement in the war they would be available for American occupation. In any event advance bases would be established on a scale hitherto unattempted.

Bureaus were instructed to proceed at once with the procurement and assembly of materials. In particular the

Bureau of Yards and Docks now moved into the procurement of advance base materials on a large scale. Contracts were awarded to the George A. Fuller Company and Merrit-Chapman and Scott Corporation for the purchase, fabrication, crating, storing, and marking of material and equipment with its main base of operations at Temporary Aviation Facilities at Quonset Point, Rhode Island, the forerunner of the Advance Base Depot, Davisville. The equipment of the new shore facilities was to be roughly the equivalent of that contained in destroyer and seaplane tenders, and the allowance lists for these vessels formed, therefore, the basis for planning and procurement of materials. "Galapagos units" were also used as a guide, and in addition there was an extensive reworking of the various lists by the bureaus, which resulted in extensive modification and elaboration of the earlier allowances, particularly in a greater proportion of base construction materials furnished by the Bureau of Yards and Docks in addition to the technical equipment furnished by the other bureaus.

The emphasis upon base construction equipment furnished also an opportunity for the large-scale development of items of special design which had hitherto been languishing for want of funds and support. Early in 1940, two planning officers in the Bureau of Yards and Docks, Commander J. N. Laycock and Lt. Commander E. S. Huntington, had taken up the problem of rapidly projecting supporting shore facilities into a broad area of naval operations such as the Pacific. The solution, they believed, lay in the design and development of highly specialized, prefabricated and portable equipment capable of mass production and adaptable to varying conditions. During 1940 they undertook the experimental design of certain units, among which were the Quonset Hut, an adaptation of a British model; portable stills and generators; and a prefabricated pontoon. This last was a hollow steel unit, 4′x7′x4′ in dimensions, and capable of combination into an indefinite number of larger units such as rafts, small dry docks, landing stages, and bridges. Its widespread though unauthorized use as a shower tank in the Pacific Area helped to provide us with perhaps the best-washed army in the history of tropical warfare. Commander Laycock tried without much success during 1940 to secure funds for further experimentation and for placing a few orders with industry which might pave the way for tooling for large-scale production. Funds were not available. The inception of the United Kingdom base program, however, opened the way to a larger effort, and Commander Laycock and his associates were given free rein.

As it developed, the United Kingdom program proved useful in many ways not originally contemplated. Other base development programs were getting underway, and since shipments from Quonset to the British Isles did not proceed as rapidly as expected, the practice developed of drawing on Quonset for materials needed urgently in other quarters. Most of the diversions were small and were generally made without prejudice to the United Kingdom program. But between August and October, six shiploads of materials were sent to advance bases in Nova Scotia, Newfoundland, and Brazil, and smaller items of critical importance were made available for Iceland, the Aleutians and even the Pacific islands. Quonset became, as a result, an important depot for the assembly and shipment of advance base materials.

Another by-product of the program was the formation of the first specialized advance base units of personnel. No authority existed in 1941 for the formation of Construction Battalions, and it was necessary to rely for the construction of the bases themselves upon Irish and British labor. For personnel to man the bases when completed the Navy drew sparingly from its more experienced rates and around these nuclei grouped seamen, mostly fresh from boot camp, who were given specialized training for the tasks they were to perform. Most of the personnel thus gathered and trained were to be rushed to Pearl Harbor for more urgent work there immediately after the beginning of war. In this role they were of great value; and at the same time their earlier assembly and training had provided a useful pattern of experience.

In one respect, the United Kingdom program did not provide a pattern of experience useful for the future. Since the project was carried out under the terms of Lend-Lease and since the Neutrality Act still forbade the employment of American ships for that purpose, shipping had to be provided by the British. Thus the many lessons derived from the procurement, design, and assembly of advance base materials did not extend into the field of providing transportation or of coordinating advance base movements with the procurement and operation of shipping. But in matters pertaining directly to advance base construction the preparations for the British bases were of incalculable importance. In them and in the earlier programs of smaller scale lay the seeds of method and the precious backlog of materials by which a much greater task was to be carried out, and without which our situation at the outbreak of war would have been profoundly more perilous than it was.

The first of the naval bases to be established in the Pacific after the outbreak of war was a fueling station on the island of Bora-Bora in the Society Group. The expedition itself was not large, consisting in all, of approximately 3,900 Army troops as a garrison, and 500 naval personnel to construct and operate the tank farm, which was the principal object of the expedition. It met no resistance from the enemy and was never attacked. It was not destined for expansion into a major base, and its subsequent role in the history of the Pacific campaign was minor. Yet "Bobcat" as the expedition was called in code, has a significance of its own, for it was conceived and dispatched under the most exacting conditions; it brought immediately into sharp focus the many difficulties inherent in the establishment of Pacific bases, and provided, therefore, a small but highly concentrated capsule of experience for the future.

The expedition had its origin on Christmas Day, 1941, when Admiral King requested that a study be made of the site for a fueling base in the South Pacific. On December 30, the selection of Bora-Bora was recommended. On January 4, the first rough plan of the expedition was issued in the form of a memorandum from Admiral Turner to his Army counterpart, General Gerow, the Assistant Chief of Staff for Plans. Between that time and January 27, when the expedition sailed, personnel and material were assembled, ships selected and armed, and loading carried on in three separate ports. It was a joint undertaking necessitating close coordination between the two services. Moreover, the Navy's part of the expeditionary force was not at the time it was ordered, a unit in being; it was the immediate precursor of the first Construction Battalion and had to be organized out of green and untrained personnel on entirely new lines of command. Material had to be assembled from points all over the country. That the expedition was able to sail from Charleston only two days behind schedule was, under the circumstances, a considerable achievement in itself.

The Joint Plan for Operation Bobcat, issued on January 8, could never have been executed within such a brief space of time had it not been for the prior existence of the United Kingdom project. The major portion of the base and construction equipment was drawn from the reserves at Quonset. Officers in the Navy Department who had gained experience working on the British bases guided and directed the assembly for Bora-Bora. The concept of advance base units of personnel served also to provide a general framework for the organization of the naval unit.

Participation in the preparation of the expedition followed the same general lines that had applied in the previous peacetime movements. Bureaus, the Office of Naval Operations, and field agencies all joined in a loose and informal association whose cohesiveness was provided by the urgency of the task and determination to see it accomplished rather than by any formal lines of authority or organization. The principal agencies were the Bureau of Yards and Docks and the Base Maintenance Division of CNO, acting under the general guidance of Admiral Turner of the War Plans Division. Plans, as prepared by Naval Operations, had summarized most of the materials to be procured and assembled by the bureaus and had stipulated also that materials would be loaded in the order of priority of their use at destination. More detailed loading plans were prepared by the Naval Transportation Service, whose responsibility it was to provide shipping for the expedition. The importance of correct loading by those who planned and directed the expedition was clearly understood. But assembly of materials at the loading points, particularly at the Naval Supply Depot, Charleston, was so hurried and confused, the ships ultimately made available so unsuited to the loading plans previously drawn up, and shipments so poorly marked and unidentifiable, that it was impossible to accomplish an orderly loading in the desired manner.

Selection of vessels for the expedition was also attended with difficulty. Of the six vessels required, the Navy itself could provide only three, and the remainder had to be furnished by the Maritime Commission on hurried notice. They were unarmed, one turned out to have been damaged and required a substitute, and all were lacking in the slings and cargo nets requisite for discharging, a fact discovered only upon arrival at Bora-Bora. Stevedore labor at Charleston was singularly inefficient, and there developed as well many details of arrangement between the Army and Navy commanding officers, which, together with the work in progress in arming the civilian vessels, impeded the loading operations. Even so, the convoy would have been able to meet its scheduled date of departure on January 25, had it not developed at the last moment that the substituted vessel, the *Arthur Middleton*, required ballasting to compensate for the weight of the armament installed.

The difficulties and confusion encountered at Charleston were mild, however, compared to those experienced upon the arrival of the expedition at Bora-Bora. Discharging was carried on without reference to priority. All cargo had to be lightered ashore with hastily assembled pontoon lighters and a few small boats. Materials were so unidentifiable that crates and boxes had to be broken into indiscriminately in search of urgently needed items. Many of the personnel, both Army and Navy, were drawn away from their primary duties in order to make up in stevedoring manpower for the disorderliness of the loading. On February 28, eleven days after arrival, five of the six ships were less than one quarter unloaded; six weeks later two of the ships had still not completed discharge. Delayed turnaround, the greatest evil of the shipping effort, had thus begun to take its toll of shipping. The effect of bad loading on the progress of the base itself was succinctly stated by Commander Sanders, the naval commander: "I believe that we could have saved three to four weeks . . . if the ships had been properly loaded. . . ."

Lack of information as to the exact nature of the terrain led to errors in planning which produced even greater delays. Naval sources of information were exceedingly scanty, the only map of the island being a French publication of the mid-nineteenth century. After the expedition had sailed, the Army uncovered in its Washington staff, a second lieutenant who had visited Bora-Bora, and he was flown to join the expedition en route. His services during the planning stages would have been of far greater value than they were to prove later.

Errors of particular importance concerned the water supply, the condition of roads and bridges, and the topography of the area in which the tank farm was to be constructed. Distilling equipment was insufficient, and naval construction forces were compelled to undertake an extensive water supply project before they could begin upon the fuel tanks. Vehicles drawn from the reserves assembled for the United Kingdom bases proved entirely too heavy for the undeveloped roads of the islands, and bulldozers and graders had been inadequately provided. The land bordering Trevanui Harbor rose sharply from the sea without any intervening plateau so that fuel tanks had to be placed upon the hillside on small shelves blasted out of solid rock.

Administrative difficulties also plagued the expedition almost from its inception. The senior officer of Bobcat was the Army commander, and it was provided, therefore, that except for the period while troops were actually embarked, he should exercise unified command. The primary purpose of the expedition, however, was the establishment of a naval fueling base, and it followed that this purpose was not always clearly kept to the fore in the direction of activity on the island. The Joint Plan had provided, moreover, that subsistence for the total force once landed on the island would be provided by the Army commander, but some time passed before his relation to the Commanding General in the Central Pacific had been properly established and maintenance shipments provided. Meanwhile, although rations were adequate, the ubiquitous Spam of later fame became the principal item of diet.

The difficulties, large and small, encountered in the establishment of Bobcat could be recited at length. In sum, they represented in minuscule many of the problems which had to be surmounted in the construction of all advance bases in the Pacific. Bora-Bora illustrated clearly the importance in planning advance bases of accurate and comprehensive information on the character of the task ahead. The inadequacy of personnel and equipment so pointedly apparent in this case led to broader thinking in the planning of other expeditions. The importance of transport and of prior assembly of materials before loading was also made clear, and all difficulties served to bring out the necessity when possible for a longer period of preparation between the strategic conception of a task and its logistic accomplishment. It illustrated, finally, the urgent necessity of greater cohesiveness in the administrative structure and procedure of the Navy's logistic organization.

If the expedition to Bora-Bora was in many respects a "comedy of errors," it was not a failure. The delays in unloading the convoy and in erecting defense installations made it particularly susceptible to attack, but happily no such attack was made. Meanwhile, an advance base position had been assumed in the Pacific providing us not only with one link in the chain to Australia, but also with a practical lesson for application in the future. Bora-Bora was an invaluable rehearsal for larger undertakings. The highly developed technique of 1944, under which the installation of a huge establishment like Guam was smoothly carried out, had its origin in the bungling of Bora-Bora.

The Joint Plan for the Bobcat expedition had scarcely been issued before studies were under way for the establishment of additional bases which would complete the link to Australia. The originating concept of these bases was twofold. Certain of the bases such as those established at Tongatabu, Samoa, and Efate in the New Hebrides involved new installations in areas where little prior preparation had been made. They had, therefore, to embody a whole initial establishment of balanced forces. Others, such as Nandi and Suva in the Fijis, Noumea, New Caledonia, and Auckland, New Zealand, were intended to augment and strengthen the positions already in the hands of our Australian and New Zealand allies. In these cases, except for Fiji, the development was carried on not on the basis of a single plan conceived at the beginning, but gradually, as new requirements and conditions unfolded. All, however, were to be carried out on a scale considerably greater than that of Bobcat.

Formal notification of the intent to establish bases at Efate, Samoa, and Tongatabu was issued by the Chief of

Naval Operations on March 6, with instruction that convoys should be ready to sail from the East Coast in three weeks and from the West Coast in four. Actually, verbal instructions had already been issued, and the formation and execution of the plans were under way.

All three of the bases were defined as "advanced operating positions" and were clearly parts of a larger pattern developing. For Tongatabu there was required "a protected anchorage and fueling base" to serve also as "a staging point for Army and Navy aircraft operations in the Samoa-Fiji area"; for Efate "a protected anchorage and a strong outpost of land aircraft," serving also for aircraft staging and support in the Fiji-New Caledonia area. For Samoa the plan called for "four strong mutually supporting defensive positions." Tongatabu and Efate would be joint Army-Navy operations; in Samoa the garrison would be made up of Marines.

The procedure for assembling and directing the new expeditions was substantially that which had been employed in the case of Bobcat, though it is notable that certain refinements and improvements had been made. Planning and direction were more centrally concentrated under the Chief of Naval Operations. Particular emphasis was laid upon the necessity for assembly of materials at the loading points as much in advance as possible and for the observance of priority in loading. A further refinement was the division of each movement into three separarate waves or echelons to sail at monthly intervals. Personnel complements and material allowances were considerably increased, and the organization of individual components was, needless to say, vastly improved. The first Construction Battalion, which was divided between Tongatabu and Efate, was a relatively mature assembly compared to the motley little band which was bearing the brunt of labor at Bora-Bora.

The preparation of these three base expeditions had one characteristic in common with Bora-Bora in that all were primarily retail undertakings. Although the projects were carried on concurrently and the convoys, when ready, actually joined at sea, each base was planned as an individual unit. Outfitting lists were made up in minute detail—a process subject to error and entailing delays, which obviously would not serve when the development of advance base movements moved into high gear.

The developments at Noumea, Auckland, and the Fijis began on a small scale at about the same time that the expeditions were formed for Efate and Tongatabu. Throughout the first six months plans were shifting constantly, and although most of the positions to be assumed were fixed in advance the size and character of each fluctuated constantly in the development of plans. By April, however, the decision had been reached to establish a major naval base at Auckland, and to locate there the headquarters of Vice Admiral Ghormley, the South Pacific Commander. Orders were issued creating a Service Squadron Six for the South Pacific Force even before Admiral Ghormley had been designated as Area and Force Commander. The expansion of facilities at Auckland during the first half of 1942 was thus more rapid than at Noumea, but it was to be the latter upon which by the end of the year the greatest effort was concentrated.

The rapid and unforeseen acceleration in the development of these bases was the result in part of increased United States participation in their defense, in part of increased naval activity as at Noumea, and finally of a growing recognition of the need for greatly augmented facilities to support the Solomons offensive launched in August. In the case of the Fijis a plan was drawn and a full expedition dispatched. In Noumea and Auckland, however, no basic plan was provided, and these two bases which were to assume major proportions developed, therefore, without the benefit of an original definition of their purpose and scope. Auckland was destined to be the principal staging point for the Guadalcanal offensive. Noumea had in store an even greater role as the headquarters of the South Pacific Command, an important staging area, and the distributing center for the entire South Pacific Area.

In organizing and directing the shipments to Noumea and Auckland a new and experimental procedure was adopted by the Navy Department, which reversed in part the tendency toward concentrating control under the Chief of Naval Operations. In order to expedite deliveries to tidewater loading points and to provide a greater degree of flexibility, bureaus were authorized to direct shipments on their own responsibility. The procedure did eliminate a certain amount of administrative delay, but it had several unfortunate consequences. The Bureau of Supplies and Accounts, whose responsibility it was to route shipments within the United States concentrated too heavily upon the port of San Francisco with the result that, as shipments increased, the facilities of the Twelfth District were hard put to keep up. Advance notice to the Commandant of goods arriving for transshipment was not adequate, moreover, and it was therefore necessary for the Office of Naval Operations itself to keep watch on prospective shipments by the bureaus and notify the District Commandant. Under this arrangement, however, information in the hands of Operations was necessarily more scanty than it would have been if the shipments had been kept under its surveillance and control from the beginning. The lack of information on cargo movements, together with the constant addition to facilities destined for Noumea, had also a serious effect on the ability of the Naval Transportation Service to estimate accurately the merchant shipping requirements of the Navy. We shall shortly consider the problem of shipping in greater detail, but it may be noted in passing that this lack of information was to prove one of the greatest obstacles to effective coordination between shipping and supply.

By the end of the first six months of war the initial steps had been taken in the assumption of positions and in the establishment of our advance base system in the South

Pacific. The Battle of the Coral Sea had been fought, and although that engagement had not brought to an end the threat of further Japanese penetration to the south, it was possible for the high command to withdraw most of the fleet forces from the South Pacific for concentration against the anticipated thrust at Midway, relying principally for defense in the South Pacific upon the island defense installations already provided.

Certain characteristics inherent in the establishment of these first advance bases stand out in retrospect. Although they all responded directly to one obvious strategic imperative—the maintenance of our lines to Australia and the containing of Japanese forces within the Central Pacific—the working out in detail both of the strategic concept and the logistic support had been extemporized. The pattern as it emerged represented a sum of individual steps taken with only a hazy and incomplete notion of what was ultimately to emerge. That feature is reflected as well in the manner of assembly and preparation of the individual bases themselves. The process as exemplified in the Bora-Bora expedition was essentially retail; each individual base was tailormade. If subsequent efforts proceeded more smoothly than the first, improvement was more the result of a constant application of experience than of a change in basic technique.

Secondly, the construction of most of these bases had been made possible only by the reserves of material accumulated at Quonset before the war. By the time provision had been made for the bases at Efate, Tongatabu, Samoa, and Fiji, these reserves were exhausted. Whatever other advance bases might be established must be provided for out of new resources, procured after the beginning of the war. Upon the soundness and accuracy of advance planning, therefore, would depend the possibility of laying out new bases and augmenting the facilities of those already established.

Finally, the direction of these efforts had been carried out largely in the Navy Department, in detailed planning and supervision of projects which would ordinarily be the duty of theater or field agencies. Much of the credit for successful execution of these plans belongs of course to field agencies such as the Advance Base Depot at Davisville, the Naval Supply Depot at Oakland, and the Port Director in San Francisco. Their work, carried on under the most difficult conditions, showed the wisdom of a system which gave considerable freedom of action to decentralized operating agencies.

In subsequent efforts this retail character of effort in the Navy Department was to give way to an operation which was wholesale, based more on long-range planning and upon the creation of stockpiles from which theater commanders might draw to meet their specific requirements. The development of methods and techniques for operating on a wholesale basis, however, was just beginning.

This initial accomplishment had been characterized by many errors of planning, direction, and execution. Its faults derived principally from lack of experience and from the want of proper coordination of effort. Yet in the main the effort was successful. With inadequate resources, with limited guidance in terms of strategic aims, and in great haste the foundations of the South Pacific campaign had been laid both for defense and for subsequent offense.

Transportation

On December 7, 1941, when the attack was delivered at Pearl Harbor, one of the Navy's principal logistic tasks as defined in Joint Army-Navy War Plans was to "Provide sea transportation for the initial movement and continued support of Army and Navy forces overseas. Man and operate the Army Transport Service." By these two succinct sentences the Navy was committed to one of the major logistic responsibilities of our military effort. During the First World War the transportation of men and materials overseas, together with their protection en route, had been the principal mission of the Navy. It had been performed with out-standing success. Under the present alignment, however, in which the Anglo-American alliance was pitted against German, Italian, and Japanese naval power, it could not be expected that the American Navy would be as free as before to concentrate upon a logistic task. The assignment of this mission to the Navy in the War Plan of 1941, recognized, therefore, a principle of long standing in "Joint Action" policy—that sea transport of military forces should be performed under naval auspices. But it had also to reckon with the likelihood that it would be regarded as a task of secondary importance.

The contrast between conditions in the First and Second World Wars applied not only to the strategic situation but also to the shipping position of the United States in the total allied war effort. In the first war, the British merchant marine was the principal shipping resource of the Allies. Not only did it carry most of the burden of imports into the United Kingdom; it supplied as well many of the wants of the allied powers. Several million tons of British shipping were allocated to French services, and in the movement of American troops overseas slightly over 50 per cent of the load was borne by British tonnage. In 1941, however, the position of the United States was relatively that of Great Britain in the first war. We did not, in 1941, have a tonnage in any way comparable to the British merchant fleet. But there devolved upon the United States, nevertheless, the responsibility for supplementing the shipping resources of the United Nations. Out of American tonnage built or building was to come the surplus capacity by which United Nations deficiencies were made up. For Lend-Lease shipments to Great Britain and Russia; for the import of strategic materials and essential civilian commodities into the United States; and for various other legitimate war purposes, United States shipping resources were subject to a greater proportion of non-military demands than in the first war. In two basic respects, therefore, conditions in 1917, when the Navy had played a major role in the national shipping effort, and those of 1941 were in sharp contrast.

The outbreak of war found the Navy wholly unprepared to assume the transportation task which had been assigned to it. The Naval Transportation Service, the organization under the Chief of Naval Operations responsible for overseas shipping, was a small, under-staffed, and highly subordinate agency, existing almost entirely on paper. It had no clear concept of its own mission and even less notion of the relation which must be established between the Navy's shipping organization and its other services of supply. Its plans were incomplete, and liaison with the Army, for whom it was to act as a carrier, was undeveloped. Certainly no channels or procedure existed between the Army and the Navy by which Army plans for overseas movements could be translated into terms of a naval shipping program. The Navy had at this time, moreover, only a few cargo vessels and transports, the major portion of which were assigned not to the Naval Transportation Service, but to the fleet's "Base Force" as ships of the train. So great was the shortage of naval personnel that the few vessels the Navy could secure either for the Naval Transportation Service or the Base Forces were manned only with the greatest difficulty.

Prior to the war the Naval Transportation Service was also unable to acquire the practical operating experience necessary to establishment of its position in the eyes of either the Navy or Army as the responsible agency for shipping. Naval Regulations assigned responsibility for transportation of property to the Bureau of Supplies and Accounts and of personnel to the Bureau of Personnel. The Naval Transportation Service was described as an agency which would come into operation during wartime. In actual practice, overseas shipping for the Navy during the years immediately preceding the war was done, in most cases, either by commercial shippers or by vessels assigned to the Base

Forces. Bureaus responsible for the shipment of material had little occasion to deal with the Naval Transportation Service. It is indicative of the prevailing condition that at a hearing of December 9, 1941, before the House Committee on Merchant Marine affairs, the Navy was represented by an officer from the Bureau of Supplies and Accounts who opened his testimony with the statement, "All Navy transportation is handled by the Bureau of Supplies and Accounts." The statement was substantially correct.

With the Army the relation of the Naval Transportation Service was even more tenuous. Immediately after the assignment of shipping responsibility to the Navy in the War Plan of 1941, an agreement had been reached between the respective Secretaries under which vessels of the Army Transport Service would be taken over promptly and commissioned in the naval service. Difficulties arose at once, however, in carrying out this agreement, particularly because of the shortage of naval personnel available for manning the ships. Many of the Army cargo vessels were old, and since the Navy was loath to waste precious personnel upon vessels unsuitable for employment in dangerous waters, only a few cargo vessels were transferred. In the case of transports a difficulty arose over the need for keeping the vessels in constant employment. Under current policy the Navy required combat loading transport vessels sufficient to lift several divisions of Army and Marine forces off each coast immediately after the United States became involved in war, and it was understood that certain of the Army transports would be converted to this use. During the autumn of 1941, however, since Army troop movement schedules required that every available vessel be kept in constant service, it could not spare the vessels for the period required for conversion. Ultimately the issue was settled by compromise, but it may be said that the Navy's inability to furnish alternate vessels for Army use had fostered, on the part of the Army, a sense of the need for self-reliance.

The agreement between the services had provided as well that the Army would continue to acquire vessels for current needs which would subsequently be turned over to the Navy for manning. This it continued to do, but since transfers could not be accomplished very easily during this period, the result in December 1941 was that the Army had on hand as large a block of tonnage as the Navy's. The responsibility of the Navy for the movement of Army forces, moreover, was to become operative only after war had begun. Army needs in excess of its own shipping resources prior to the war were supplied almost entirely by the Maritime Commission. Between the Army and Navy no procedure had been worked out and refined in practice by which the terms of the War Plan could be implemented in wartime.

In justice to the few officers then in the Naval Transportation Service it must be said that they labored strenuously and against great odds to bring the Naval Transportation Service to a war footing. Recommendations were made repeatedly, for example, that it should take over from the Atlantic Fleet Base Force the transport service for bases then building in the Atlantic and Caribbean. But since this would have involved shifting vessels from the Base Force to the Naval Transportation Service, the recommendation was not approved.

In other directions the efforts of these few officers bore greater fruit. In September 1939, when war began in Europe, steps were immediately taken to establish in the principal ports of the United States a system of naval port directors to act as field agencies of the Naval Transportation Service in all matters pertaining to the procurement and operation of merchant shipping. Detailed instructions were issued to them. In the two major ports, New York and San Francisco, the officers selected, Captains F. G. Reinicke and M. C. Davis, were well chosen. They made themselves familiar with the waterfront organization, secured terminal facilities, and developed their own plans and procedures.

During the first two critical months of the Pacific war, it was Captain Davis's office in San Francisco that bore the brunt of the emergency shipping and logistic effort.

In October 1939, a procedural agreement was worked out with the Maritime Commission under which requisitioned vessels could be transferred to the Navy. Since the Maritime Commission was the only agency empowered by law to requisition vessels during an emergency, an understanding between it and the Navy was of first importance. The agreement, however, was purely procedural, and it did not immediately affect the Navy's efforts to acquire merchant vessels. The declaration of emergency under which the Commission's authority became operative was not made until more than a year later. Meanwhile, the Navy was compelled to purchase vessels from private owners in a rising market, in which the most suitable ships were frequently not for sale. Even after the proclamation of emergency, the Maritime Commission adopted the practice of screening Navy requests for merchant vessels against the total needs of the national mobilization effort, and on several occasions refused to transfer vessels requested.

It may be added, too, that the War Plans did not envisage that all the merchant shipping employed by the Navy during the initial stages of the war would be manned and commissioned in the Navy. Most of the ships originally put into military service would be secured on a time-charter basis and operated by the Navy, after arming, with their original civilian crews. Gradually, as personnel became available and conditions permitted, they would be manned by naval crews. This procedure was thoroughly understood by the port directors, and district war plans included instructions for the rapid mobilization of merchant vessels in collaboration with the Maritime Commission. When war broke out, some of the port directors such as the able and energetic Captain Davis in San Francisco sprang rapidly into action and began procuring ships to meet the urgent

needs of Hawaii and other beleaguered positions in the
Pacific. As he later described the situation, "It was something of a honeymoon and lasted about six weeks. Then
the Maritime Commission woke up and started the allocation of ships." "But by that time," he added, "the immediate needs of the Navy at Pearl Harbor had been fulfilled."
The statement illustrates not only the manner in which the
Navy's decentralized system responded quickly to the emergency of war. It illustrates also the danger inherent in isolated actions of this kind and the failure of the central administration, both in the Navy and in the government at
large to formulate a concrete program of action embracing
the larger aspects of the shipping problem.

In sum, the outbreak of war found the Navy assigned a
responsibility which it had no adequate means to discharge.
Lacking prestige, organization, experience, and facilities,
the Naval Transportation Service was prepared only in its
field agencies. At the center, upon which the whole projected system depended, it was all too ill-prepared.

The want of proper organization to administer shipping
was not confined to the Navy. In the broader field of national organization, no effective steps had yet been taken to
deal with demands from many sources upon available merchant tonnage. In February, 1941, the Maritime Commission had been directed by the President to assume responsibility for the national shipping effort, and had set up a
Division of Emergency Shipping which had begun tenta-
tively to allocate available shipping to various claimants.
The major portion of American tonnage, however, was still
in private hands, and the organization and operation of the
division was on a limited scale. Both in the field of military
shipping and on the higher level of national administration
the outbreak of the war found, therefore, a vacuum into
which various cross-currents of policy immediately began to
penetrate.

In order to meet the pressing need for some central policy

organization in shipping matters the President directed on December 8, 1941, the formation of a Strategic Shipping Board, composed of Chairman Land of the Maritime Commission, General Marshall, Admiral Stark, and Mr. Harry Hopkins, to "establish policies for and plan the allocation of merchant shipping to meet military and civilian requirements, and coordinate these activities of the War and Navy Departments and the Maritime Commission." But it rapidly developed that the board as constituted lacked both the unity to conceive policy and the authority to enforce it. Before a week had passed a movement was under way to substitute for it a single agency to direct the mobilization, and control the allocation and operation of shipping. Meanwhile by verbal agreement between the Army and Navy the provisions of the War Plan under which the Navy was to provide shipping for the Army had been temporarily suspended.

On February 7, 1942, the President signed Executive Order 9054, creating the War Shipping Administration and bringing under a single authority the control and operation of all United States merchant shipping except for naval auxiliaries, transports owned by the Army and Navy, and vessels engaged in coastwise service. The origins of the Executive Order are obscure, but it appears to have received its original impetus in the Navy in a suggestion of Admiral Turner that a ministry of shipping be established. General Marshall had regarded this proposal as extreme, but had agreed that "there must be some agency endowed with absolute powers over the allocation of shipping and the establishment of priorities." Drafting of the order had been a joint effort in which the Army, the Navy, the Maritime Commission, and the Bureau of the Budget all participated.

In the evolution of the order, several significant issues had arisen which later affected the pattern of shipping administration carried out by the War Shipping Administration. One of these issues turned upon the question of whether or not the War Shipping Administrator, who would obviously be Admiral Land, should be responsible to a Board of Directors. The Navy had envisioned such a board of directors as the real policy group with the Administrator acting as its executive agent. Both Admiral Land and Mr. Hopkins objected to this limitation upon the authority of the Administrator, and it was therefore provided that while he should "collaborate with" and "maintain close liaison with" the military and civilian agencies, his "decisions shall be final with respect to the functions and authorities so vested in him."

Secondly, the Executive Order provided that the War Shipping Administrator would "allocate vessels under the flag or control of the United States for use by the Army, Navy, other Federal Departments and agencies, and the governments of the United Nations." In order to safeguard the primacy of the military interest, the original draft had included a qualification that the Administrator should comply with the decisions of the Secretaries of War and Navy as regards their requirements. Once again, Admiral Land, supported by Mr. Hopkins, objected that this would unduly subordinate the central civilian authority to the military services. The final draft of the order stated simply that the Administrator should comply with "strategic requirements."

Within the defined area of his authority, namely, the operation, purchase, charter, requisition, and use of merchant vessels, the authority of the War Shipping Administrator as stated in the Executive Order was not seriously qualified. Admiral Land was instructed to report directly to the President. He was to act both as War Shipping Administrator and as Chairman of the Maritime Commission, thus bringing under a single authority responsibility for both the construction and operation of merchant shipping.

The authority of the Administrator over merchant shipping, however, was not in fact absolute. With the creation of the Combined and Joint Chiefs of Staff, and under them of military transportation committees whose task it was to define "strategic requirements" in terms of merchant tonnage, there was created a counterweight to the authority of the Administrator which in practice served to maintain a working balance between the civilian and the military interest. Secondly, while the War Shipping administration was to control the operation of shipping, responsibility for the loading and unloading of vessels remained with the military services. Finally, the Executive Order of February 7 was no more than a grant of authority. Before it could become effective, there was necessary an extended period during which actual working procedures could be developed and understood. Within the interstices of this developing procedure there was room for compromise.

The effects of the establishment of the War Shipping Administration upon the Navy's role in war shipping were considerable. Many tasks of considerable magnitude which would have fallen upon the Navy were thereby assumed by the civilian administration. The Navy was relieved, for example, of the vast range of activities such as manning, fueling, and repair, which were corollaries to ship operation. It was relieved as well of the tremendous task of mobilizing and procuring vessels which would have been necessary had the Navy been required to create a merchant fleet on the scale hitherto contemplated. Procurement of merchant vessels by the Navy was confined after the first few months to meeting its needs for fleet auxiliary vessels, and that task itself was considerably simplified by the fact that the War Shipping Administration had already mobilized under government control the vessels previously in private hands.

On the other hand, civilian operation of merchant shipping for military purposes raised the problem of providing effective coordination between ship operation and its protection by the Navy. The organization and training of naval armed guard units to be placed aboard merchant vessels became a major task. Port Directors were required as well to give careful indoctrination to merchant masters in communications, convoy organization and procedure, and routing. As experience was gained in the organization of convoys and in the handling of merchant vessel traffic this liaison between the civilian operators and the naval organization was developed; at the outset, however, the task presented many complications.

A more significant result of the establishment of the War Shipping Administration was the readjustment which followed in the relation between the Army and Navy. The Navy had subscribed to the creation of a civilian shipping authority under the assumption that the suspension of the Joint Action policy, under which it was responsible for Army overseas transportation, had been only temporary. Even though responsibility for vessel operation had been placed under civilian auspices, it had expected that the military requirements for tonnage allocations would be combined into a single program and presented to the War Shipping Administration by the Navy, as the responsible agency for military shipping. On February 26, 1942, therefore, Admiral Stark wrote to General Marshall suggesting that the principle of Joint Action be revived as of the first of May, when the Navy would assume responsibility for securing and directing the employment of shipping necessary to meet all military requirements. Admiral Stark enclosed a plan of organization drawn up by Admiral Taffinder, the Director of the Naval Transportation Service, under which the proposed procedure would operate.

The reply of General Marshall left no doubt as to the Army's attitude toward a revival of the Joint Action principle. Stating that he could not concur in the plan of Admiral Taffinder, "in which the question of operating the overseas transportation of the Army by the Navy is reopened," General Marshall affirmed that "this matter was disposed of by Executive Order No. 9054. . . . The solution offered by the Executive Order," he concluded, "is most satisfactory to the Army. It is believed that the creation of the Maritime Commission and now of the War Shipping Administration promises a much better use of our shipping in time of war than has ever obtained in the past. It is therefore felt that this question is settled."

In assuming this position, it must be said, the Army was being neither arbitrary nor inconsistent. From the beginning, it appears, it had conceived of the Navy's responsibility for overseas transportation as limited solely to the operation of merchant vessels, i.e. to their manning, navigation, and husbanding, but not as extending to the scheduling and direction of their employment. The movement of materials it regarded as an essentially indivisible process, governed from point of origin to destination by the exigencies of the military situation. Navy operation of shipping except for considerations of protection should not in any way restrict the Army's control over the flow of supplies, of which shipping itself was merely an instrument. The Army would perhaps have preferred to have the Navy operate shipping because of the greater degree of security which might be expected from naval crews. But since the task had been shifted to the War Shipping Administration, it followed from the Army's point of view that its immediate relation was now with that agency rather than with the Navy.

In wartime, when the determination of shipping routes and services is necessarily fluid, the distinction implied here between traffic management and carrier operation is obscured to a greater degree than in normal commercial practice. Had army shipments prior to the war been carried out in the manner contemplated in the War Plan, Army and Navy together would have been exploring in practice the twilight zone between ship operation and supply control, not setting up separate and competing services. In any event, the establishment of the War Shipping Administration removed from the Navy its responsibility under the War Plans for Army overseas transportation.

The confusion over control of the employment of shipping derived also from a second assumption made by both services as to the manner in which allocations would be made by the War Shipping Administration for military use. In approving the allocation of merchant shipping by a central civilian authority, there can be no question, both services assumed that allocations would be made on a long-range basis, a minimum of six months, which would leave to the military agencies the scheduling of employment of the vessels allocated. Under broad allocations of tonnage, the movements of vessels would thus be controlled by military shipping agencies and would be governed by the exigencies of supply programs without active intervention by the War Shipping Administration. Original estimates of their merchant shipping requirements reflected this assumption.

Almost from the beginning, however, the War Shipping Administration took a different line. The shortage of tonnage available to meet the total requirements of the war effort was so great, it insisted, that no system could be applied which did not guarantee the maximum constant employment of all vessels. This it believed, could be achieved only by the establishment of a single pool of tonnage out of which all requirements—military and non-military—could be met with the greatest flexibility. Vessels which carried a military lift on the outward voyage might then be diverted to the import of critical materials or essential civilian commodities on return. Only by a master schedule of employment comprehending all legitimate needs could wasteful voyages in ballast be avoided. Under this schedule, allocations to one claimant or another would be made upon the basis of a single voyage, and vessels would rotate from one service to another in order to secure the greatest number of sailing days for all vessels. The segregation of a large block of tonnage for permanent employment by one claimant, it maintained, could only result in less tonnage available for all.

The issue between broad, long-term allocation and the assignment of vessels by single voyage dominated the early months during which the new system of shipping administration was being elaborated into working procedures. Both services felt themselves unduly restricted by the necessity of calculating in terms of single voyages, for if the system of pool shipping provided necessary flexibility in the overall employment of shipping, its effect upon military supply and distribution procedures was exactly the opposite. Acceptance by the Navy of the pool principle was given in an exchange of letters between the Secretary and the War Shipping Administrator on April 7 and May 7, 1942, in which it was agreed that the Navy would cancel all charter agreements entered into prior to the formation of the War Shipping Administration, return the vessels to the Administration, and henceforth, except for accretions to its auxiliary fleet, rely upon the system as outlined for meeting its overseas shipping needs. The Army's adherence to the system was reached in a formal agreement of June 13, 1942, between Major General Somervell and Mr. Lewis Douglas, the Deputy War Shipping Administrator.

Henceforth Navy requirements for merchant shipping to bases and staging areas would be met in large measure by the allocation to the Naval Transportation Service of civilian-manned vessels under the control of the War Shipping Administration. A very few commissioned vessels would remain under the employ of the Naval Transportation Service, but for the most part its operating role had been assumed by the War Shipping Administration. Commissioned vessels of all types, the "fleet auxiliaries," would generally be assigned to the Service Forces, where they would be employed in deliveries directly to the fleet, or, in the case of vessels designed for assault uses, would be assigned to the Amphibious Forces. No hard-and-fast line could be maintained between these categories, but they represented in general the division of tasks upon which the assignment of vessels was premised.

The necessity of calculating its requirements in terms of specific sailings, and of presenting its requirements to the War Shipping Administration sufficiently far in advance to enable it to make allocations, demanded of the Navy more refined planning than it was able to accomplish under the early conditions of the war. Estimating shipping requirements meant, of course, the determination in volume and weight of all kinds of materials which would be available at tidewater within a given period of time. It meant also that the requirements by destination as well as by assembly and loading points must be known. Had the Navy had a broad, long-term allocation of tonnage, it would have been possible for it to operate to a greater degree "on the cuff," matching ship schedules to tonnage availabilities as they developed. Under the system set up by the War Shipping Administration, however, a higher degree of accountability was required, making it necessary for the Naval Transportation Service as the Navy's shipping agency to forecast in considerable detail the periodic requirements for tonnage.

The development of bases at Noumea and Auckland and subsequent unplanned accretions in strength at pre-established bases, however, raised serious difficulties in the estimation of merchant shipping requirements, which were greatly increased by the practice of leaving responsibility for the supply of materials almost entirely to the separate bureaus. As a result, the Naval Transportation Service had little or no information upon which to calculate the Navy's shipping requirements. This situation was further complicated by the fact that the Naval Transportation Service had no responsibility for or authority over the movement of naval materials to tidewater by rail or other inland transportation. These fell within the province of the Bureau of Supplies and Accounts.

The organization of railroad and other forms of domestic

transportation had been undertaken almost immediately after the outbreak of war with the establishment on December 17, 1941, of the Office of Defense Transportation. In the case of the railroads, however, the issue of operating control was not seriously raised. Operation was wisely left in the hands of the private companies with necessary coordination supplied by the American Association of Railroads. In April 1942, the Office of Defense Transportation put into effect a system of apportioning available railroad capacity to meet the needs of the military services, Lend-Lease programs, and the civilian economy. Its original plan was to issue individual permits for the release of all shipments under specific programs, but this detailed control was quickly recognized as too cumbersome. Accordingly, it was agreed that each of the services would receive a "block" of permits to cover its own needs, which it would administer as it saw fit.

Navy administration of railroad transport was assigned to the Bureau of Supplies and Accounts on the logical ground that having closest contact with the actual flow of Navy goods it could best route shipments, provide storage, and supervise the goods in transit. On the same principle the Bureau of Supplies and Accounts in turn had delegated to other bureaus a fairly free hand over the movement from contractors to naval depots of the technical material under their individual cognizance. With the exception, therefore, of planned initial movements carried out under the immediate direction of the Chief of Naval Operations, knowledge of what materials would accumulate for shipment at tidewater points could be had only from the ports themselves on the basis of advance shipping notices or reports of material already on hand. This lack of central control or knowledge of the movement of materials within the country was to become one of the most significant features of the Navy's system of material distribution.

Transportation was thus from the outset a divided and

decentralized operation. Close articulation of its many inter-dependent phases and the close coordination of all transportation with supply programs depended upon an interchange of essential information which did not yet exist.

Throughout the first year of the war, the Navy experimented with methods of drawing together the necessary information, but generally with little success. In mid-January, the Naval Transportation Service made a preliminary calculation of Navy shipping needs for the remainder of the year. At that time, however, little could be known of the prospective deployment of forces overseas throughout the coming year, and it is not surprising, therefore, that the original estimate was a grossly inadequate representation of the Navy's true needs. Again at the end of February, as the War Shipping Administration began its operations, the Navy was requested to estimate its needs for the remainder of the year. This time, its calculations were based presumably upon forecasts from the bureaus of the material they would be able to make available for shipment during the coming months. But it rapidly developed that not all bureaus had submitted estimates. Before a week had passed, urgent Navy requirements for the month of April alone had increased by 50,000 tons or 5 shiploads the estimated figure.

The problem involved was by no means simple of solution. Essentially, it derived from the fact that the pattern both of strategy and of logistic support was still unfolding. Most of the shipments in excess of forecasts were for base development projects in the South Pacific and for stockpiles at Pearl Harbor, the ultimate scale of which no one could then have foreseen. Materials were urgently required, however, and if they were to move forward rapidly, bureaus must be left free to act quickly, without waiting for detailed authorizations of shipments from a central office not yet organized to clear business rapidly. The Navy was faced, therefore, with a choice of two alternatives. It could institute a system of detailed movement control over shipments to tidewater, in which a central file of information would be constantly maintained, but in which shipments themselves would be delayed. Or it could rely principally upon the tidewater ports for reports as to the cargo on hand for shipment and develop its shipping requirements from these. For advance planning purposes, the latter method was obviously inadequate, but during these critical early months the more loosely administered method offered the most immediate benefits. The decision was made, therefore, to base shipping estimates upon weekly cargo availability reports from each of the principal continental ports, and not to attempt a detailed, centralized control of domestic shipments and routing. This lack of control or knowledge of the movement of materials within the country was to become one of the most significant features in the Navy's system of material distribution.

Logistic Support in the Theaters

THE conduct of logistic support within the theaters was no less critical a factor in the successful conduct of the war than the greater effort of mobilization, production, and distribution within the United States. Theater logistics were necessarily on a smaller scale than the total economic effort of the nation. They represented only the distillation in terms of weapons and supporting military elements of the national effort. But as the link between our forces and the continental support system, bearing closely upon the employment of forces in combat, theater logistics were of the greatest importance.

In the Pacific, as everywhere, during these early days, the immediate problem was to provide something out of relatively nothing. Specifically, the organization of logistic support within the theaters may be regarded as turning upon three principal problems. It was necessary first to organize the use of all supporting facilities, whether already in the theater or flowing into it from the United States, into a single, coherent pattern. This meant, of course, coordination between the various services and their forces already within the theater. It meant that supplies must be jointly administered, and that media of transport, whether under the control of the Army, the Navy, or the War Shipping Administration, must be utilized in support of a common effort. In short, the ideal of a common striking force, utilizing all arms in their most effective combination, must be realized as well in the furnishing of logistic support.

The second major problem was to establish effective liaison with the supporting establishment in the United States through which logistic requirements, accurately reflecting the military situation, could be transmitted rapidly to the ultimate sources of supply. So great was the inevitable dispersion of effort in the United States not only between the services and civilian agencies, but within each service itself, that to realize the first aim of unified theater logistics as well as to give military direction to the mobilization of resources, an effective liaison was essential.

The third major problem, more important during the initial phases of the war, was to make efficient use of all local sources of support available in the islands or in the hands of our Australian and New Zealand allies. Their resources, needless to say, were limited, and it has already been pointed out that the islands themselves offered perilously little of the basic necessities of life. But the total of local resources, small though they were, could supply an important margin of support.

The primary essential to the coordination of military and logistic effort within the theaters was provided early in April in the establishment of two unified theater commands under Admiral Nimitz and General MacArthur. Within an area broadly defined as the South, Central, and North Pacific areas Admiral Nimitz was directed to exercise unified command of all armed forces which might be assigned. Within the Southwest Pacific Area, roughly comprising

Australia, New Guinea, part of the Solomons, and the Bismarck Archipelago, General MacArthur assumed a similar command. Under Admiral Nimitz as Commander in Chief in the Pacific Ocean Area, it was also provided there should be established a Commander South Pacific Area who would bear responsibility for the conduct of operations in that area.

The agreement upon unified command was in its terms and concept primarily military. No specific instructions were given as to the responsibility for logistic support of the united forces, but it was a natural implication that responsibility for logistic support in an operational area would be comprehended within the duties of command. The development of a unified system of support was to require many months of experiment and elaboration, and it did not follow immediately that unified command over the employment of forces would lead to unified support either in the theaters or on the mainland, where shipping and supply agencies of the services still operated independently of each other. Conversely, however, no progress could have been made toward coordinating logistic support without overall unity of command.

Turning for the moment from the broader aspects to the problem of naval logistic support, it is important to examine the condition of our naval supporting forces at the outbreak of the war. Upon the Base Force, Pacific Fleet, devolved the principal task of supporting the Pacific Fleet in war. Both in war and peace, however, so long as the fleet was based on Pearl Harbor this responsibility would be shared by the Navy Yard and other facilities of the Fourteenth Naval District. The concept upon which the Base Force was organized was that of a train providing a mobile floating base which could be moved forward progressively behind the operating forces as they extended their range of operations. In September 1941, when the Base Force was extensively reorganized, responsibility for the "establishment, support, and security of advance bases" was assigned to one of its train squadrons, but for lack of base equipment and of emphasis upon construction of shore support facilities this aspect of its task had never been actively prosecuted. When war broke out, there were in the Pacific Fleet neither reserves of materials nor responsible organization for the establishment of advance bases.

The lack of facilities, however, was not limited to those necessary for the establishment of advance bases. Requests to Congress and reports of the Secretary, Chief of Naval Operations, and the Commander in Chief of the Pacific Fleet had reflected for many years a chronic insufficiency of auxiliary vessels necessary to enable the Base Force to carry out its mission of supporting the fleet at sea or of creating a mobile base. The total auxiliary force available in December 1941 was 61 vessels of all types, of which the greater number were minecraft and fleet oilers. In cargo and provision ships and in transports, the Base Force was notably deficient.

The problem of liaison between the Base Forces and the continental shore establishment had been considered at length early in January 1941, and there had followed the gradual establishment of a Subordinate Command of the Base Force with headquarters in San Francisco. This command was formally placed in commission in June. Its duties were both operational and logistic. It carried on liaison with the Pacific Coastal Frontier and the Naval District organization, for example, for the routing and protection of shipping, for the assembly and loading of advance base materials and other supplies in Base Force vessels, and for the care and administration of the vessels themselves while in coastal waters. Its general function was best described by Rear Admiral Calhoun, then Commander of the Base Force, as a "fountainhead of the service of supply for the entire Fleet." As an arm of the fleet itself, it would presumably be best informed as to current needs and could speak with authority in expediting shipments and determining priorities.

The most important fact about the support of the Pacific campaign during the first year, however, was that both the Base Force headquarters at Pearl Harbor and to a lesser degree the Subordinate Command in San Francisco were by-passed by direct contact between the South Pacific Command and logistic agencies in the United States. Communication and the flow of supplies proceeded directly between the South Pacific on the one hand and coastal agencies and the Navy Department on the other. For this there were many reasons. Except for limited raids in the Central Pacific, based on Pearl Harbor itself, the main effort of the United States was concentrated in the South and Southwest Pacific. Out of our original defensive effort there were developed, moreover, the campaigns in the Solomons and New Guinea which until the Gilberts offensive in late 1943 were our principal offensive undertakings in the Pacific. The South Pacific was remote from Pearl Harbor. To have routed communications and supplies via Pearl Harbor would have consumed time and effort; shipping would have been wasted. The early task, which was one of improvising support out of all existing sources could only be done on the spot.

It must be kept in mind, moreover, that few resources existed in Pearl Harbor for the support of the South Pacific campaign. That fact we have noted in the concentration in the Navy Department of direction of the initial establishment of bases. Material had to be assembled, shipping mobilized, personnel organized, and plans laid all within the United States. The total task involved a far greater effort than could be supported by existing channels through the Base Force headquarters in the Central Pacific. The expanding volume of shipments soon overtaxed all administrative agencies on the Pacific Coast, and though the Subordinate Command expanded with the rest, its early growth was hardly commensurate with the size of the task. The organization and channels developed for the support of the South Pacific were therefore almost entirely new and extemporized.

In April 1942, even before a South Pacific Area Commander had been designated, the South Pacific Service Squadron was formed with headquarters at Auckland. Captain M. C. Bowman was directed on the 14th of that month to proceed by air to Auckland and there make preparations for a major naval base, with headquarters for the Area Commander. Several days later, a "task force" consisting of one repair ship and a destroyer as a temporary escort was ordered to Auckland to serve as a nucleus of the base. Plans for the establishment of South Pacific advance bases had already set in motion the movement of harbor defense equipment and other base materials to Auckland, and meanwhile Captain Bowman began making arrangements for the use of docks, storage, and repair facilities already available in New Zealand. Supplies of fresh food in New Zealand were ample for all forces initially established in Auckland. A few converted tuna boats and several lumber steamers were made available to supply food from local sources to the outlying bases.

On June 1, 1942, the Vice Chief of Naval Operations announced the formation of a Joint Purchasing Board whose mission was to purchase from local sources in New Zealand all available provisions and other supplies in order to conserve on shipping from the United States. Actually, purchase of local supplies had been going on for several months by various commands and services in the New Zealand area. The formation of the Purchasing Board was designed to centralize this procedure under a single agency. It was intended also to complement the work of a similar agency, the General Purchasing Board, which had previously been established in Australia under General MacArthur.

It was already obvious, however, that the main burden of

supplying forces and establishing bases in the South Pacific would be borne by the United States. Original Joint Plans for base expeditions had made general and tentative arrangements for the continued support of both Army and Navy forces, and had provided in certain instances (such as petroleum products and provisions) that one service should be responsible for the maintenance of all forces. The various joint plans did not, however, constitute a general supply procedure, nor did they stipulate in any detail the channels through which supply would be furnished.

In April, the Army directed that its forces in New Zealand and the South Pacific area should be supplied directly by the Port of Embarkation, San Francisco. Meanwhile, the Navy was also defining the procedures for supply. In April, the Commander of Service Forces Pacific which had replaced the old Base Force outlined a plan to the Service Squadron South Pacific, under which the latter would become the center for all requests from bases in the area. These it would screen and forward to the Subordinate Command in San Francisco and the Commandant of the Twelfth District. Where possible, the movement of supplies would follow the same channels in reverse. Certain exceptions were made, however, in the case of bulk fuels and ammunition, where requests would be made upon the Service Force Headquarters in Pearl Harbor. In May this procedure was formally instituted. It remained now for the supply of both services to be organized into a single plan following the lead taken in the establishment of joint purchasing agencies.

The need for some general plan covering supply from the United States for joint forces in the South Pacific was felt increasingly as initial stocks began to run low and the problem of replenishment increased. Accordingly, on July 15 by agreement between Admiral Horne, the Vice Chief of Naval Operations and General Somervell a "Joint Logistic Plan for the Support of United States Bases in the South Pacific Area" was issued. Listing all bases and codifying all supplies of common use under five general classes, it stipulated in each case the service which would be responsible for furnishing common items for both services. Provision was also made for the centralization of all requisitions and distribution of supplies through the headquarters of the Commander South Pacific Area, either under naval auspices or under the authority of the Commanding General. In either case, all requests submitted from bases, by either Army or Navy commanders, would be screened through the Joint Purchasing Board before they were forwarded to the United States to see if they could be satisfied from local sources. The control of shipping into the South Pacific Area was vested in the Area Commander.

The Joint Logistic Plan for the South Pacific Area was a simple and rudimentary scheme for the coordination of requirements and supply of all services. With the beginning of the campaign in the Solomons and the increase in forces concentrated in the South Pacific Area which followed, it was to require further development. For the moment, however, it served to eliminate much of the confusion which had arisen in the hurried establishment of joint bases during the first six months of the war. It provided at least a cornerstone in the development of joint maintenance and supply procedure in the Pacific.

CHAPTER III

THE BEGINNINGS OF METHOD

July 1942-March 1943

URING the second six months of 1942 and the early months of 1943, the progress of the war on all fronts greatly expanded the task of furnishing balanced logistic support. Having blocked out our defensive position in the Pacific and having passed to an organized effort in the Atlantic submarine warfare, the Navy was preparing now to assume a limited offensive in the South Pacific and to assist in the beginnings of offensive action in the European theater. In August, with extremely limited resources, the campaign in the Solomons was launched. In November, the North African campaign, known as Operation Torch began. Coincident with these two specific operations there was a steady build-up of American forces in the British Isles, an intensification of the anti-submarine warfare in the Atlantic, and an acceleration of the raiding activity of fleet task forces in the Central Pacific.

This history will be concerned primarily with campaigns in the Pacific, in which the Navy was most concerned. But it was rapidly being demonstrated in many lines of activity that no single phase of the war could be divorced from any other. In determining requirements, in allocating materials and forces, in assigning shipping to the support of current operations and to the preparation for others, situations within one theater, which might seem to bear only upon local conditions, in fact bore heavily upon the whole. The assumption of the offensive and the acceleration of activity of all kinds made a maximum demand upon almost all existing support facilities. The result was that imperfections in organization and procedure which obstructed the most economic utilization of resources could not be hidden.

Although the operations undertaken during the latter half of 1942 were on a limited scale as compared with those which followed, they were sufficiently grand in relation to existing means to place the system under severe strain.

In retrospect it is possible to discern during this period the emergence of the two primary problems of military logistic effort—the determination of logistic requirements in terms of strategic plans, to serve as a guide to procurement, and the distribution of materials once they had been procured and had passed into the logistic support system. At this time, however, such a simple and systematic summary of the task was impossible to make. A multitude of other problems only slightly less general in their application to the total task were slowly developing out of the military and logistic situation into which we had been impelled. Within the Navy Department, the central organ of direction, there was a growing need for more effective organization. Between the theaters and the continental supporting system stronger liaison was needed—more clearly defined channels by which both essential information and physical support could pass. Within the theaters themselves the problem of coordinating efforts between and within the services was emerging.

These general conditions were reflected in many concrete problems which pressed for solution. The system of planning logistic requirements required overhauling. No clear distinction had yet been drawn either in practice or theory between strategic and logistic planning. Nor was it yet possible under existing organization to disentangle the planning of logistic programs from their execution. Confusion at the source was reflected, moreover, down through the entire system. The procurement and distribution of aircraft, ships, auxiliary vessels, construction equipment, ordnance, fuel, spare parts and all the other materials required depended directly upon the effectiveness of the planning system.

The advance base program, which in its Lions, Cubs, and

Acorns accounted for the major part of organized overseas shipment of all kinds of materials, required further elaboration of its planning and distribution procedures before the methods utilized within the United States for procurement and assembly could answer the specific needs of the theaters. The shipping situation, aggravated by urgent demands from many directions upon our limited resources of tonnage, was growing steadily more serious. Difficulties were arising in the system of allocation and control, and these pointed to the need for a more explicit understanding among the Army, the Navy, and the War Shipping Administration. These difficulties were increased by auxiliary problems both in the theaters and in the United States—the coordination of Army and Navy shipping programs to the theaters, the limited discharge capacities at Pacific destination, the need for a system of control over the movements of vessels once they had been dispatched to the theaters. Within the Navy there was a continuing need for better coordination between shipping and supply and between shipping and internal transport.

Finally, it was essential to build up within the theaters the means and organization for assuming some of the task of direction which had hitherto been borne by the central administration. Short-term requirements could best be determined by theater agencies themselves. Priorities for movement of materials must likewise be determined on the spot. In all phases of activity the character of the military task must be imparted to the supporting effort.

The history of the first six months of war had shown a remarkable capacity to extemporize in our economic and military system. A system of defense, at first insecure, but subsequently strengthened, had been established in the Pacific. But we were now embarking upon an effort in which extemporizing would no longer suffice. To accomplish the tasks set forth, it was essential that the host of interdependent and contributing elements—planning, assembly, transport, and utilization—be brought into coherent relation with each other. Not only through formal organization, but also, and more importantly, through the development of sound methods and concepts within the organization, the energy being generated must be harnessed and directed toward the accomplishment of our military aims.

Logistic Planning

AT the outbreak of war, partly because of external and substantive conditions and partly for want of suitable organization, centralized, long-range logistic planning had been impossible. Certain initial goals for procurement had been set, but they had served almost exclusively for procurement purposes, had been very roughly calculated, and had overlooked or deferred many important categories of material. For the assembly and distribution of materials, particularly of advance base assemblies, there was almost no advance planning upon which implementing agencies could depend. Thus the original plan to procure and assemble materials and personnel for 4 Lions and 12 Cubs had served a useful purpose in setting a goal for production. Once the materials had been assembled, however, bureaus and other agencies had little to guide them in moving the units forward.

In no small part this condition of affairs arose from the continued need for reorganization within the Office of Naval Operations. The Division of Plans under the Chief of Naval Operations had dwindled steadily, until shortly after the Executive Order of March it was composed of only a few officers, who were largely out of touch with the main current of events. Plans continued to be formed for the most part in the office of the Commander in Chief, or failing that, by bureaus and other agencies responsible for their execution.

Between the Office of Naval Operations and that of the Commander in Chief there was, moreover, no clear distinction even in theory as to the division of planning responsibilities. Most of the work of Naval Operations during the first few months had been the supervision of the execution of plans.

The terms of the Executive Order of March assigning to the Vice Chief of Naval Operations "all necessary authority for executing the plans and policies" of the Commander-in-Chief and Chief of Naval Operations had suggested that a distinction would be drawn, not between strategy and logistics, but rather between planning and execution. It was, therefore, along these lines that the thinking of Admiral Horne, the Vice Chief, and Rear Admiral Farber, the newly appointed Assistant Chief of Naval Operations for Maintenance, was directed.

On June 17, Admiral Horne recommended to Admiral King that the Vice Chief should concentrate on the execution of plans and directives, leaving planning itself to the Commander in Chief. On June 29, this proposal was amplified by a second recommendation which drew the distinction clearly on the basis of planning and execution and recommended the abolition of the Plans Division under the Chief of Naval Operations. Planning in Naval Operations should be limited to matters of execution and should be coordinated by the Assistant Chief of Naval Operations for Maintenance, Admiral Farber.

This recommendation was not approved by Admiral King, who held that both of the higher offices had substantive functions requiring the maintenance of planning offices. A dividing line was drawn between the two by a directive of July 1 which defined the planning functions in each office. Under the Commander in Chief would be: plans for current operations and plans for future operations including the number and type of vessels, troops, merchant ships, and materials required. He would also fix "requirements as to location and facilities of advanced bases for the support of present and future operations." The Chief of Naval Operations was defined as "Chief of material practicability" and was held responsible for "Logistic and other necessary planning for Naval Districts and the Shore Establishment," for the coordination of plans of material bureaus, and for the execution of all logistic plans.

The basis of distinction in this division of responsibility could hardly be called that between strategy and logistics. It appeared rather to be between the shore establishment and the fleet. On this basis, it concentrated all kinds of planning pertaining to fleet activity under the Commander in Chief, while that pertaining to the continental shore establishment was assigned to the Chief of Naval Operations or in effect to the Vice Chief.

The directive of July 1 did not, however, affect the actual distribution of tasks within the Navy Department. It is of interest primarily because it showed the impossibility at this early date of drawing a clear distinction between the planning of operations and the planning of their material support. In actual practice, logistic plans continued to be drawn within the Navy Department much as before; under the Commander in Chief, by the bureaus, and to a certain extent by the Office of Naval Operations. The distinction between the fleet and the shore establishment, although it is clearly indicated in theory, could not be maintained in practice.

In July and August, as the problem of supplying Pacific operations and of maintaining base installations grew, the strengthening of the plans agency under the Chief of Naval Operations became necessary.

The whole situation of logistics planning was reviewed once more, beginning in September, when the management engineering firm of Booz, Allen, and Hamilton, which had previously made management studies of the Navy Department, was requested to make a survey of Naval Administration and particularly of the Office of Naval Operations. Their final report was issued on March 15, 1943, but because of the urgency of the problem, they were asked to make interim reports and recommendations, which they did on November 5 and December 24. On the basis of these interim reports a number of changes were made in the administration of the Navy Department, among the most important of which was the establishment of a Logistics Plans Division under the Chief of Naval Operations.

The great virtue of the Booz investigations was that they approached the problem of organization on a purely functional basis, unencumbered by traditional notions of naval organization. From this functional approach the proper relation of logistics planning and strategic planning was drawn. Concentrating upon the weakness of the planning agency under the Chief of Naval Operations their first report of November 5 found three serious conditions resulting:

"(1) . . . . Logistic situations and possibilities have not been fully or properly represented to F1 (the Cominch) Planning Section in their strategic planning and in their makeup of operational plans. (2) Under these circumstances there has been no real integration and coordination of logistic plans with strategic plans. In such a situation strategic plans may be made that are not logistically feasible, or it may require so long to determine logistic feasibility that the value of strategic planning is seriously impaired. (3) Because Op-12 (the CNO Plans Division) has been unable effectively to plan logistic operations, the Division has been to a critical extent by-passed in the dissemination of logistic planning information which derives from F1 and from Operational plans. This has made it necessary for the project divisions in Naval Operations such as Base Maintenance to do individual project planning. Thus there has been no central control of logistic planning and good coordination of the efforts of logistic agencies all the way down to the material and service bureaus was next to impossible."

Paradoxically, the Booz report demonstrated that if the aim was to secure the most effective correlation between logistic and strategic planning, the combination of these two functions within a single office was not desirable. Logistic planning, it suggested, must be established as a separate function, contributory to strategic planning, but not necessarily of it, before it could be performed properly under the necessary single control.

Several other significant points were made by the Booz report. The effectiveness of logistic planning would depend upon two sources of information. First, it must have advice as to strategic plans and probable operations on which it could determine the character, volume, and timing of the material support required. Secondly, it must have adequate information as to the status of all material projects from which it could supply to strategic planners a well-informed judgment on logistic or material feasibility. Logistic plans should be the link, in short, between the definition of strategic aims and intentions and the execution of plans for the procurement, assembly, and delivery of material. To this end, it recommended that, in the reconstitution of a logistics plans division under the Chief of Naval Operations, it should be made up of officers directly representing the material bureaus, which alone had information as to the status of material programs. A much simplified presentation of this functional relation can be seen in the figure opposite.

Another point, which followed very closely the idea of separating planning and execution recommended by Admirals Horne and Farber, was that the supervision of material programs, once they had been broken down by the Plans Division into separate projects, should be divorced from the planning function. For this purpose they recommended the establishment of a projects section under the Assistant Chief of Naval Operations for Maintenance which should take the logistic plan as broken down by the Plans Division and supervise its execution by the project divisions of Naval Operations, such as Fleet Maintenance, Base

THEORETICAL EVOLUTION OF A LOGISTIC PLAN

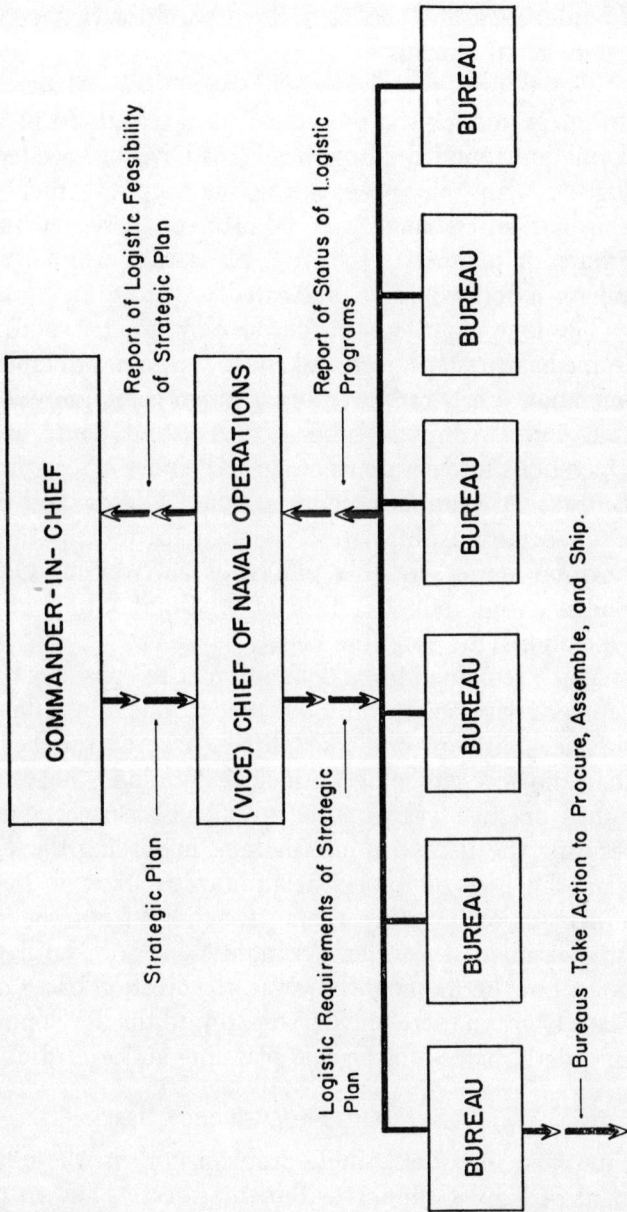

COMMANDER-IN-CHIEF

(VICE) CHIEF OF NAVAL OPERATIONS

Report of Logistic Feasibility of Strategic Plan

Report of Status of Logistic Programs

Strategic Plan

Logistic Requirements of Strategic Plan

BUREAU

BUREAU

BUREAU

BUREAU

BUREAU

BUREAU

BUREAU

—— Bureaus Take Action to Procure, Assemble, and Ship.

Maintenance, and the Naval Transportation Service, and by the material bureaus.

The Booz report laid great stress upon what it called an integrated logistic procedure, having as its focus and information center the Logistics Plans Division. Strategic and logistic plans, it saw as being built up together with a constant interchange and adjustment between the two groups of planners. Upon the plans thus formed all subsidiary action would be predicated.

The first report was made on November 5, and almost immediately steps were taken to put its principles into operation. Early in November, a progress section was organized under Admiral Farber, the Assistant Chief of Naval Operations for Maintenance. In December officers from the Bureaus of Supplies and Accounts, Yards and Docks, Ordnance, and Ships were assigned to duty in the Plans Division under an able officer, Rear Admiral Oscar C. Badger, who took the title of Assistant Chief of Naval Operations for Logistic Plans.

Much remained to be done in order to carry out the concept as envisioned in the Booz report. The establishment of the new division embodied little more at the beginning than the acceptance of a principle. Working that principle out in practice was to prove a difficult task, particularly in securing the necessary information, in placing the Logistic Plans Division in proper relation with strategic planners, and in divorcing its planning functions from the project supervision of the other Assistant Chief of Naval Operations. For the moment, however, the creation of a Logistics Plans Division represented a step toward the development of an orderly process of logistic planning and execution.

Assemblies and Advance Bases

THE most important single problem both in the establishment of logistic support within the theaters and in the organization of supporting elements within the United States continued to be the development of advance base units. Within these major units as originally conceived—the Lions, Cubs, and Acorns—were most of the supporting elements that were to be provided for our combatant forces. The term major naval bases comprehended airfields, piers, supply and fuel depots, reserves of equipment, roads, dry docks, and construction facilities, to mention but a few of their components. In their organization and assembly, their delivery to destinations overseas, and in the use made within the theaters of the materials made available lay the key to logistic support during this early period of the war.

As the program developed during the latter half of 1942, the problem was one of adjusting the existing advance base units as previously conceived, to the particular needs of the theaters. By July 1, 1942, according to schedule, one Lion and three Cubs were in large measure ready to be shipped forward. Shortly thereafter, Cub No. 1 began its movement to Espiritu Santo in the New Hebrides, where Rear Admiral Byrd, after a special investigation of the South Pacific Area, had recommended the establishment of an additional advance base. Lion No. 1, however, a much larger unit, was detained on the West Coast for almost six months, while an unplanned Cub No. 13, not scheduled for assembly or shipment until many months later, was improvised out of personnel and materials assembled for Lion No. 1. Early in 1943, Lion No. 1 also began its movement to Espiritu Santo, where upon arrival it was extensively reformed to meet the peculiar needs of the base.

The experience of Lion No. 1 illustrates clearly the difficulty in adapting the advance base units as procured and assembled to the shifting and special requirements of the forward areas. Few of the Cubs which were sent out followed exactly the lines on which they had originally been assembled. Units had been added, and some had been taken away. Repeated requests were received from area commanders that Lions and Cubs be reshuffled in their composition, emphasis generally being placed upon the formation of smaller and more flexible assemblies. A typical dispatch from the theater to the Navy Department was one of July 1942, "Requirements (specified in a previous message) involves 2 Cubs split 3 ways." Frequently new units were being formed either within the theaters or in the United States designed for special purposes and cutting radically across the lines of Lions, Cubs, and Acorns.

Not all advance bases in the South Pacific, moreover, were established as the result of planned expeditions. Auckland's development proceeded rapidly by unplanned accretions. The case of Noumea was even more outstanding. Instructions issued in May to Vice Admiral Ghormley as Commander South Pacific had indicated that no basic plan for the establishment of a base in Noumea would be provided. The principal activity there, it was contemplated, would be under the Army, the Navy furnishing harbor defense and a port director and staff. In June 1942, when Admiral Byrd made his inspection, no great increase in the Navy's activities at Noumea was foreseen. In August, however, with the beginning of the Solomons campaign, the importance of Noumea as a supporting base began to increase rapidly. In September, Admiral Ghormley called attention to the expanding activity in the harbor and in particular to the urgent need for personnel and equipment to unload ships and handle cargo on shore. The Chief of Naval Operations immediately took measures to provide essential equipment. Between the Commander South Pacific and the Chief of Naval Operations there then developed a rapid interchange, in which the Area Commander indicated by almost daily dispatch the increasing requirements of the base and the Chief of Naval Operations reported the measures which had been taken. On October 17, Admiral Ghormley recommended the establishment at Noumea of a base of 20,000 men, more than double the size of a Lion.

The same process of accretion was going on in some degree

at all bases in the South Pacific. New airfields were laid out, supply depots expanded, boat pools, repair shops, hospitals, recreation centers, docks, power plants—the whole equipage of supporting shore establishments—were constantly added.

Under these conditions it was impossible to contain the distribution of advance base units and materials within the limits of the Lion, Cub, and Acorn assemblies as originally conceived. The original concepts had served a useful purpose in fixing a goal for procurement and in stretching production facilities to the maximum. But in the task of distribution they were too large and cumbersome. Some more flexible system was required—one under which, without going back to a wholly retail procedure, the specific needs of the theaters could be met.

In order to forestall the dissolution of assembled Lions and Cubs into completely dispersed and heterogeneous smaller units the Chief of Naval Operations had directed that no personnel or materials were to be transferred from previously assembled units without his authorization. In some cases, as in the formation of Cub No. 13 this authorization was given. But there is also reason to believe that to meet the requirements for the great volume of unplanned shipments, bureaus having custody of earmarked materials were compelled to draw upon the Lions and Cubs as reserves. In actual practice Lion and Cub assemblies were coming to be used as stockpiles out of which smaller units were formed for distribution purposes. Unless the concept of wholesale procedure was to go no farther than procurement and assembly of units, leaving their distribution to an ungoverned retail process, new units of distribution, adaptable to the needs and conditions in the theaters had to be developed.

The manifest need for a viable tool for distribution of advance base materials was supplied by a "Catalogue of Advance Base Functional Components" promulgated by the Base Maintenance Division of Naval Operations on

March 15, 1943. The catalogue was comparable in many respects to those issued by a mail order house such as Sears, Roebuck or Montgomery, Ward, yet it had one very important difference. The items listed were not the individual tools of support required to establish and operate an advance base; neither were they complete advance bases, large or small, representing all the tools already assembled. They were rather "tool chests" or components built up on functional lines, each designed to fulfill a necessary function at an advance base. Taken together, they represented the sum of individual units constituting a major base but they could be selected individually, combined, and regrouped with relative ease so that advance base assemblies could henceforth be tailored fairly exactly to the varied and changing requirements of the theaters.

Just how this remarkable tool of administration came into being can probably never be determined precisely. In part it derived from the repeated practice of theater commanders of asking for modifications in the larger base units. In part it developed out of the practice of bureaus and forwarding agencies of pilfering the larger units for special purposes. It was also a natural extension of the practice of forming specialized units to meet unexpected requirements. The Construction Battalion was a natural forerunner of the functional component, as were Carrier Aircraft Service Units (CASU's), Base Aircraft Service Units (BASU's), and other specialized combinations some of which had their genesis in peacetime maneuvers before the outbreak of war. Out of these suggestive prototypes, various officers in the Office of Naval Operations, with the assistance of certain of the bureaus, gradually conceived the notion of organizing all base components along functional lines and setting them forth in catalogue form.

The origin of the concept for use in the establishment of advance bases may be traced back as far as the Rainbow War Plan of July 1940, which put forward the idea of "Base

Units, designated and grouped along functional lines," but that plan appears to have lain unheeded during this time while the functional component was being worked out in practice. Early in December 1942, Captain R. W. Cary, Director of Base Maintenance, urged the organization of units along purely functional lines with the end in view of abolishing Lions and Cubs altogether. From that time forward until the first publication of the catalogue in March the work was prosecuted vigorously. No formal authorization or directive sponsored it, but various bureaus, particularly Ships, Aeronautics, and Yards and Docks, showed a keen interest in the project.

In developing the catalogue a distinction was drawn between primary and secondary components. Thus units for such purposes as airplane maintenance or repair, fleet supply, tank farms, landing craft, communications, or ship repair formed generally the primary group. To these could be added in the proportion required for the primary components the housekeeping, medical, and to a certain extent the construction units. Given, therefore, the primary functions which a base unit was called upon to perform, it was possible to assign at once the essential units and their subsistence and service groups. Since requirements for bases were generally conceived by strategic planners in terms of their task assignments, the system was excellently adapted to bridging the gap between operational requirements and material programs of support.

Many other advantages were inherent in the catalogue. The catalogue itself was a brief, concise description of 79 functional components arranged under 14 major groupings. Supplementing it there was an abbreviated volume of advance base outfitting lists containing allowances transposed into terms of functional components from the original lists for Lions and Cubs. This in turn, was supplemented by a far more voluminous catalogue of allowances, which by the end of the war ran into 479 volumes, weighing 250 pounds, and indicated the requirements of each component down to the last wrench and cotter pin. For assembling agencies this latter was a necessary instrument, but it was not essential to the purposes of the planner or the area commander, who could define their requirements briefly and accurately by reference to the catalogue and the abbreviated outfitting list.

The original catalogue published in March was a crude and experimental document, but during succeeding months many refinements were made. In the second edition, for example, certain of the bureaus totalled up the weight and cube of components for which they were responsible, and this great aid to shipping agencies was extended subsequently to all components. Gradually, all components were assigned to the bureau having principal interest in its materials so that their procurement and assembly was woven into the basic bureau structure of the Navy. The list of components developed from the original 79 to nearly 250, including such diverse units as oxygen generating plants, typewriter repair, malaria control, sawmill, and gardening units in addition to the primary components such as ship and airplane repair. Needless to say, successive refinements were also made in the equipment, packaging, personnel training, and other elements making up the individual components.

The original Lions and Cubs were not entirely abolished as Captain Cary had anticipated in December. They continued to be discussed as larger units and in a number of cases, where a major installation was required, they were assembled and shipped. But the essential factor of flexibility was supplied by the functional components. Henceforth, whether for establishing a new base or augmenting facilities already established, the functional component catalogue supplied a common language which could be understood and applied both in the theaters and the United States. It was one of the outstanding achievements of the war.

Transportation

PROBABLY no phase of the logistic effort felt more strongly the impact of expanding operations than did the organization for overseas transport. As the year 1942 drew to a close, the shipping situation became increasingly tense. The problem was essentially one of inventory—the growing discrepancy between the requirements for tonnage for all purposes and the amount available. Yet there were many contributing factors which conspired to aggravate the natural condition of shortage. Two factors in particular—the increasing proportion of tonnage under military employment and conditions in the military administration of shipping—acting together, placed severe strain upon the relations between the military services and the civilian shipping administration.

By December 1, the shipping requirements for the South Pacific area and the Mediterranean alone were already twice the military requirement for all theaters of war only eight months before. The portion of total available United States tonnage allocated to or controlled by the Army and Navy, which in March had been 22 per cent had now risen to approximately 50 per cent. Tonnage available under the War Shipping Administration had risen during the same period, it is true, from 5,865,000 deadweight tons to 10,725,000 deadweight tons. Approximately half of this increment represented gains from new construction not cancelled out by losses; the remainder had come from the assumption of control over shipping still in private hands, a source which by this time had been completely exhausted. Moreover, it is noteworthy that the losses of United Nations tonnage during November, when the landings were made in North Africa, reached the highest figure of any month of the entire war. Totalling 1,202,000 deadweight tons, they exceeded the gain from new construction by 261,000 tons and marked the first month since June that a net loss had been suffered. These basic inventory facts do not explain entirely, however, the extremity of our shipping position at the end of 1942. The difficulties of meeting even the minimum requirements for shipping were greatly increased by the circumstances under which shipping had to be operated. Evasive routing lengthened the voyage time, while the necessity of matching vessels of disparate speed in single convoys and the days lost by loaded vessels awaiting convoy sailings added also to the total turnaround time in almost all services.

Still another factor which complicated the operation of military support shipping was the difficulty of securing a "full and down" loading of vessels, the maximum utilization of cubic and weight capacity. The character of military cargo and the many special circumstances governing its flow did not permit the standard of capacity utilization that would be considered necessary in a commercial operation. Capacity was, in fact, not being utilized, and in many cases this failure was one which might be remedied by better administration on the part of the military services. But at the same time the War Shipping Administration, thinking largely in terms of commercial standards and goaded by the necessity of meeting all the demands of the national effort, took perhaps too rigid a view of the problem.

Finally, a good deal of difficulty was being experienced in matching the outloading capacity of United States ports with an equivalent discharging capacity on the other end. Military exigencies directed cargo to many new and outlandish places where port capacity was either nonexistent or utterly inadequate. In December 1942 the consequences of this fact were beginning to be seriously felt. Ships were banking up in idleness at receiving ports such as Noumea and Murmansk, waiting their turn to be unloaded. Once unloaded, because of the shortage of ships within the area, they frequently had to be retained for local shuttle service.

All of these factors, coming acutely to a head at the conclusion of the year, served simply to accentuate the basic issue which had underlain the administration of shipping since the beginning of the year. That issue, stated in essence, was the extent to which unity of control over shipping and its ancillary functions required the assumption by the civilian agency of responsibility over matters primarily of military concern. It is not necessary to review in detail the progress of relations revolving around this issue. The War Shipping Administration had insisted upon a rigid adherence to the rotating pool system which took too little account of the pressing needs of the theaters for local shipping. It had insisted upon a rigid definition of the term "fleet auxiliary" in transferring vessels to Navy control. It had even sought to bring the Joint Purchasing Board in New Zealand under the cognizance of the civilian Combined Shipping Adjustment Board as "essentially a shipping problem."

For its part, the Navy, faced with the responsibility for protecting all shipping, had regarded the War Shipping Administration's operating control as more or less probationary and had toyed with various formulae which would have shifted operation of shipping in military services back to its control. In October the Secretary requested Mr. Walter Franklin, Vice President of the Pennsylvania Railroad, to review the Navy's transport organization and make recommendations for its improvement. The Franklin plan, delivered to the Secretary on November 13, called for the assumption of operating control over all military shipping by the Navy. This plan was discussed at length between the Army and Navy. Whether or not the War Shipping Administration was informed of the Franklin recommendation it is impossible to say, but it is clear that the War Shipping Administration was highly suspicious of Navy policy during this period and that mutual confidence between the two agencies was breaking down.

The issue came to a head in December, when the War Shipping Administration secured from the President a directive authorizing it to control the loading of all military cargo

except for assault purposes and to bring into its pool of shipping the combat loading and other assault vessels of the
Navy when they were not employed in combat operations.
Such an arrangement would have projected the War Shipping Administration deep into the province of military conduct of the war on a level coequal with the Army and the
Navy. Strong representations were made to the President by
the Joint Chiefs of Staff, and the directive was rescinded. No
change was made in the basic alignment of responsibilities.
The net effect of the controversy was a clearing of the atmosphere and a more determined effort on the part of all
agencies to work within the system as originally defined. In
January 1943 an important step was taken in the establishment in San Francisco of a Joint Army, Navy, War Shipping
Administration Committee for Ship Operation whose purpose was to work on a regional basis, exchanging cargo, assigning ships and piers, simplifying vessel itineraries, and in
general coordinating the shipping programs of Army and
Navy in the interest of more economical utilization of tonnage. It was to prove a useful instrument for logistic coordination between the services.

Meanwhile, during the autumn of 1942, the Navy was increasingly aware of defects in its own administration of shipping. The Booz report noted that "Naval Transportation
Service Operations are curtailed by the fact that the division
has to perform its functions within the limits imposed by an
outside Government agency, the War Shipping Administration." But beyond its comments on the lack of information in the Office of Naval Operations as a whole, its investigation did not bear closely upon the problems of overseas
transportation. Mr. Franklin's report covered the transportation problem more fully, tracing the transport operation
through most of its ramifications in the tidewater terminals and overseas. His recommendations, however, were tied
closely to the proposal to assume operating control, which
never came to fruition. Improvement in transport organiza-

tion had to be made, therefore, in small and limited stages and not by a major reorganization of shipping control and administration.

The most persistent difficulty from the beginning had been the inability of the Naval Transportation Service to secure the information essential for estimating the Navy's requirements for merchant shipping. The first effective solution to this dilemma was reached on October 5, 1942, when the Commander in Chief directed that an estimate should be prepared of Navy shipping requirements for all purposes during the period from December 1942, through June 1943. For the first time by this directive the disclosure to the bureaus of information on operational plans was authorized. For the first time, therefore, they were in a position to inform the Chief of Naval Operations of the probable requirements by *destination* of naval cargo and personnel. By drawing a distinction between requirements for the establishment of bases (which would be furnished by the bureaus) and requirements for the maintenance of bases and forces afloat (which would be furnished by the Commander in Chief Pacific Fleet), Admiral Horne was able, also for the first time, to draw theater agencies into participation in the determination of requirements.

The estimate prepared under the directive of October was the most complete and exhaustive guide to shipping requirements that had yet been assembled. It comprised as well in all its parts a valuable schedule for all logistic activities. But it had one serious defect, in that it was only a single estimate and did not initiate a continuing procedure of assembling information on logistic movements. It was inevitable that changes in either the logistic or strategic outlook would outmode the estimates for the latter months of the period.

A second measure was directed toward the establishment within the theaters of a more efficient system of port directors through which shipping could be controlled, discharge facilities developed, and the turnaround of vessels expedited. The port director system within the United States had been established well before the war and had proved generally adequate for its task. Little provision appears to have been made in War Plans, however, for the establishment of an overseas port director system either to direct the movements of vessels or to establish and operate stevedoring service.

Port directors had been provided in the plans of early 1942 for the establishment of bases, but in most cases their functions were limited to directing the movement of vessels within the harbor and to the issuance of routing and communications instructions. They were not staffed or organized to deal with stevedoring problems, nor had any system of reporting been established between them and the Naval Transportation Service by which the latter could be kept informed of congestion in the harbors and regulate the movement of vessels from the United States accordingly.

The deficiency in stevedore organization derived from the Navy's anticipation that its efforts in the Pacific would be primarily afloat and that shore installations would be largely under Army auspices. The Navy's extensive base establishment had clearly not been foreseen. The lack of an efficient system of ship movement control, which was a constant irritant between the War Shipping Administration and the military services stemmed from a host of conditions. It was part of the price of decentralized organization. It reflected as well the failure to comprehend the great scale and critical importance of the shipping effort.

The situation was summed up in the report of Mr. Franklin: "One of the most important parts of the Naval Transportation Service does not appear to exist today, i.e., representation . . . at the ports of discharge. Great economies in the use of ocean tonnage can be accomplished by the establishment of Naval Transportation Service offices, properly coordinated with the staff of the commanding officer at the important ports of discharge. Where port directors have been assigned to foreign ports, they are not properly tied into the headquarters of the Naval Transportation Service at Washington." In brief, once a vessel left the shores of the United States, the Naval Transportation Service had almost no knowledge of its subsequent location or employment.

This condition was amply demonstrated in the growing congestion at Noumea during September and October, which was duplicated on a smaller scale at all bases. On October 13, the Vice Chief of Naval Operations wrote to all theater commanders requesting that they establish port organizations under base and force commanders, whose principal task would be to expedite the turnaround of cargo vessels and transports. Port director units were added to the list of functional components then evolving, and on October 14, the Bureau of Yards and Docks, which was responsible for the administration of Construction Battalions, was directed to organize special battalions for stevedoring operations.

The effects of these measures could not be felt immediately. Congestion in Noumea, for example, continued to increase through December and January until at one time as many as one hundred vessels were awaiting discharge. Moreover, the system of port directors was not, in fact, "tied into" the headquarters of the Naval Transportation Service. Port director units tended to be absorbed into the larger advance base units, and where a local commander found more urgent use for personnel, transfers were made and the unit lost its identity. Finally, it may be pointed out, these measures were palliative and could not seriously affect the larger issues of supply which governed the employment of shipping. The development of effective shipping control procedure depended upon the evolution of logistic machinery as a whole.

The Basic Logistic Plan

CONGESTION in the ports of advance bases was a natural and inevitable concomitant of the increasing tempo of the war.

At the same time it was symptomatic of various weaknesses in the system of support, which must be remedied if the requirements of impending operations were to be met. Since tonnage was chronically short, shipping conditions were the first to reflect weaknesses in the system at large. For this reason, therefore, the effort to secure a general reform in logistic procedures had its historical origin in the problems of shipping.

The Franklin plan, submitted to the Secretary on November 13, contained a broad survey of transport organization broken down into its principal phases: movement of materials within the United States, loading at the tidewater terminals, and movement by sea including the operation of merchant vessels. These problems had been considered, moreover, not only in their relation to the logistic organization of the Navy, but also upon the broader basis of coordination of logistic activity between the Army and Navy. Mr. Franklin recognized clearly that the heart of the problem lay in the coordination of activity in theaters of joint operation. Whatever was done, therefore, in the organization of transport would depend upon coherent direction from the theaters based upon a clear concept of unified logistic effort.

For transport, Mr. Franklin recommended that movement by rail continue to be controlled separately by each service; that materials for all overseas establishments of the Army and Navy be loaded by the Army through its ports of embarkation with certain exceptions in the case of construction materials then loaded through advance base assembly depots at Davisville and Port Hueneme. Supplies for the fleet would continue to be loaded aboard Service Force vessels at the Naval Supply Depots. All vessels would be operated by the Navy. Within the theaters unloading of all cargo would be under Army supervision except in special instances. Most important of all, priorities of shipments would be determined on a joint basis by the theater commander.

Shortly after its submission the basic recommendations of

the Franklin plan were drawn up into a "Plan to Consolidate Supply and Transportation of Overseas Forces of Army and Navy," and delivered to the Army for its consideration. General Somervell's reply to Admiral Horne was enthusiastic. "It is my opinion," he stated, "that we must go even further than proposed in the Navy paper in the initial effort to consolidate the two transportation services and to eliminate duplications and conflicts." General Somervell then proposed a completely unified transportation system under the command of the Army Services of Supply, in which the Army would be primarily responsible for the movement of materials to tidewater, loading, storage en route and at the ports, and the Navy for manning, repair and operation of merchant vessels as well as for their routing and escort. On December 30, an elaboration of the plan suggested by General Somervell was presented to Admiral Badger by General W. D. Styer, Deputy Commander of the Service of Supply. General Styer's plan did not add much to the basic principles outlined by General Somervell, but there was one notable deletion in the scheme. Probably because of the crisis then pending in affairs with the War Shipping Administration, the suggestion that the Navy should take over and operate merchant shipping for military purposes was deleted. Discussion of joint logistic organization thus began to pass from the field of shipping in which it had originated to the broader field of over-all organization.

General Styer's plan for unified supply and transportation services suggested a fairly complete consolidation of Army and Navy logistic organization both within the theaters and in the United States. On January 7, 1943, Admiral Badger, Director of the Logistics Plans Division, presented an alternate plan which suggested that coordination rather than consolidation between the two services be attempted. Progressing from the theaters back to the sources of support within the United States, his remedy for the problem of joint effort moved in diminuendo.

Having studied the general problems of joint logistic support and the Franklin and Army proposals, Admiral Badger concluded that there was urgent need for "closely coordinated, possibly, unified Logistic Planning and Supply systems" within the overseas theaters of joint operations. There should also be "full and complete coordination of effort . . . through a suitable coordinating organization" between Army and Navy transportation agencies. Between the military services and the War Shipping Administration, he saw the need for "cooperation and mutual understanding."

At the same time, Admiral Badger's studies indicated, he said, "(a) The inadvisability of effecting drastic changes in the internal organizations of the War and Navy Departments, or in the duties and responsibilities of those agencies of the Army and Navy which handle the procurement, storage and transportation of personnel, material and equipment within the continental limits of the United States. . . ."

Between the two services agreement had thus been reached on placing logistic planning and operation within the theaters upon a joint basis under the control of the single theater commander. Between the theaters and continental agencies there should also be a single priority list by which the latter would be guided in loading and shipping materials forward. The Navy did not desire, however, a thorough consolidation of transport agencies which would place the control of internal transport and storage upon a joint basis. It believed that tidewater agencies should be coordinated and that complete consolidation of logistic effort and organization should be confined to the theaters, where unity of command was exercised.

The distinction drawn here between coordination and consolidation was real, and it would be profitable to pause for a moment and consider its basis. The real roots of difference between the Army and Navy rested in two fundamentally different systems of distribution organized for the support of different kinds of fighting forces. Of all forces operating in the overseas theaters, Army ground forces were the least mobile both in their tactical deployment and in their composition. Tactical units of known size and character remained over relatively long periods in known locations. Their requirements for maintenance, therefore, could be determined fairly exactly on the basis of fixed tables of allowances and reckoned in tons per man per month. They were supported locally by established depots built up gradually as increased forces were deployed, between which and the United States it was possible for supply to be carried on largely on a wholesale basis. Given these factors, it was possible for the Army Services of Supply to operate as a centralized organization, fully integrated in all the sequential phases of the movement of supplies. Supplies moved in a relatively unbroken flow from large depots in the continental "Zones of Interior" through ports of embarkation to established depots overseas. Over all the process a very real measure of control was exercised by its headquarters in Washington.

Naval forces, on the other hand, had necessarily to be more mobile in their composition and deployment. Within certain limits task forces varied according to the requirements of a particular operation; their area of operations was broad and uncertain. Support, therefore, had to be organized with the greatest possible degree of flexibility. If possible, the Navy would have preferred to render all its support to the fleet through the medium of floating and mobile base forces and train, capable of moving behind and with the striking forces, setting up and taking down its shop as occasion required. Forced to depend upon shore installations, it had still to aim at the widest and most flexible dispersion of supporting elements. The alternative would have been duplication of large facilities in various potential areas of operation. Naval forces, moreover, were reckoned in terms of ships rather than men. New types were constantly being added to the operating forces whose maintenance requirements were at best uncertain and whose allowances had also to be flexible. In contrast to the Army's system, naval logistic organization was decentralized, less fully integrated, leaving maximum freedom to local agencies, combining, for example, storage and issuing facilities together at tidewater, where they would be in a position to meet the demands of the fleet with the greatest promptness. Until the Navy had sufficient freedom of action to determine the basic direction of its effort, sufficient control of the sea in forward areas, and sufficient reserves of material to establish major advance bases and depots, the argument could be supported that it was best served by a looser system of control.

For purposes of joint effort, therefore, coordination alone was possible for the Navy without a wholesale reorganization of its system. At any level of operation—at loading points, for example—it was possible for naval agencies to adapt their methods to those of the Army. Had such agencies been consolidated, however, they would have had to work upon the same basis, either centralized or decentralized. Conversely, in the case of the Army, to have adapted its operation at any single level would have required a sacrifice in the degree of centralization and integration under which it operated.

Out of this basic incompatibility, from which sprang the Navy's unwillingness to consolidate continental agencies of distribution and the Army's unwillingness to delegate greater authority, for example, to the ports of embarkation, was hammered out a compromise solution, the "Basic Logistical Plan for Command Areas Involving Both Army and Navy Operations," issued on March 8, 1943, over the signatures of Admiral King and General Marshall. Its main provisions were directed toward coordinated logistic effort within the theaters from which, it was hoped, would stem coordinated direction for the guidance of logistic agencies within the United States.

To each area commander the Basic Plan granted full control and responsibility for all logistic services within the areas under his command. To exercise such control he was directed to establish either a joint logistic-supply staff or to arrange for joint staff planning and logistic operation. Specifically, each commander was charged with keeping Army and Navy agencies informed of future requirements and of the readiness and adequacy of all service facilities and personnel, determining levels of supplies to be maintained in the area, arranging for the supply of common items to both services by a single agency, and arranging for the interchange of emergency logistic support with other area commanders. Systematic information would be supplied by the area commander on needs for all military forces, the priority of Army and Navy shipments arranged in a single list, on storage and discharge capacities, and on items obtainable locally which could be screened out of requisitions on mainland sources. Based upon this information and acting with identical priority lists, Army and Navy seaboard shipping agencies were charged with necessary coordination to meet combined requirements of both services in the allocation of shipping and the loading and routing of ships.

The broad importance of the Basic Logistical Plan was two-fold. In the first place, as it intended to do, it provided the means of coordination of theater logistics. Obviously, the degree to which that coordination would be effective depended upon the measures taken to establish joint logistic planning and operating agencies. In the South Pacific, considerable progress had already been made in that direction. In the Central Pacific, some tentative steps had been taken early in the war towards joint organization, but they had all been small. Implementation of the new plan, moreover, did not follow immediately in the Central Pacific area. Not until somewhat later in the year, when major operations were closely impending, was a suitable joint logistic staff developed. In the Southwest Pacific, the degree of coordination between the services remained smaller throughout the war than in any of the theaters involved. In the Atlantic where no unified commands had been established, the fleet commander was at first unwilling to adapt his procedures to fit the concept of the Basic Plan; subsequently he acceded and an adaptation suitable to the widely dispersed effort in the Atlantic was applied.

The key to the plan for joint logistic effort lay in the joint priority list. For planning and execution within the theater it was the central factor. To the extent, therefore, that the joint list reflected the relative needs of various units within the theater irrespective of service, continental agencies would be guided in procuring, assembling, and shipping the personnel and materials necessary for a joint military effort. Upon its accuracy and refinement would depend the responsiveness to military exigencies of the continental supporting system.

This fact brings out a second major factor in the development of logistic procedure introduced by the Basic Logistical Plan. By its terms the principal responsibility for determining logistic requirements was shifted from the central command to the field commands under which operations were to be carried out. The desirability of such a delegation of responsibility had long been recognized in principle, but in actual practice it had been the Naval Transportation Service, acting through the San Francisco port director, that had determined shipping priorities, the Base Maintenance Division of Naval Operations that had conceived and directed the establishment of bases, and various offices under the Commander in Chief and in the bureaus that had determined the forces required, the levels of supply to be maintained, and the schedules and deployment of various supporting troops and services. To a far greater extent than ever before, therefore, the theater commander was charged with providing guidance and direction for the various logistic programs necessary for the accomplishment of his strategic directives.

Within the framework of the Basic Logistical Plan, planning responsibilities were more precisely defined and distribution could be more efficiently managed. The groundwork was laid for a better control of shipping employment and for the extension of the advance base system onto a scale only dimly foreseen. These possibilities, it should be pointed out, were inherent in the Basic Plan, but they were potential rather than actual. Much required to be done before the possibilities of the system were realized. Yet it brought both services abreast of the problems with which they were confronted. It moved them nearer the solution of their joint problems, and at the same time it opened the way for the Navy to the solution of its own problems of logistic organization and procedure. The Basic Logistical Plan provided, therefore, the cornerstone of method and authority upon which the structure of Pacific logistic support was ultimately to be built.

CHAPTER IV

BUILD-UP FOR THE OFFENSIVE

IN the broad chronology of the war the summer and autumn of 1943 offer little of major interest to the operational historian beyond the landings in Sicily and the beginnings of the campaign on the Italian mainland. In all other theaters of the war, although pressure was maintained and minor advances in position were made, the tempo and scale of our operations remained upon the same plateau. The conclusion of the Guadalcanal campaign in February 1943 was followed by slow, bitterly contested advances into New Georgia and the Central Solomons. In the Southwest Pacific, naval forces assisted in the advance to Lae and Salamaua. In the North Pacific, Attu was regained and Kiska occupied. Around these positions the activity of air and surface forces was steadily intensified. Yet the objectives of the Pacific operations of 1943 were limited. Although carried out in pursuance of directives of the Joint Chiefs of Staff, they were supported in large part by resources already built up within the area or flowing to it without noticeable effect upon the widening channels of normal supply. Except for the Mediterranean landings, no major campaigns undertaken introduced large incalculables or committed logistic resources on a high priority basis.

In contrast to the level plateau of operational history, the summer and autumn of 1943 was a time of mounting logistic effort. The fact that operations in the Pacific could be supported from local resources and through already established channels of supply bears witness in itself to the growing capacity of the logistic support system. From the hand-to-mouth condition of 1942 we had progressed to a position of relative abundance. The Solomons offensive begun at Guadalcanal, for example, could now be extended while at the same time reserves were accumulating both in the theaters and in the United States for the support of the great operations to come. In this swelling volume of goods and services—surplus to the needs of the moment—lay the genesis of a new kind of logistic effort.

The major problems of logistics during 1943 continued to be the production and procurement of goods and services. But in the progress in that direction already achieved and in the pattern of operations impending there was foreshadowed the need, particularly in the system of distribution, for something more than the simple, direct action techniques which had served in the early phases of the war. During 1943, therefore, the extension of physical means of support was accompanied by a renewed interest in naval organization, in which once more the search was undertaken for a formula which would reconcile conflicting interests and jealousies of long standing and at the same time meet the requirements of the emerging problems of logistic support.

The year 1943 witnessed a great increase in the physical structure of support in the Pacific. Geographically, the overseas shore establishment remained substantially within the limits already under our control at the end of 1942. Noumea and Espiritu Santo in the South Pacific continued as the main foci of services and supply, at which support was rendered to the growing fleet forces and through which supplies were distributed in the area as a whole. Throughout the year their growth was phenomenal.

Hawaii, too, began to assume an importance it had not enjoyed during the first year of war. As efforts were concentrated upon preparations for 1944, stockpiles and military population grew, operational training was intensified, and supporting forces were assembled and put into readiness for the beginning of the Central Pacific offensive. Warehouses and fuel and ammunition depots spread out in the areas surrounding Pearl Harbor and the new airfields at Barbers Point and Kaneohe Bay. New piers and dry docks were installed. Between December 1942, and the end of 1943 the number of vessels of all types actually on hand under the Service Forces in the Central Pacific increased almost five-fold from 77 to 358. Pearl Harbor was on the way to becoming the mighty base a complacent America had assumed it to be in 1941. The increase of vessels under the Service Forces was also preparing the way for a return in part to the concept of floating base support which might be expected to give to the striking forces greater range and mobility.

The build-up of forces overseas during 1943, great as it was, was still slight by comparison with the expansion of the naval establishment within the United States. Deliveries of war materials and the recruitment of personnel during 1943 represented in most categories the greatest percentage increase of any period during the war and a substantial total in actual volume and numbers. During the year, for example, naval personnel, excluding the Marine Corps and Coast Guard, had increased by more than a million to a total of well over two million. Deliveries of vessels reckoned in numbers were twice as great as in 1942. In tonnage they were three times the total of 1942 and only slightly behind the figure of 1944. In navy yards, training stations, ports and depots, the conclusion of the year found the material and logistic effort within the United States approaching its peak, bringing forth the fruit of the first two years of the nation's war effort.

Under these conditions the systematization of the Navy's logistic procedure was imperative. Only by a more precise definition and elaboration in working procedures of the concepts outlined in the Basic Logistical Plan could the Navy hope to keep under satisfactory direction and control the flow of goods and resources now beginning to issue forth from the production machine. That effort had to be carried on simultaneously in the three principal areas of logistic responsibility—the Navy Department, which supplied broad direction and guidance for the overall conduct of the logistics of war; the theaters, which supplied direction for specific operational and maintenance purposes; and the continental supporting establishment which performed the actual labors of procurement and distribution in response to the dictates of both long range and short range programs.

The Navy Department

THE problem of systematizing the central direction of logistic effort had its roots in the continued weakness of the Office of Naval Operations. Primarily this was a problem of organization, the full explanation of which must await a detailed study focused not upon logistics alone but upon all the problems of the relations among military commander, bureau chief, and civilian secretary which have run as a major theme through naval administrative history. Yet it is necessary and possible, even with the limited evidence presently available, to sketch the main outlines of organizational development within the Navy, for it was organization in its broad sense that set the limits within which effective coordination of the logistics task could be achieved.

The authority granted to the Chief of Naval Operations in the Executive Order of March 1942 over the "preparation, readiness, and logistic support of the operating forces" had marked the farthest point of advance in the long and subtle contest for control between the professional and civilian. Yet it was by no means a complete victory, for the Executive Order had been signed by the President only after the Office of Procurement and Material had been separated from the jurisdiction of the Chief of Naval Operations and established within the Secretary's office. Until the new authority had been implemented, moreover, by the development of staff and organization within the Office of Naval Operations itself, which was competent in fact to assume the burden of direction, the Executive Order must remain a paper instrument. An attempt by Admiral King in May 1942 to strengthen the Office of Naval Operations by the creation of three Assistant Chiefs—for Air, Personnel, and Material—who would also be respectively the Chiefs of the Bureaus of Aeronautics and Personnel and the newly created Chief of Procurement and Material had been frustrated by the President's refusal to go to such limits in the integration of material matters under professional control. Throughout succeeding months the Office of Naval Operations had limped along, as the Booz report indicated, lacking the personnel, information and prestige necessary to discharge its mission. Instead of making progress, it had lost ground, frequently losing its ablest personnel to the headquarters of the Commander in Chief and delegating functions it had not the means to perform to the bureaus or to field agencies of the continental shore establishment.

Much of that decentralization had been necessary and unavoidable under the conditions of 1942, but by the beginning of 1943 it had been carried too far. The truism offered by Admiral Badger in March that "Decentralized effort is effective only when the various agencies are provided with guidance sufficient to promote intelligent use of initiative" had a very real application to the performance of the logistics task within the Navy Department.

In May 1943 Admiral King renewed his efforts to effect a reorganization of the Navy Department which would provide a strong Office of Naval Operations. This time he proceeded with greater caution, avoiding, for example, the identification of bureau chiefs and Deputy Chiefs of Naval Operations and paying homage to civilian authority in his plan by assigning to the Under Secretary, the Assistant Secretary, and the Assistant Secretary for Air respectively "all matters relating to Naval material, personnel, and naval aviation." At first glance, such a provision might appear to insinuate civilian influence more completely into the affairs of the Navy Department, but in proposing to place under the Vice Chief three Deputy Chiefs for Air, Personnel, and Material, over whom would be a fourth Deputy charged with plans and general supervision, he had provided a counterweight of military organization which would more than offset the concession to civilian influence.

If Admiral King's intention in extending his reorganization scheme to the secretarial level had been to make it more palatable to the President, it did not succeed. Sources of opposition to the plan were not lacking in the Navy Department, bureau chiefs in particular offering a formidable phalanx of opposition reinforced by close associations with the Congress and in some instances with the White House. But the real opposition to the proposal was the President himself, who knew too well the intricacies of Navy Department relationships not to perceive the true direction of the reform. Although the plan came to him with the endorsement of both Admiral King and Secretary Knox, he refused to approve more than the establishment of a Deputy Chief for Air.

The ultimate outcome of Admiral King's attempt to strengthen the Office of Naval Operations was the establishment of the Deputy Chief of Naval Operations (Air) in a relation to the Vice Chief which can be described only as ambiguous. Asked by the House Appropriation Committee in March 1944, about his relation to Admiral McCain, the Deputy Chief for Air, Admiral Horne remarked, "He has a peculiar situation. He is my deputy for Air. He works under me. But he is an excellent man and Admiral King also leans on him a good deal. . . ."

The "peculiar situation" of Admiral McCain referred not only to his divided responsibility to Admirals Horne and King. Part of Admiral King's intention in suggesting the creation of an office for air logistics under the Chief of Naval Operations was undoubtedly to bring air planning and program direction more closely under the control of central planning and directing agencies. In bringing the office into being he had responded to an insistent popular demand for elevating air matters and air men to a higher position in the counsels of the Navy Department. But the aim of integration had not been achieved.

Since the authority of the Deputy Chief for Air was delegated directly from the Secretary and was defined for air logistics in terms identical with those which defined the powers of the Chief of Naval Operations over all logistics, the Deputy Chief was within the Office of Naval Operations, but not essentially of it. In major matters, he must refer to Admiral Horne, but within and between their respective offices the problem of integration still remained. In planning and executing logistic programs no real integration of air under the general divisions of the Office of Naval Operations was accomplished.

The Logistics Plans Division of CNO, for example, did not determine aircraft requirements. The old confusion, only slightly mitigated, persisted in matters of materials for air bases, personnel requirements, carrier complements and other matters which could not be isolated from overall programs. Its responsibility for comprehensive advance planning, therefore, could not be fully discharged. It did not have in its organization a real staff of air men capable of evaluating the needs of air programs. It did not have the genuine contact with the conditions from which air needs derived. The progress sections under the Assistant CNO for Maintenance were even less well equipped to deal with the execution of air programs. Out into the field organization for logistics and the channels of distribution the same schismatic weakness was extended, complicating the performance of the logistic task.

The lack of jurisdiction over planning and execution of programs was not limited, of course, to aviation logistics alone. Over many other categories of equipment entering into logistic support the Office of Naval Operations continued to have little or no control. In fact, it may fairly be said that only in the realm of advance base materials, and that by virtue of the component system developed in 1942, did the planning and progress divisions of Operations exercise any real measure of direction. In ships, ordnance, personnel, and general supply as well as inland transportation the control of the Chief of Naval Operations varied from a casual contact to almost no contact at all.

In lieu of establishing a proper identity between lines of functional and administrative responsibility, the Navy had to resort to committee procedure in many cases to achieve the necessary coordination. Thus, for example, an Auxiliary Vessel Board established shortly before the war exercised cognizance over all auxiliary vessel programs, and a District Craft Development Board exercised cognizance over yard and harbor craft. Committee procedure, however, was cumbersome. It represented coordination among several agencies as distinguished from central direction by a single authority. While committees and boards might reconcile disagreement and provide a forum for the interchange of information, they were dependent for the execution of policy upon the agencies represented. They were stopgap remedies, which themselves multiplied confusingly within the loose-jointed naval organization. For the most part bureaus and field agencies remained autonomous, not only in the proper sphere of execution, but also in that higher level of planning and policy where a single direction should have been supplied.

With the failure of Admiral King's scheme of reorganization of May 1943, efforts to increase the power of military direction over logistic programs through organic reorganization came to an end. Early in the spring of 1944, Secretary Knox appears to have considered a proposal to abolish the Office of Naval Operations and substitute for it a Chief of Naval Logistics in the person of Admiral Horne on a level coequal with the Commander in Chief. Such a plan would have had the merit of giving to the Chief of Naval Logistics the real control over material programs which had long been

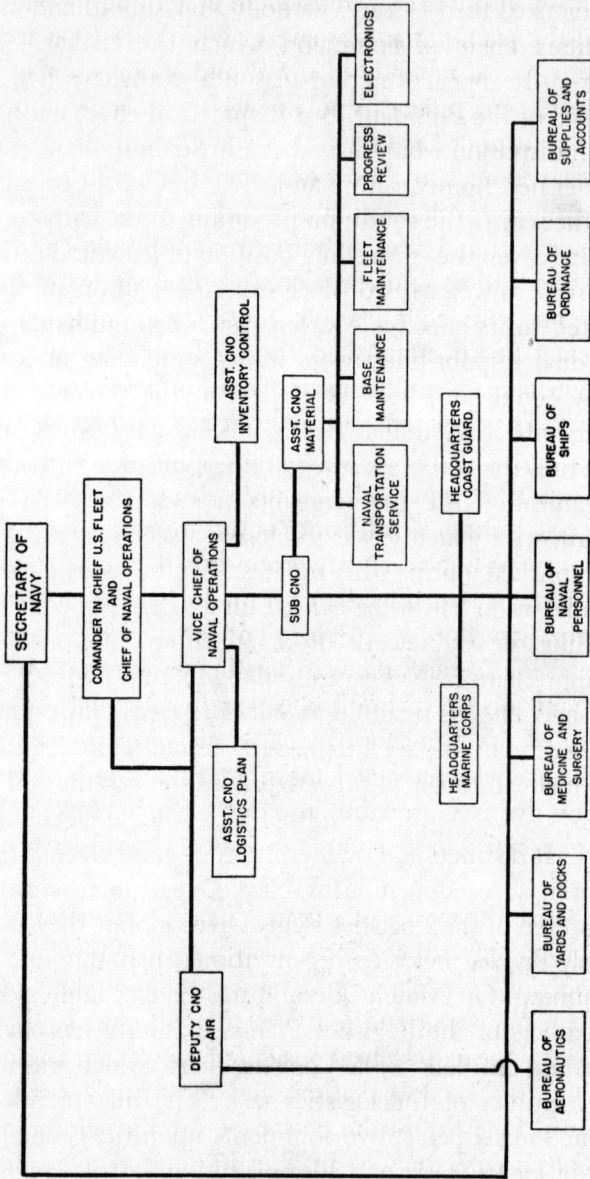

ORGANIZATION OF PRINCIPAL LOGISTICS AGENCIES
IN THE NAVY DEPARTMENT 1942-1946

recognized as necessary, without that subordination to the military chain of command which the civilian Secretary feared. It appears for that reason also to have had the approval of the President. But its practical effect upon logistic administration would have been little more than a reversion under new nomenclature and with the benefit of experience to the schismatic condition prevailing in the early months of 1942. Given the controlling position of logistics in the spring of 1944 as well as two years' experience of organization unsuited to its effective coordination, the arguments in favor of dual responsibility were more compelling at least than they could have been in 1942. But the project came to a halt with the sudden death of Secretary Knox in April. Neither the complete integration of aviation into the naval organization nor the reorganization of the Navy Department, with which it was so closely associated, was to be accomplished during the progress of the war. Logistic administration had to be carried on and developed, therefore, within the framework of organization laid out in 1942. Minor changes in organizational structure might be accomplished, but the basic alignment of responsibility and control was not to be altered. Progress toward better integration must be made through improved procedure, liaison and persuasion.

That distinction, however, was not at all clear at the time. During succeeding months, Navy Department reform efforts centered in the Logistics Plans Division, but they were curiously divided between organizational planning and logistic planning. On March 30, Admiral Badger addressed to all members of the Logistics Plans Division a lengthy memorandum entitled "Basic Logistic Plans" which was intended as a primer of the logistics task. The memorandum contained many perceptive comments upon the general character of logistic tasks and administration, but its language was obscure, and in itself it failed to draw a clear distinction between task and organization. The aim it suggested was to set up a Basic Logistics Plan, but it did not make clear whether the "Plan" would be a substantive schedule of logistic requirements or simply an outline of procedure under which a substantive plan would ultimately be formed. Eschewing any intent to tamper with organization and procedures within the bureaus and other procurement agencies and stating "that the approved Naval construction program is to be considered as requiring no change for the successful pursuit of the war as now foreseen," Admiral Badger set as his goal simply "the development of clear and comprehensive instructions as to the interchange of information between all logistic agencies." These instructions, developed in systematic form, would be published as Part I of the "Basic Logistics Plan." What would constitute subsequent "parts" was not indicated.

The systematizing of logistic information was a necessary and preliminary step to the establishment of better coordination. In August, on the basis of reports submitted by the various bureaus and offices of the Navy Department, Admiral Horne promulgated a schedule of information and reports as a guide to all agencies in the dissemination of information. The schedule made some additions and deletions in the reports already being made, but in the main it represented a reworking and classification of existing information. All information was broken down into three general classes—Basic Logistics Information, or the sum of components derived from the established or planned strength of the fighting forces; Area Logistics Information, which indicated the status of supply and readiness within the area; and Shipping Information, which indicated the schedules and priority of area requirements as well as the availability of cargo for shipment from the United States. The first heading would constitute presumably that information dealing with the establishment of stockpiles and the creation of forces within the United States. The second would indicate the status of area reserves and serve as a source of usage factors and rates of consumption. The third would supply the necessary link between the two, providing the guidance by which the rate of flow would be governed.

The three-fold classification of information fitted that broad division of responsibility between the theaters, the Navy Department, and the continental establishment which was slowly emerging in practice. It also opened up several areas, among which the most important was shipping, where systematic advance planning had been frustrated by lack of information. It provided in general the basic pattern of interchange of information under which the Navy operated during the remainder of the war.

Yet the Survey of Information had certain weaknesses and limitations. By concentrating simply upon the orderly arrangement of reports, many of which did not pass through CNO, it missed the opportunity to penetrate into the form and character of reports themselves and to set up in them certain uniform features which would make possible the synthesis of information from all sources for high level purposes. Without some such synthesis it was impossible for the Office of Naval Operations to become the true nerve center of logistic administration.

Secondly, the survey was directed only toward the interchange of information among agencies subordinate to Admiral Horne. One of the major weaknesses in the system, however, was the sparsity of information on strategic plans and operations which was made available by the Commander in Chief. Within the Office of Naval Operations only Admirals Horne and Farber regularly had full knowledge of plans being formulated under the Commander in Chief. Admiral Badger, by virtue of former service under Admiral King enjoyed a favorable position, but the remainder of the Division Directors under the Vice Chief were forced to depend upon such information as they could secure informally. The situation of bureaus and field agencies was even worse. Until the close of 1943, despite two years of experience, the assumption was adhered to by the Commander in Chief that information need pass in only one direction—from logistic agencies to strategic planners.

Finally, it must be repeated that the interchange of information did not affect the distribution of administrative responsibility. The attempt was consciously directed toward tightening logistic administration through better information alone without disturbing the existing pattern of operation or authority. Unless the Logistics Plans Division, which had assumed responsibility for defining the flow of information, was to enter the field of administrative direction and designate also the agencies responsible for action in various instances, there could be no guaranty that the flow of information would be brought in harmony with the pattern of action responsibility within the logistic system.

The Continental Establishment

IN fairness, it must be pointed out that the limited objectives of the informational survey described above had been set at a time when two schemes of organic reorganization had been under consideration. The first was that effort to reorganize the machinery of the Navy Department which has already been described. The second was a plan to reorganize the Naval Districts, which were the basic administrative divisions within which operated the continental supporting establishment. Both projects were of importance, for if within the Navy Department power and responsibility tended to flee from the central Office of Naval Operations to the bureaus, it must be remembered that each bureau in turn presided over an elaborate system of subordinate agencies in the field, within which the process of decentralization was carried even farther.

Over all the activities of the continental shore establishment the District Commandant, responsible directly to the Chief of Naval Operations, was intended to supply regional coordination and a link between headquarters and the field.

Since the outbreak of the war, however, the plight of the district organizations had become even more serious than that of the Office of Naval Operations. Organized primarily for local defense purposes, they had failed to keep pace with the growing pressures of the logistic task. Within the districts lines of command were steadily blurred by the weed-like growth of new activities for transporting, procuring, storing, assembling and training which had been established either by the Navy Department or by theater commands. Between the districts there existed no effective means of cooperation in logistic matters, which continually overflowed their geographic limits. Hampered by the limited application of Naval Regulations and suspended between Washington and the theaters, they were the step-children of the naval organization. Suspended also between operational duties carried out under the control of the Sea Frontier Commanders and the growing burden of logistic activity, carried out under no higher regional authority whatsoever, the districts were divided, confused and impotent.

Far from being able to coordinate and direct activities within their districts, commandants were often hard put even to keep up-to-date catalogues of the agencies over which they supposedly presided. When, for example, the Commandant of the Third District in New York attempted in the summer of 1943 to list all the activities within his District, he was forced to consult the New York Telephone Company for complete information. Seventy-seven agencies were discovered whose previous existence had not been known to the Commandant.

On the West Coast, where the Navy's major effort was concentrated, the confusion of agency and responsibility was greatest. Activities of the Bureau of Yards and Docks were carried on largely through its Advance Base Assembly Depot at Port Hueneme and coordinated for the coast as a whole by a Director of Pacific Theater Yards and Docks set up in 1942. Naval Supply Depots at Oakland, Seattle and San

Diego looked to the Bureau of Supplies and Accounts for their direction rather than to District Supply Officers. At Oakland in 1942, for example, the commanding officer had held out strenuously against the efforts of the District Commandant to place all loading under the supervision of the District Port Director. Only the superior aggressiveness of Captain Davis, the port director, had prevented a serious division of loading responsibility within the port of San Francisco. The Fleet Air Wing Command, West Coast, established in 1942 by the Fleet Air Commander with subordinate commands in Alameda and Seattle exercised jurisdiction over aviation personnel, maintenance, and supply. Service Forces Pacific, the principal agency of support within the theater, was represented by its subordinate command in San Francisco.

Many of these agencies, it is true, supplied regional coordination for certain major categories of activity. In shipping, which occupied a focal position for all activities, the San Francisco Port Director had established a central booking office for all cargo and had assumed the role of regional shipping director for the West Coast. With the establishment of the Joint Ship Operations Committee early in 1943, that element of coordination was fortified and extended to include both Army and Navy shipments. But even the Port Director's Office, which was certainly the strongest of the regional agencies and operated with relative autonomy, was limited in its scope.

In general the pattern of regional logistic activity was one of many separate autonomies over which district organization had almost ceased to exercise any influence. The resultant in terms of logistic effort was increased overhead, waste of personnel and material, and, worst of all, the impossibility of carrying out the policies and programs of the central command, even to the limited extent that comprehensive direction was supplied by the Navy Department.

As early as September 1942 Admiral King had discussed

with Admiral Hepburn the possibility of a study of district organization looking to its reform. In February 1943, when the problem was referred to the Vice Chief of Naval Operations, Admiral Badger was charged with a study of the Twelfth District, whose headquarters were in San Francisco, with a view to applying to all districts whatever scheme of reorganization could be developed there. In June still another commission headed by Rear Admiral Wright was assigned under a somewhat broader precept to investigate district and logistic administration in the Fourteenth Naval District in the Hawaiian Islands. Through the spring and summer of 1943, Admiral Badger's study was carried on, and in August a proposed General Order was prepared.

The General Order embodied a broad scheme of district reorganization developed along functional lines and intended to create within the districts a full-scale logistic organization and staff with direct responsibility over all procurement, supply, distribution, training and other supporting activities within the District. Under a Vice Commandant, charged with logistic supervision and coordination, district organization was intended to duplicate in smaller scale that of the Office of Naval Operations. Certain of the larger districts would be charged with coordination of contiguous district activities on a regional basis. Between this organization and the Office of Naval Operations a direct contact was to be established.

The proposal for a wholesale and drastic reorganization of the Naval Districts necessarily gave pause to many naval officers. Despite its obvious inability to meet the demands of war, the concept of the district was woven deep into the fabric of naval administrative thinking. Tradition regarded the district as inviolable. Caution militated against radical changes during the war. Fears were raised that the entire continental establishment might cease to function while changes were being effected. Nevertheless, fully cognizant of the sweeping character of the changes proposed, Admiral Horne endorsed the reforms, as did Admiral King and Secretary Knox. But once again the project of reorganization foundered upon the ancient issue between civilian and military authority. Considering that control of the bureaus by the Chie: of Naval Operations was as dangerous within the districts as within the Navy Department, the President steadfastly refused to sanction the proposed General Order. Subsequently upon the findings of the Wright Commission, a reform of the Fourteenth District very similar to this General Order was carried out by direction of the Commander in Chief. But in the Continental District organization as in the Navy Department, the development of logistic procedures was constrained to move within existing organizational forms.

In November the Secretary returned once more to the problem of district logistic organization and directed the establishment within each district of an Assistant Commandant for Logistics. But the substance had fled from the earlier proposal of reform. Although the Commandant was charged with logistic responsibility in terms very similar to those of the General Order, the necessary machinery to develop effective logistics control was not provided. The powers of the Assistant Commandant were defined as advisory and coordinative. The appointment of the Commandant of the Twelfth District as the Pacific Coast representative of the Vice Chief without providing him also with the means of control was a solution in name only. The situation of the Navy's continental supporting establishment remained substantially what it had been.

Just why the measures actually taken should have fallen so far short of the original effort is difficult to determine. The moral effects of the President's refusal may be imagined, but that alone does not explain the apathy and the paucity of accomplishment which followed. A more satisfactory explanation appears to lie in the limited resources in able personnel then at the disposal of the Vice Chief of Naval Operations. Organizational proposals had been generated in the newly formed Logistics Plans Division, which appears to have been the only agency under the Vice Chief in a position to develop such plans on a comprehensive basis. But organizational planning was not the true function of the Logistics Plans Division. Theoretically, at least, it had been established to formulate logistic plans, and it could enter into the field of administrative direction only at the expense of its primary planning function. In fact, neither in the development of a comprehensive plan of logistic requirements nor in the field of administrative reform did the organization under Admiral Badger make very great progress during this period. Distracted between two fields of endeavor, it was wholly successful in neither.

Still a third explanation may be sought in the personality and leadership of Admiral Horne and in the character of the office over which he presided. In experience, professional accomplishments, and personal temperament Admiral Horne was better suited to the difficult role in which he had been cast than perhaps any other naval officer could have been. Placed at the cross-roads of civilian-military pressures, he had a remarkable capacity for recognizing the many sides of the Navy's administrative problem and for reconciling its many contradictions in harmonious working relationships. Forced to persuade the Chiefs of Bureau, he persuaded successfully because of the confidence they reposed in him. In an atmosphere where personal temperaments frequently clashed Admiral Horne managed to preserve an attitude of calm objectivity and realism. When, for example, the Secretary asked his opinion of the scheme to make him Chief of Naval Logistics, he replied that he could "make it work" either way. If placed under the Secretary on a level equal with Admiral King, he said, he would still receive his direction in strategic matters from the Commander in Chief. If left in his present position, he could continue by persuasion rather than by formal authority to administer the logistic activities of the Navy Department.

Aided by a photographic memory, rapid comprehension and broad understanding of the problems with which he dealt, Admiral Horne was able to do his own work without the aid of elaborate staff organization. He had created amidst the confusion and contradiction of the Navy Department a personal system in which without reference to forms of organization the unresolvable was resolved and direction was supplied. It is significant that in the spring of 1943 he chose as his principal subordinate Rear Admiral W. S. Farber, an officer thoroughly schooled in the incongruities of the Navy Department whose ruling purpose was similarly to "make it work."

Those very qualities of tolerance, breadth and patience which fitted Admiral Horne so admirably for his task defined also the limits to which reform of logistics administration could be pursued. Not disposed to push issues à outrance, he worked always within the limits of the possible. He did not pursue reform for itself. Nor did he desire to jeopardize the confidence he enjoyed among the Chiefs of Bureau by reaching down into the bureaus even in search of functions which properly belonged in the Office of Naval Operations. Finally, he was limited by the magnitude of his task to considering problems only in their broad aspects. Detailed matters quite naturally had to be left to subordinates.

Unfortunately one of the significant areas of the possible was the quality of the personnel Admiral Horne had to assist him. Subordinate echelons in the Office of Naval Operations were ill-suited to carry forward without benefit of system and organization the direction supplied by Admiral Horne. With a few exceptions the office was manned by men not chosen for their administrative abilities but because they could be spared from the "more important" duties of command. Industrious and well-intentioned, they lacked as a group that kindling quality of the mind upon which in subordinates a personal system must rely. They formed a lackluster environment in which all too frequently the ruling principle of "make it work" which guided policy at the higher levels emerged at the operating level as "let it work." To have altered this condition would have required qualities of ruthlessness and stubbornness which Admiral Horne did not possess.

Logistic Development in the Theaters

THE problem of logistic administration within the Pacific theater was at once simpler and more complex than that of the continental United States. It was simpler because in the Basic Logistical Plan of March 1943 the direction had already been marked out. Within the theaters, moreover, there was no need to resolve those persistent and insoluble problems of civilian and military responsibility which beset the continental establishment and the Navy Department. The theater was the undisputed province of the professional. Nor was it necessary after March 1943 to worry about the basic authority under which coordination of logistic activity between the two services could be accomplished. If a method remained to be worked out, at least the general aim had been defined and authority provided.

On the other hand, the very necessity of integrating all forces and their logistic support within the theater raised problems of detailed procedure and direction whose solution bore directly on the success or failure of operations. Theater logistics demanded both in planning and execution a degree of refinement far greater than was required in the United States. Working with limited resources in men and materials, compelled to operate in areas where few facilities for distribution existed and where physical limitations were severe, the theater logistician performed a difficult and exacting task.

The major logistic problems confronting the Commander

in Chief Pacific Ocean Areas during the remainder of 1943 were substantially those already defined. Within the area he must provide the machinery for a maximum pooling of Army and Navy resources, eliminating duplicating services, emphasizing common stockpiles and the interchange where possible of other goods and services. He must, in short, provide a single plan for the utilization of all resources made available to the area and provide under the plan the machinery for assuring its execution.

A second problem confronting the area commander was the development of machinery by which he could supply to logistic agencies within the United States the guidance necessary in moving forward men and materials in the proper quantities and at the proper time. The importance of a joint priority list had been emphasized in the Basic Logistical Plan, but it may be added that its importance was not limited to joint priority. Within the Navy's logistic system itself no system of priority of shipment had been developed which took its direction from, or referred in more than a perfunctory way to, the status of need in the theaters.

Finally, upon the theater commander there was devolving more and more the responsibility for planning not only specific operations but also their logistic support. The obvious purpose of this build-up of forces in the Hawaiian area was to enable it to act as an advanced point of distribution. Once operations in the Central Pacific had begun, Pearl Harbor like Noumea in the South Pacific, would be a principal staging and forwarding point. Between it and the target areas into which we proposed to move there must be created a retail distribution system suitable in the first instance for the support of assault operations and secondly, for the rapid development of operating and supporting facilities.

Until the close of 1943 this phase of logistic support in the Central Pacific was minimized. Military operations in the South Pacific continued to occupy the center of the stage. Satellite bases immediately around Pearl Harbor such as Midway, Palmyra and Canton were of minor importance compared with active and growing establishments like Efate, Tulagi and Espiritu Santo in the South Pacific. Priorities on critical materials were higher in the South Pacific area, where equipment passed more quickly into operational use. Until the Central Pacific offensive had been launched, shipments to Pearl Harbor were absorbed by the base itself, either as reserves for coming operations or for the maintenance of its own base facilities.*

Planning activity also was limited by the relative inactivity within the Central Pacific theater. Unlike planning in the Navy Department, where requirements were set in terms of long-range programs without close reference to specific operations, theater planning could not proceed until strategic objectives had been firmly defined by the Joint Chiefs of Staff. Navy Department planning, moreover, was directed primarily toward procurement, whereas theater plans were for purposes of distribution. Looking essentially toward the consumption of supplies in military operations, they represented a draft upon the continental reserves already procured and assembled. They were short-range, concrete and necessarily more detailed and exact than the broad program planning of continental logistics.

Throughout the greater part of 1943 no specific operations in the Central Pacific were approved by the Joint or Combined Chiefs of Staff. Although on the basis of discussions in May 1943 the Combined Chiefs included the

---

* During the first six months of 1943 shipments from West Coast ports were: to Central Pacific 707,557 short tons; to South Pacific 856,645 short tons. Of the Central Pacific total 500,647 or approximately 70 per cent were construction materials. Shipments of construction materials to the South Pacific were only 281,000 tons or 30 per cent. On the other hand, shipments of combat and ordnance materials and petroleum products, two categories which indicate a high degree of operational activity, were: *Combat and ordnance materials*: Central Pacific 34,000 short tons; South Pacific 100,000 short tons: *Petroleum products*: Central Pacific 15,000 short tons, South Pacific 214,000 short tons.

seizure of the Marshalls and Carolines among assumed undertakings for 1943 and 1944, they added that "no firm plan for this operation exists" and that "a firm estimate of requirements cannot be made at this time." Until the conclusion of the Quebec conference in August, campaign logistic planning hung in abeyance while attention was concentrated almost exclusively upon regulating the flow of shipments between the mainland and Pearl Harbor.

Among the principal measures directed by the Basic Logistical Plan had been the establishment under the theater commander of either "unified logistical-supply staffs consisting of both Army and Navy officers" or of "joint staff planning and operations on the part of the respective Army and Navy staffs within his jurisdiction." The alternative proposed here was between a single staff operating as an integrated planning unit and a committee procedure in which coordination of planning would be sought between separate Army and Navy staffs. So far as the Pacific Ocean Area was concerned, however, the alternative was only apparent. If the result of staff planning and direction was to be a single, joint priority list for the movement of personnel and materials from the United States, sooner or later the theater staff would have to devote itself to joint logistics.

On April 6, immediately after receipt of the Basic Logistical Plan, Admiral Nimitz promulgated his own Basic Logistical Plan for the Central Pacific Area, and on May 20 a similar plan for the South Pacific was published by Admiral Halsey. Both plans chose the less radical alternative and established Joint Logistical Boards composed in the Central Pacific of the Commander Service Forces, the Commanding General Hawaiian Department and the Commandant 14th Naval District; and in the South Pacific of the major type commanders under Admiral Halsey. Under each of these boards was established a Joint Working Board and a Joint Secretariat. But for all the apparent emphasis upon joint logistics, the establishment of joint boards did not alter substantially the composition of staffs and the methods of procedure already prevailing within each theater.

Under Admiral Halsey actual practice in joint logistic planning and operation had already developed beyond the terms of the plan. Pursuing a campaign which was largely amphibious in nature and in which fleet forces played at best a sporadic role, and engaged constantly in the conduct of active operations which combined all services, he had already developed in practice a unified logistics staff. By grouping his various type commanders into a Joint Logistics Board he had done nothing more than give formal recognition to what was already a fairly closely knit operation.

In the Central Pacific, however, the problem was one of creating joint organization and working procedure where separate staff organization was already well established and where there was not as yet any combined operational activity which could serve as an impetus to unification. Unification was also hampered by the fact that members of the Joint Working Board and Secretariat continued their full-time duties on the separate staffs from which they came. The inclusion of the commandant of the district moreover, gave to the Joint Board a hybrid quality which did not obtain in the South Pacific, for it threw into what should have been an evolving operating agency an organization whose character was derived largely from peacetime continental practice. The fact that it was included at all reflected simply general confusion in the working establishment at Pearl Harbor between the functions of the district and of the Fleet Service Force organization.

Meanwhile, a joint priority procedure was being developed. On May 26 a directive signed by Admiral King and General Marshall provided for the monthly promulgation of a joint priority list for the movement of personnel to the Central, South and Southwest Pacific Areas. On July 20 Admiral Horne provided a working procedure under which the personnel priority list was to be developed and applied. In doing so he extended the meaning of personnel to include "unit shipments predominantly cargo but including personnel" so as to embrace the shipment of functional components which at this time at least constituted a fairly large proportion of overseas shipments.

The system in its general outlines provided for the tabulation of units available for shipment two months hence for the information of the area commander. He would then indicate on the list of available units furnished him the relative order of priority in terms of his current requirements and consolidate these in a joint list for both services. When priority lists had been received from all Pacific area commanders, they would be combined into a single master list which would be issued to shipping agencies for their guidance in making shipments.

The joint priority list was limited only to organized assemblies of personnel and material sufficiently under the direction of the Chief of Naval Operations and the bureaus to permit of their tabulation two months in advance. To the increasing volume of unorganized shipments, flowing in response to requisitions from the theaters, it had no application. Nevertheless for component units, which formed at least the major elements entering into base expeditionary forces in their early and critical phases, the joint list provided a method of orderly planning and distribution upon a joint basis.

In Pearl Harbor itself, however, the growing abundance of new materials had given rise to unauthorized projects of construction and utilization which outran all efforts to control them through the Joint Logistic Board, the workings of the Joint Priority List, or in the separate agencies under the District, the Commanding General, and other type commanders. With many separate agencies able to requisition upon mainland sources without close scrutiny from command headquarters, with confusion and duplication of responsibility persisting between the District and Fleet logistic agencies, and finally, with a growing number of Construction Battalions and other service units being held in reserve for future operations but available for the moment to carry out locally inspired projects, the build-up and utilization of resources threatened to get entirely out of hand. In June the Bureaus of Ships and Yards and Docks combined to issue a warning to the Vice Chief of Naval Operations that conditions in Pearl Harbor were rapidly approaching a state of critical disorder. With the endorsement of the Vice Chief, the Naval Inspector General, and the Assistant Secretary, Admiral King immediately authorized the commission under Rear Admiral Carleton Wright, previously mentioned, to investigate logistic facilities in the Fourteenth District and to report upon current and proposed projects from the point of view of the logistic support of present and future fleet activities.

In August, after an extended investigation, the Wright Board submitted its report. Having no better information on strategic prospects than did theater planners, the board did not find it feasible to determine the adequacy of logistic facilities beyond the end of 1943. Comments were confined, therefore, to an analysis of existing logistic organization and to projects approved for 1943.

In general, the board found that a satisfactory beginning had been made in the interchange and pooling of facilities as prescribed by the Basic Logistical Plan, but that much remained to be done. "Conscientious efforts . . . should be made to achieve as nearly as possible a thoroughly unified supply service covering all comparable items of common use and all similar logistic services. Up-to-date lists of combined facilities should be compiled; and continued attention should be devoted to developing the interchange of services."

The Joint Logistical Board required the addition of more full-time officers to its secretariat before it could become "a potent executive agency of the area commander for the furtherance of the joint war efforts." Investigation disclosed that the board had taken no steps to provide for additional hospital facilities for impending operations, had not anticipated the need for additional district craft, had been of no assistance to the area commander in preventing the back-up of naval personnel on the West Coast, and had neither originated nor processed any of the logistic reports which were customarily submitted from the area to the Vice Chief of Naval Operations. It might have added that many reports stipulated by the Basic Logistical Plan, such as information on the availability of storage by types and localities and data on discharging capacities at ports of destination, had not yet been furnished to mainland agencies.

In its investigation of the Fourteenth District, the Wright Board found much the same conditions that had been discovered in the investigation of continental districts. "Within the Fourteenth Naval District," it said, "there is no logistic office or agency per se. Its absence now and in the past has resulted in lack of long range planning and in faulty coordination of logistics. . . . Our Naval organization for the handling of logistical matters has not been developed to solve adequately the problems presented by all-out war."

As already stated, the Wright Board recommended a plan of reorganization for the Fourteenth District very similar in form to the General Order which had been disapproved by the President. Their recommendations were immediately executed by a directive from the Commander in Chief. Similarly specific reforms for the improvement of inventory and the reduction of excess or unbalanced stocks in the district were carried out by the bureaus under the direction of Admiral Horne.

The investigation of the Wright Board served not only to point out many deficiencies in area and district logistic organization, but also to bring to the attention of the Area

Commander himself the importance of logistic matters. It must certainly have contributed in part to the reorganization of the area staff which followed in September. In fairness to the Area Commander, however, it must be pointed out that the Wright report coincided closely with the conclusion of the Quebec conferences in August, which provided Central Pacific forces for the first time with definite operational objectives and the impetus toward closer unification which had hitherto been lacking.

On September 15, Admiral Nimitz announced the dissolution of the Joint Logistical Board and the creation in its stead of a Logistics Division of the Pacific Ocean Area Joint Staff. The creation of the Logistics Division was, in fact, but a part of a general move to create a joint staff in all categories of activity within the theater. Under designations J-1 to J-5, joint staff divisions containing Navy, Marine Corps, and Army members were established for Plans, Intelligence, Operations, Logistics and Analysis. Fleet staff divisions were not entirely abolished, and in some cases as in Operations and Plans they coincided in membership and function with the Joint Staff divisions. There was also in the Fleet staff a division for Aviation which had no exact counterpart in the joint organization. Even with these modifications, however, the establishment of a joint staff organization represented a notable advance in the development of unified theater command.

The joint staff benefited as well from the recrudescence of planning and preparatory activity for the operations which had been decided upon in Quebec. Early in October, it brought forth operational and logistic plans for the attack upon the Gilbert Islands scheduled for mid-November. The assault upon the Gilberts may be regarded as the starting point, for the development of joint operational effort in the Central Pacific. For the first time Central Pacific forces had now a focusing point for joint effort.

Summary of Two Years of Logistic Effort

THE history of naval logistics during the first two years of the war exhibits a curious schizophrenia. Seen in terms of administration and of adaptation of organization to an unaccustomed task it is by and large a story of frustration and stasis which contrasts markedly with the record of actual logistics accomplishment. On the one hand, efforts to lend substance to the nominal authority of the Chief of Naval Operations over the bureaus and working establishment of the Navy by the creation in effect of a General Staff organization had been successfully defeated. Throughout the Office of Naval Operations as a whole, cognizance of logistics functions was thinly distributed, and control over the working establishment was frequently vitiated by lack of information or understanding.

Three examples chosen from many will serve to illustrate this point. In December 1942 a Logistics Plans Division had been established for the purpose of translating strategic aims into logistic programs, but thus far it had extended its planning function only into the province of advance base component materials and exercised little governance over personnel, landing craft, combatant ships, aircraft or auxiliary vessels. No comprehensive plan or control procedure, holding all these subsidiary programs in balance with each other, had yet been developed. Limited energies and resources of talent had been drained off in the supervision, as well as planning, of the advance base program and in efforts to outline logistics procedure as a whole and to indoctrinate the naval organization in the essential elements of the logistic process.

An Assistant Chief of Naval Operations for Material had been established charged with the execution and implementation of logistic plans, but with a few exceptions his cognizance over the execution of material programs was even less complete than that of the Plans Division over planning.

A third illustration may be seen in the exercise of responsibility over transport. Rail transportation of material was the responsibility of the Bureau of Supplies and Accounts. Rail transportation of personnel was the responsibility of the Bureau of Naval Personnel. Under the Secretary's office a Transportation Division supervised motor transport. The Coast Guard and Marine Corps exercised fairly complete autonomy over their own internal transport of personnel and material. Loading of naval cargo in the ports was in some cases under the supervision of the Naval Transportation Service port director; in other cases of the local Naval Supply Depot, responsible to the Bureau of Supplies and Accounts. Responsibility for overseas transportation was divided between the Naval Transportation Service and the Fleet Service Forces.

Beyond the confines of the Navy Department the situation was no better. District organization continued in its archaic form with little relation to the realities of the logistic task. Logistic effort accommodated itself naturally and necessarily to the nation's industrial geography, while district lines of command and administrative responsibility remained immutable, growing progressively more obscure and irrelevant. Throughout the naval establishment as a whole there was apparent a growing discrepancy between the forms of naval organization and the emerging character of the logistic task.

On the other hand, for all the lack of suitable organization, logistic support was, in fact, being provided to the operating forces. By the close of 1943, the United States stood on the threshold of the greatest naval and military offensive in the history of warfare. Approximately 1,500,000 Navy and Marine personnel were already deployed overseas, of whom slightly under 300,000 Navy personnel and 180,000 Marines were shore based. Naval advance base establishments, large and small, in all theaters of the war had increased by the end of 1943 from the pitiful few dozen with which we had entered the war to a total of only slightly under 250. Numerical tabulation, moreover, does not indicate the teeming activity and spectacular expansion of some of the bases like Espiritu Santo, Noumea, Dutch Harbor and the Hawaiian Islands. In November, with more auxiliary vessels available, the Service Forces had reverted to the prewar concept of floating support and established Service Squadron Four at Funafuti as a mobile base. During 1943, the first of the great sectionalized floating dry docks, capable of lifting 85,000 tons, was put in operation at Noumea, and a second was in the process of being assembled at Espiritu Santo. Naval floating dry dock capacity had increased from none at the outbreak of war to 108,000 tons at the close of 1942, and 723,000 tons at the end of 1943. Issues of fuel oil in the Pacific theater alone rose from 17,000,000 barrels in 1942, to 28 million barrels in 1943, almost twice the commercial export of gas and fuel oil in the United States in 1941. Almost all vessels damaged at Pearl Harbor had been repaired and returned in improved and modernized condition to active service. In forces and in the capacity to maintain those forces in effective striking condition in the Atlantic and Pacific the condition of the Navy at the end of 1943 gave witness to two years of unprecedented accomplishment.

Between the striking evidence of logistic achievement and the apparent lack of effective direction and logistic organization there is an obvious discrepancy, in explanation of which four possible factors may be suggested. In the first place, it is obvious that a large measure of the successful provision of support was directly the product of the nation's tremendous industrial capacity. Without minimizing the accomplishments of the Navy in directing the design and production of material and the training of personnel, it is not too much to say that the real index to the country's capacity to wage war lay in the farms, factories, raw materials, railroads and schools of the nation. The achievement of the first two years had been predominantly one of production. Whatever bad effects the lack of suitable military direction may have had upon procurement programs and activities of the Navy lie beyond the province of this study. But from the point of view of military logistics, which is concerned with the disposition of goods and services once they have entered the logistic support system, the "battle of production" was being successfully waged.

Secondly, we must consider the traditional "bureau system" of the Navy. Administrative history tends often to concern itself with matters of "coordination, integration and direction" to the exclusion of substantive effort. In vast undertakings such as the Navy's logistic effort during the war, moreover, the only suitable point of view from which to observe and assess the effectiveness of an operation is at the top. No study in management and administration could hope to do otherwise. Unfortunately, when operation is decentralized, when direction and coordination are lacking, there is a tendency to assume the absence of all effort and accomplishment. The want of effective coordination, leading to excessive overhead and to duplication and conflict of function, induces very real evils into any working system, particularly when it is laboring under a narrow margin of surplus, but it does not imply the absence of all effort. On the contrary, majority opinion in the Navy has held traditionally to the tenet that decentralization of effort conduces to greater accomplishment and economy as well as to the flexibility considered necessary for the support of naval forces. That assumption has been for many years the foundation of the bureau system.

Over the course of many years bureau chiefs had consistently answered the argument for a General Staff by pointing to the record of successful bureau accomplishment, ringing the changes upon the "historical fact that the Bureau System has successfully fought the Mexican War, the Civil War, the Spanish War and the World War." In 1943 the Chief of the

Bureau of Supplies and Accounts had added to the traditional arguments a pertinent comment which undoubtedly reflected the view of most officers in the Navy: "The erection of another barrier of control over the Bureau [by establishing a kind of General Staff] with undefined powers of supervision and direction is merely setting up a control over these bureaus which is considered unnecessary and which will have the effect of establishing a slowing up process by abolishing direct action and contact."

Lacking consistent military direction the bureaus had in fact carried on the business of the Navy; had designed, procured, assembled, and shipped the necessary materials for support. Possessing money, legal authority and concrete tasks to perform; having superior information, more competent personnel, and within their separate provinces a more highly developed method and organization, the bureaus of the Navy Department contained in themselves all the elements necessary to create, expand and maintain the working establishment of the Navy. Where sufficient impetus and direction from above were lacking, the bureaus could and did set their own goals for procurement, mark out the pattern of distribution, establish field agencies and maintain contact with theater commanders. Like water flowing beneath the frozen surface of a stream, the workings of the bureau system were hidden, but not essentially impeded by the overlay of authority in the Office of Naval Operations. Thus far, if for no other reason than by default, the bureau system was on the way to adding one more war to its oft-cited record of achievement. If at times decentralization led to confusion and disarticulation within the logistic process as a whole, there are relatively few instances in which a charge of apathy could be maintained against the bureaus. Their sins were of commission rather than of omission, and the need for supervision and coordination derived in most cases from the surplus of energy and effort which poured through the bureaus from the nation as a whole into the support of naval forces.

Thirdly, although the true sources of energy were the bureaus, one must not discount entirely the personal system of Admiral Horne, for if it did not challenge the ultimate distribution of responsibility within the naval establishment, it did succeed in practice and through informal association in providing the necessary minimum of cohesion in the logistic system and the necessary contact between civil and military functions of the Navy. Of his own position, Admiral Horne has remarked. "The Bureau Chiefs were good men; they trusted me, and they did what I asked them." That description is undoubtedly accurate. The evidences of Admiral Horne's influence are not to be found in the study of formal organization nor in the exercise of directive authority. But there can be no question that within a system traditionally dependent upon the spirit of cooperation among the Chief of Naval Operations, the Secretary and the Bureaus, he exercised through persuasion and mutual confidence a very real measure of influence.

Finally, it should be observed, that despite the chronic and sometimes critical shortage of shipping, despite the lack of adequate interchange of information between the theaters and the continental establishment, despite evidences of confusion and waste within the districts and even in the theaters, the problem of the first two years had been preeminently one of production and procurement, in which the basic relation was between the civil part of the naval establishment and the civilian economy. Under the established division of civil and military responsibility the principal field of action of the Chief of Naval Operations was to be the distribution of resources already procured for consumption in military operations. During the first two years of war that problem had gradually developed, but always within the shadow of the task of production. By the close of 1943, the first phase of our logistic effort had come to an end. Henceforth, in the shifting emphasis from production to distribution the military logistic system was to receive its major test. Taking its direction not from the industrial capacity of the nation, but from the military situation, logistic effort would be constrained to move more and more within the province of military imperatives in which effective military direction would assume paramount importance.

CHAPTER V

LOGISTICS IN TOTAL WAR

Two events occurring in June 1944, only nine days apart but on opposite sides of the globe, signalled the inception of our major offensive against the Axis. On June 6 Allied invasion armies landed on the shores of Normandy, breaching the walls of "Festung Europa" and launching the drive which had as its objective the capture of Berlin and the destruction of the Nazi Third Reich. On June 15 an American invasion fleet launched the assault upon the Marianas Islands on the threshold of the Western Pacific, from which fleet operations could be extended into the waters of the Japanese homeland and planes of the Army Air Forces could attack the homeland itself.

The Marianas offensive was in fact only the high point of a series of thrusts begun in November 1943, with the invasion of the Gilberts and continued in February and March with the more rapid and expeditious occupation of Kwajalein and Eniwetok in the Marshalls. It was followed in September by the invasion of Palau, in October by the rapid succession of operations beginning at Leyte which led to the reconquest of the entire Philippine archipelago, and ultimately by the Bonins, Okinawa and the preparations for attacks upon the coast of China and the Japanese mainland.

This series of thrusts in the Central Pacific is our main interest, because it was within this unfolding strategic pattern that the naval logistic support system was developed in its most complete form. But it is important to note as well that Central Pacific operations were carried on in close relation to an equally accelerated schedule of advances in the South and Southwest Pacific. In February 1944 forces under General MacArthur invaded the Admiralty Islands, setting the stage for the development at Manus of one of the Navy's major bases in the Pacific. The Admiralties were followed by Hollandia and a succession of thrusts forward along the coast of New Guinea including Wakde, Biak, Noemfoor, Cape Sansapor and Morotai.

The schedule of amphibious operations, moreover, gives no indication of the almost unceasing activity of fleet task forces throughout the Pacific area as a whole, which by the close of the year had brought Formosa and the Ryukyu, Bonin and Volcano Islands under the range of carrier aircraft guns and bombs. Between the close of August and the beginning of November, for example, Task Force 58 or 38 was almost constantly at sea, much of the time engaged in active operations. At the end of that time it was still capable of engaging the Japanese fleet in the decisive battle for Leyte Gulf. During these two months planes of the fast carrier task forces had expended 6,000 tons of bombs, 331 torpedoes, 7,752 rockets and immense quantities of fuel and provisions. During November, its third consecutive month away from base, the carrier force took up the air bombardment of Manila in preparation for the landings on Luzon. Having completed this task, it was able at the beginning of 1945, after one month's return to base, to begin the series of operations prior to Iwo Jima and Okinawa which ranged through the Western Pacific from Hong Kong to Tokyo.

Between the series of movements toward the Philippines from the South and the Central Pacific thrust there was necessarily close correlation in strategic planning and timing. Both offensives were predominantly amphibious and relied upon covering support from both air and sea forces. The initial phases of each assault required large concentrations of amphibious craft, assault shipping and bombardment and carrier task forces. Time schedules of operations in both theaters had to be closely correlated to allow for the maximum interchange of available amphibious and striking forces and for the allocation of shipping by the Joint Chiefs of Staff for the support of both theaters. Major task forces and especially fast carrier groups were thus in constant employment in support of widely scattered landings, supplementing these covering activities with frequent strikes against enemy positions in advance of target areas.

In many cases, moreover, operations in the Central Pacific were staged and supported in part in the South Pacific. Such was the case in the Gilberts, the Marshalls and the Marianas. The Marianas assault was staged in three principal areas—the South Pacific, Pearl Harbor and the United States. Thus from the start of 1944 offensive operations in the Pacific fitted increasingly into a single pattern of attack. With the beginning of the Philippines campaign at Leyte the need for close correlation of activity in all areas, hitherto occasional, became normal. In many respects operational and logistic methods and organization varied greatly between the two principal commands in the Pacific. Each relied primarily upon its own resources and its own channels of support from the United States. But in the allocation of shipping and in the deployment of fleet and amphibious forces they bore a close relation to each other which must be observed in the strategic and logistic developments of the Central Pacific.

The launching of a full-scale offensive in all theaters of war in 1944 brought the accompanying logistic effort into its mature phase, a phase in which three dominant factors—distance, magnitude and uncertainty—conditioned the character of logistic effort. The constant lengthening of our lines of communication is the most obvious of the difficulties with which logistic support had to contend. Its effects were felt in the lengthening of voyage times and the consequently greater requirement for cargo tonnage, in the remoteness of established repair facilities from active operations and in the distance, sometimes as great as 5,000 miles, between staging areas and objectives.

The increased magnitude of operations and the expanding

volume of shipments from the United States were no less important than the factor of distance. Total shipments of naval cargo to the Pacific alone increased during 1944 by 62 per cent over those of the previous year to a grand total of 5,522,000 long tons. The increased volume of shipments was directed more and more into undeveloped areas, where storage and discharging facilities were limited or non-existent, where land areas were small and where the pressure of combat operations obstructed the orderly distribution of materials. They continued to be shipped largely from the West Coast, where transshipment facilities were already hard pressed. In its relation to the capacity of channels of distribution the expanding volume of shipments was thus one of the outstanding factors in the logistic effort of this major phase.

The third factor seriously affecting the character of logistic effort was the accelerated tempo and uncertainty of all activity, whether operational or logistic. As never before, the war had now become a war of movement. Its duration depended directly upon the mobility of operating forces and hence upon the rapid projection forward of base facilities, staging areas and airfields. Theoretically the schedule of operations was determined by logistic feasibility, and in practice this was substantially so. But with striking forces already available in superior strength, with troops, aircraft and other operational components now being produced in quantity, the tendency of strategic planners was to place the most optimistic construction upon estimated capacity to provide and transport logistic support in accordance with the schedule of operations.

After beginning the Central Pacific campaign in late 1943 in the traditional manner developed at the War College and in successive War Plans, operational planning in 1944 took on a highly flexible and opportunistic character. Target dates were constantly advanced. Eniwetok was attacked one month, Palau one and one-half months, Leyte two months and the Marianas two and one-half months ahead of original plan.

Frequent changes in strategic and tactical objectives likewise affected logistic plans and schedules. The landings in the Admiralties, originally undertaken as a reconnaissance in force, developed rapidly into a full-scale effort and drew heavily and without prior notice upon the reserves of naval base materials and components. As late as March 12 the Joint Chiefs cancelled a projected assault upon Truk, preparations for which had already begun, and substituted an assault upon the Marianas with the target date set for barely three months later. The Palau operation was modified even after the assault had begun. For tactical reasons landings on Babelthuap and Yap were abandoned after some of the forces for Yap were already embarked and en route. The result was that more than half of the advance base materials planned and assembled for installation in the Palaus were diverted elsewhere. Landings on Leyte had originally been scheduled for December 20 following an assault upon Mindanao on November 15. On September 15, however, after air attacks by Task Force 38 and the 5th Air Force had exploited weaknesses in the Central Philippines, the Joint Chiefs of Staff authorized General MacArthur to carry out landings on Leyte on October 20, eliminating Mindanao from the strategic plan. Fortunately forces diverted from Yap could be added to those already available for the operation. The effect upon logistic movements, however, particularly upon later echelons, of these constant shifts in strategic and tactical plan was considerable.

Production requirements for many advance base components were determined in some cases as much as two years in advance. The advance air base unit known as Acorn, for example, was over eighteen months in the process of procurement, training, assembly and shipment. Firm statements of merchant shipping requirements were required by the War Shipping Administration three months in advance so that requirements of one area or service could be fitted into the broad pattern of requirements for all phases of the total war effort. These are but a few examples of the intricate and extended preparations in all phases of logistic activity which were affected by constant fluctuations in operating plans and schedules.

Of the justification for this policy of opportunism in the conduct of operations there can be no question. The development of the by-passing and attrition technique employed at Truk and Rabaul was a brilliant example of the utilization of superior air and sea power in hastening the conclusion of the war. But it would be less than justice not to point out that the execution of these tactical and strategic concepts depended entirely upon the resources and the resiliency of the logistic support system. Forced to adapt itself not only to the speed-up of operations but also to the constant flux of operational planning, which allowed little margin for advance logistic planning, the logistic system was kept under constant pressure. Any slack offered by the build-up of surplus resources was immediately taken up by further acceleration in the operational schedule, and generally the line was drawn a little tighter in the process. Operational planners, quite properly, were determined to wring out the last possible drop from the logistically feasible.

The three factors of distance, magnitude and uncertainty exercised a broad and constant governance over the character of logistic effort in its mature phase. Just what that effort comprehended in more concrete terms can best be understood by examining the requirements for logistic support of all kinds in the conduct of the Pacific war. Broadly speaking, logistic requirements could be divided into two main groups. The first group, "operational" requirements, included all those elements employed or expended in active operations against the enemy, whether for the support of fleet or task forces, landing operations, garrison forces, or for the development of operating and logistic base facilities in the forward areas. Operational requirements included a multitude of elements, and they retained the designation "operational" during various successive phases in which the conditions by which they were determined varied widely.

To carry out an assault upon an enemy-held island position there was required first a naval task force to prepare the way for assault by air and surface bombardment, to cover and screen the landings themselves and to secure the lines of communication between the objective and its base of supplies. Fleet forces operated in close concert with expeditionary forces, but they did not constitute an integral part of the expeditionary force. Their requirements were not determined with close reference to it and only in part to the planned operation. Battleships, carriers, personnel afloat and lesser combatant types represented in a sense the capital plant of naval striking forces, whose maintenance requirements were fairly stable and could be calculated without reference to particular operations. Aside from battle damage and collision repairs, certain critical accessory material such as electronic equipment, and varying fuel and ammunition requirements the maintenance of basic task force units could be predicated over a fairly long period on knowable and established usage factors. The variable factor in fleet maintenance was not so much what the forces would require at a given time as where they would be when supplies or maintenance were necessary.

Expeditionary forces, consisting of landing and amphibious forces and all service and supporting units accompanying the assault, constituted the most variable factor in the determination of operational requirements. The total operation of seizing, reducing and developing an enemy-held position fell broadly into two phases. In the first or "assault" phase logistic requirements derived directly from the size and character of the expeditionary force itself. Upon this basis were determined requirements for landing craft, assault shipping, ammunition, water, rations, gasoline, medical supplies and other items of combat equipage which had to be landed with assault troops. Certain operations calculated on the rapid seizure and repair of airfields, and for this reason there were frequently included among assault echelons Construction Battalions and advance Acorn units. At Palau and in the Admiralties, for example, the speedy renovation of captured airfields exercised an important influence on tactical developments. In all cases the speed with which land-based air operations could be begun determined the time when supporting carrier aircraft could be withdrawn for other operations.

Beachmaster parties and stevedore troops were also included in early echelons. Initial assault waves, needless to say, were predominantly combat forces, but as amphibious technique developed and landing operations became more massive, there was an increasing admixture of service and supporting units in the early echelons of movement which made up the assault phase.

Supply during the assault phase was entirely automatic. As defined by Cincpoa (Commander in Chief Pacific Ocean Areas) in November 1943, automatic supply was "a system of supply in which the entire impetus is from rear to front. Each element in the supply chain must push supplies forward, without requisitions, requests or reports from forward units to be served . . . by periodic shipment of fixed quantities of supply." Determination of these fixed quantities and the periods of shipment were the major items of theater logistic planning for the assault phases of operations.

Upon the completion of combat operations, and frequently while they were still under way, the assault phase began to give way to the garrison or "build-up" phase, whose objective was the rapid conversion of the newly seized territory to two uses: first, an operating base for continued operations, predominantly air but also surface and submarine; and second, a logistic base serving as a supply and distribution center, repair base and staging and rehabilitation area.

Between these two functions there was in the early stages no clear line of demarcation. The rapid movement forward of all forces required that each objective seized become quickly the *point d'appui* of further advances. Thus the governance upon logistic activity imposed first by the tactical situation gave way imperceptibly to the influence of strategic factors and the general pattern of logistic support.

The garrison period was in reality one of rapid construction which followed generally the Base Development Plan laid out in advance by the Joint Staff Planners under Cincpoa and attached as a logistic annex to the operating plan. It was during this phase that most of the advance base functional components were delivered and established, that airfields were built and expanded, roads, storage warehouses and port facilities constructed. It was this phase, therefore, that constituted the most critical period in the logistic development of the new position.

Once shipment of construction and component materials was largely completed there followed the shipment of supply materials such as provisions, general stores and spare parts required to bring stocks at the new base up to authorized levels. Shipments of components and materials stipulated in the Base Development Plan continued to be automatic, but during this garrison period the transition was begun toward non-automatic or requisitioned supply, which was the outstanding characteristic of the second broad class of requirements generally defined as "maintenance."

One other feature of operational support deserves attention before we pass to the maintenance phase of theater logistics. Up until the inauguration of the Central Pacific offensive the principal and frequently sole reliance for the support of fleet forces had been the development of shore-based facilities. Base development continued to be the chief reliance during the Central Pacific campaign, but because of the greater distances between objectives and staging areas, the smallness of land areas in the mid-Pacific, and the rapidity of forward motion, it was impossible to rely solely upon the development of shore facilities. Rapid prosecution of the Central Pacific campaign and the exploitation of Japanese weaknesses as they developed required some means of furnishing support to task forces more rapidly and more flexibly than was permitted by base development. Mobile base facilities, which could serve during the interim for the support of fleet operations and which were not rooted to an area once it had become remote from the scene of operations became, therefore, an important operational requirement.

The concept of mobile base support had long since been worked out in naval planning, but until the close of 1943 the facilities had not been available. In October 1943 a beginning was made, when Service Squadron 4 was set up at Funafuti in the Ellice Islands for the assault upon the Gilberts and Marshalls. Made up of barges, station tankers, repair vessels and various other units of service and supply, it constituted a miniature advance base for fleet support which could be moved from one strategic anchorage to another as required by the movements of the fleet. In March 1944, Squadron 4 was moved to Kwajalein, where it was absorbed into the larger Squadron 10, newly established along similar lines. Throughout succeeding months Squadron 10 expanded until by the end of the year it consisted of five major sections located at various strategic points in the Pacific and comprising hundreds of vessels. To the few barges and ships of Squadron 4 there had now been added a vast array of dry docks, stores ships, tankers, hospital ships and salvage and repair vessels which could move or be towed forward with relative ease.

By the close of 1944, however, the need was being felt for some link between the facilities offered by Squadron 10 and the widely ranging task forces of the fleet. This need was met by the organization of Service Squadron 6. Operating as a "Logistic Support Group" this unit formed part of the task force itself. It moved with the fleet, joining it at stated intervals and rendezvous points for refueling, rearming and reprovisioning. To the limited services such as fueling at sea which had formerly comprised the duties of the train Service Squadron 6 added many others, among which the most important was rearming combat ships at sea. As the war drew to a close, it was making deliveries at sea not only of fuel and ammunition but also of provisions, small stores, mail, aircraft, motion pictures and personnel. The list of supplies and services might have been extended indefinitely had the war continued. As it was, the brief career of Service Squadron 6 had demonstrated clearly the practicability of servicing combatant forces at sea and thus of keeping them operating at sea for extended periods.

Satisfaction of maintenance requirements was the crux of the logistic problem during its mature phase. For this there were two reasons. As more and more forces were deployed overseas, maintenance materials came to represent the bulk of all naval overseas shipments. Early in the war, when the primary task was the establishment of bases and the deployment of forces, initial movements constituted a larger percentage of shipments, and with this fact in mind the Office of Naval Operations had kept under close surveillance the programs for advance base functional components. As the total of ships, bases and personnel increased, however, the volume of consumption naturally increased. And as initial equipment began to wear out, the demand for spare parts and replacements rose even more rapidly. By the close of 1944 maintenance requirements constituted 80 per cent of the total shipments to naval forces overseas.

The second reason, which goes to the heart of the Navy's logistic problem, was that of the two types of requirements it was maintenance that depended most upon the decentralized system of planning, procurement, and distribution. Most of the elements entering into operational requirements were subject to a certain amount of centralized control in one part of the naval organization or another.

Planning and preparation of combat troops, ships and landing craft were fairly closely controlled in most phases by the Readiness Division of the Commander in Chief. Auxiliary vessel construction programs were under the supervision of the Auxiliary Vessels Board and received a certain amount of informal, overall supervision from Admiral Farber, the Sub Chief of Naval Operations. Advance base functional components, as indicated above, were planned and distributed under the direction of the Chief of Naval Operations. All of these elements, moreover, were included in the logistic annexes of operating plans and moved forward under comparatively orderly procedures, which, as we shall see, were continually refined during 1944. Administratively and geographically, however, the determination and satisfaction of maintenance requirements was a decentralized function lodged in the separate bureaus and in their widely dispersed and highly ramified field agencies. Maintenance support moved forward without benefit of centralized control and direction either from the Navy Department, the seaboard agencies or the theater commands.

Until the development of detailed operational logistic planning, moreover, it was difficult to distinguish maintenance and operational requirements even in the theaters. The distinction between the two had certain approximate parallels. Thus, for example, it followed the time sequence of any particular operation, early phases being operational and later phases maintenance. In the same manner it paralleled the geographical division between forward and rear areas. The most applicable distinguishing feature, and it too is only approximate, was the distinction between requisitioned and non-requisitioned items where the requisition was originated by the ultimate consignee. This fact is illustrated by the critical importance assumed by the requisition control problem as requirements for maintenance expanded.

What was required by the beginning of 1944 was a logistic support system corresponding to the pattern of actual requirements for logistic support. The logistic task was governed primarily by the imperatives of the military situation and secondarily by the factors of distance, magnitude and uncertainty. To support the tremendous undertaking of 1944 required that an ever-increasing mass of materials move in orderly flow through channels of distribution which were already approaching the limits of their elasticity. In port capacity, storage space, tonnage availability, and in the various physical and geographic limitations of land areas in the Pacific through which the process of distribution had to be carried on there was no longer a wide margin for greater volume of shipment. The Navy was now coming to the point where it must put a camel through the eye of a needle.

The solution to this dilemma lay in three basic principles, always inherent in the logistic process, but most clearly discernible when it has attained its mature phase. These are timing, motion and selection. Effective logistic support is not so much a matter of the accumulation of material as of the correctly timed distribution of properly selected equipment and specially trained men. Motion is the decisive factor to which timing and selection contribute. Just as the New York City subway system, for example, can operate only so long as its millions of daily users are kept constantly in motion, so the structure of logistic support in the Pacific could bear the burden of mass support only so long as the great volume of shipments flowed steadily and systematically from source of production to point of consumption.

Reduced to more concrete terms, motion was essential because no point in the supporting system, whether rail and shipping facilities, continental storage and terminals or area depots, provided an adequate platform for the accumulation of more than a fraction of the materials required and being made available. Timing was required to keep motion under control and to bring the furnishing of logistic support into synchronization with the necessary phasing of operational activity. Selection was required to give due recognition to the actual degrees of urgency and priority which existed in the requirements for support. Without selective techniques there was a serious danger that the flow of urgently required items of support would be impeded by, or lose its identity in, the congestion of low priority material. Throughout the remainder of the war the history of logistic effort may be interpreted as an intensified search for administrative techniques and procedures of control through which these three dynamic principles could be infused into the working logistic process.

CHAPTER VI

THE NAVY DEPARTMENT

Basic Planning

INCREASING emphasis upon the provision of maintenance support (an emphasis which characterized the mature phase of naval logistics) called attention first to the methods of basic logistic planning by which requirements were originally determined and the process of procurement set in motion. The need for improved procedures for maintenance planning had been recognized by Admiral Badger as early as March 1943 in his memorandum on "Basic Logistic Plans." Among the principal weaknesses in the system as then operating he had noted that "largely because the Navy Department is decentralized . . . requisitions are not adequately screened"; that "At the present time there is no well-recognized replenishment program mapped out whereby the operating forces can control the flow"; that "There is no directive governing the assembly and analysis of the wealth of statistical data available after sixteen months of war"; and finally, that "present procedures result in unbalanced and excess shipments and in certain shortages of shipping because of the need of guesswork on the part of many agencies." "The critical shortage of shipping requires its most efficient use and requires more accurate forecasts of shipping needs than is now feasible under existing procedures."

The survey of the interchange of logistic information and improved methods of forecasting shipping requirements had provided partial remedies for the most critical of the weaknesses in the logistic system. But no real progress had been made against the underlying decentralization that affected the entire process of planning, procurement and distribution of maintenance materials and replacement personnel. Meanwhile, procurement of personnel and material proceeded apace. By the beginning of 1944 there was a genuine need not only for more centralized planning, but also for some method of continuing review of projects in execution and an up-to-date inventory of materials already on hand against which the need for new procurement could be assessed.

Early in 1944 the Bureau of the Budget was invited to undertake a survey of logistic functions under the Chief of Naval Operations with a view to suggesting improved procedures which might be developed within existing lines of organization. The Summary Report of the Bureau of the Budget, submitted on March 11, 1944, contained a number of broad and certain specific recommendations having to do chiefly with more detailed planning of requirements and a more constant review of bureau procurement and distribution schedules by the Vice Chief of Naval Operations. Reaction to these recommendations in the Office of Naval Operations, however, as expressed by Rear Admiral Purnell, the Assistant Chief for Material, and Admiral Horne was generally lukewarm. Admiral Purnell believed that certain of the suggestions for more extensive control of bureau activities were of doubtful legality, particularly where they would involve intrusion into the fiscal responsibilities of the bureaus. In his mind there was already as much review of bureau programs as was compatible with the existing organization of the Navy Department. The weakness, he felt, lay in the lack of sufficiently advanced and comprehensive planning by the Logistic Plans Division, which was illustrated by the fact that advance base component materials then scheduled for delivery over the entire year of 1944 would be exhausted by April. The underlying cause lay in the acceleration of operational schedules by strategic planners without adequate forewarning to logistic planning agencies. This much was certainly so.

As far as the weaknesses in the Office of Naval Operations were concerned, the view of Admirals Purnell and Horne appears to imply two general assumptions: first, that machin-

ery for close and constant supervision of bureau activities
was not possible within the existing framework of organization, and second, although it was not stated, that to attempt
to set up machinery for such a review would jeopardize the
currently happy and cooperative relation between the Office
of Naval Operations and the bureaus. Admiral King took a
different view, however, holding that "the principal correc-
tions indicated . . . can be achieved within the present basic
organization framework." Stating that officers were presently
available in the Department "competent in precept and experience" to review the logistic organization, he specified
four officers by name and directed the Vice Chief to acquire
their services and establish a Logistics Organization Unit.

The Logistics Organization Planning Unit (LOPU) established on April 1, 1944, was to play a very significant part
in the future development of logistic organization both in
the Navy Department and in the continental establishment.
The unit was established with no other duties than to review logistic procedures and organization and to make recommendations for their improvement, an advantage which had
not been possessed by the Logistic Plans Division in 1943,
when Admiral Badger attempted his reforms. Even more important, however, was the character of the officers designated
by Admiral King to make up the unit. Captain Paul Pihl,
the senior member, had had considerable experience in the
Bureau of Aeronautics and later, under the Deputy Chief of
Naval Operations for Air, in aviation procurement and distribution. He possessed a keen and imaginative mind and an
appreciation uncommon among regular naval officers of highly specialized techniques of business administration. Captain
H. L. Challenger, perceptive and outspoken, had served under Admiral Badger in the Logistic Plans Division and later
on the Joint Logistics Plans Committee of the Joint Chiefs
of Staff. Captain J. D. Mooney, a reserve officer, came to the
unit, like Captain Pihl, after experience in aviation procurement and distribution. In civilian life, as vice president of

General Motors in charge of export, he had exhibited remarkable ability and aggressiveness in developing that company's overseas trade. He was the author as well of a standard work on *The Principles of Organization* in which his fertile and imaginative qualities of mind are amply demonstrated. The fourth member, Commander R. W. Yeomans, also a reserve officer, had considerable experience of theater problems as supply officer at Espiritu Santo. Together these four officers formed a remarkably imaginative and energetic group.

The mission of LOPU as defined by Admiral King covered most of the critical points in the existing logistics organization of the Navy Department and continental establishment. Specifically, three major objectives were set. First, LOPU was directed "to strengthen the logistic (surface and air) planning organization of the Office of the Chief of Naval Operations: By adoption of an orderly step-by-step system of breakdown of over-all logistic plans into ultimate bureau programs with provision for constant review of progress and degree of balance throughout. (Equivalent of Army Supply Program.)"

Second, it was to "Complete as a matter of urgency an over-all logistics plan (surface and air) for the all-out phases of the war in the Pacific based on the premises that maximum requirements will thereby be approximated and that subsequent requirements, especially for intervening phases, can be obtained by periodic adjustment."

And third, "Establish strong decentralized administrative machinery under central planning and scheduling control for efficient distribution, to include inventory and replenishment control of stocks."

On the whole, the charter of LOPU provided it with an opportunity to take under survey many of the most critical problems in naval logistic administration. From it there emerged in the unit's own work program a number of projects, and four of these became significant developments in the logistic system and organization. These were: (1) Study of the organization of the Office of Naval Operations, (2) The development of an Overall Logistics Plan, (3) The development of instruments and organization for progress review and inventory control, and (4) Reorganization of West Coast logistic agencies with a view to better control of distribution throughout the system as a whole.

On the suggestion of Captain Mooney, the first of these projects, dealing with organization, was turned over to a group of civilian management experts headed by Mr. T. P. Archer, vice president of the General Motors Corporation, and Mr. George Wolf, president of the U.S. Steel Export Company. After preliminary correspondence between Secretary Knox and Messrs. Sloan and Fairless, the respective heads of General Motors and U. S. Steel, a meeting was held in the Navy Department on April 17. There it was agreed that the group of experts, working in close cooperation with members of LOPU, should make recommendations concerning high-level problems of logistic administration and would not be regarded as responsible for the implementation of any recommendations they might make. The two companies volunteered to assume the cost of the investigation themselves.

The broad problem, as worked out in the preceding correspondence and in subsequent discussions was defined by the group itself as: "The determination of requirements (forecasting) planning, scheduling, procuring, assembling (components), transporting and the distribution of all materials and personnel in adequate quantities needed at the place and time required to support strategic plans." Studies of the group were carried on over a period of approximately six months, an interim report being issued on July 24, and a final report on October 3, 1944.

Unfortunately there is a point which can be reached in the effort to achieve a broad and general point of view where conclusions, no matter how well informed they may be, lose contact with the concrete realities which they attempt to comprehend. The Archer-Wolf report was in many respects an example of this phenomenon. It contained an excellent definition and analysis of the major steps in the logistic process. It suggested certain general principles of organization which were certainly applicable to naval logistics. It undoubtedly rested upon a good understanding of the logistic problem as seen through the eyes of men experienced in the management of export industry. But if the Secretary had hoped for expert assistance in the solution of outstanding problems of a concrete nature as stated in the group's own definition of its task, the report could only be disappointing.

The two major recommendations of the report suggested the establishment of an Organization Control Board and an Organization Planning and Procedure Unit. The first of these would be composed of "a small number of top ranking officials, headed by the Secretary of the Navy or his designated representative" and would concern itself with "all matters of policy which relate to organization planning, development, procedure and functional assignment." The Organization Planning and Procedure Unit, headed by a rear admiral would act as the working and executive agent of the Control Board and would coordinate as well the work of various Organization Planning and Procedure Units to be established in each bureau.

In justice to the Report it should be pointed out that several of its other recommendations—such as for standardization of parts nomenclature and numbering systems, the creation of a Comptroller General of the Navy, clarification of procurement responsibilities among the bureaus, improvement of current systems of establishing "use factors" and trends, and less rotation of logistic officers between sea duty and the Navy Department—were more closely related to the specific problems at hand. But even those recommendations consisted more often of the recognition of problems than of the "specific solutions for use within the naval organization" originally requested by the Secretary. Thus the two principal recommendations and many of the subsidiary recommendations made in the Archer-Wolf Report were at least once removed from concrete reality. They outlined a method and procedure for reorganization, but not for logistic administration.

The lack of immediate reference in the report to logistic problems themselves was best characterized by a story of Will Rogers told by one of the group's members in commenting upon the report at their final luncheon in October. Discussing with the Secretary the problem of combating the German submarine menace during the First World War, Mr. Rogers was reported to have suggested that since submarines couldn't very well operate in boiling water, the solution was simply to bring the Atlantic Ocean up to a steady, slow boil.

"But," expostulated the Secretary, "how are we going to do that?"

"That is a matter of detail," replied Mr. Rogers. "I outline the policy. You take care of the details."

Despite its lack of immediate application the Archer-Wolf Report did lead to constructive measures within the Navy Department. Following the two principal recommendations, the Secretary established an Organizational Policy Group and under it an Organization Planning and Procedure Unit, headed by Admiral Snyder, the Naval Inspector General. The suggestion that subordinate units be established at lower levels was not adopted, with the result that discussions of the Policy Group seldom embraced very closely the real problems of logistic administration. For it was at the lower levels, in the interstices of decentralized organization, that the problems of logistic administration and the information relative to their solution resided. Perhaps the most important work of the Planning and Procedure Unit under Admiral Snyder was the creation in February 1945 of the Requirements Review Board, headed by Assistant Secretary

Hensel, a board which sought for the first time to bridge with continuing procedure the gap between the determination of requirements defined by military objectives and the programs of procurement which resulted therefrom.

The Archer-Wolf Report offered to the Navy a fresh insight into its problems of organization and procedure seen in terms of a management problem. The methods of peacetime production and exporting, which were the yardstick of the civilian experts, cannot comprehend entirely either the magnitude or the complexity of logistic effort during war, but there are certain fundamental principles and methods inherent in the former which have application to wartime logistics, and in pointing these out the committee of experts rendered a notable service. Unfortunately it had been agreed that the Archer-Wolf group would study the problem in terms of organization within the Office of the Chief of Naval Operations. But the key to that problem of organization lay not within the Office, but outside—in that vital relation to the Bureaus, the Secretary, and the Commander in Chief, which was a matter for decision by the President and on which he had already taken a firm position.

Various other attempts at internal organization within the Office of Naval Operations were made during 1944, among which the most outstanding was a renewed effort to integrate air planning and program implementation as performed under the Deputy Chief for Air with logistic planning and implementation directly under the Vice Chief. The attempt was unsuccessful. Torn between the desire of Admiral King to see aviation logistics thoroughly integrated into the naval organization and the fear of air men headed by the Assistant Secretary for Air that integration would mean subordination, Admiral Horne was forced to compromise upon a liaison committee made up of members of the Logistic Plans and Aviation Logistic Plans Divisions. Without the introduction of leading air officers into the higher echelons of the naval organization as a whole the hope of air integration was destined to frustration. Only by bringing the air divisions bodily and in toto into the organization immediately under the Vice Chief could Admiral King's directive have been accomplished.

The development of an Overall Logistic Plan was in many ways the most critical need of the Navy's logistic system in 1944. Between the time when nuts, bolts, aircraft engines, or landing craft were delivered into the hands of operating forces and the time when the requirement for them must first be determined, there was an extended period, frequently as much as two years, during which component elements were procured and assembled by countless steps into the major end items of support. The major portion of this activity fell to the bureaus. But to plan and carry out the procurement of several million catalogue items in sufficient quantity and according to schedule, bureaus required sufficient guidance in sufficient time.

As late as 1944, such guidance did not exist. Directives of the Commander in Chief, and occasionally of the President, laid down the objectives for combatant ship and landing craft construction. The Office of Naval Operations projected requirements for advance base components and the Deputy CNO (Air) for aircraft and aviation components. But such information as could be provided even in these limited categories was incomplete and uncertain, fluctuating with changes in strategic plans. Forecast requirements for maintenance and replenishment procurement were particularly needed. Strategic and operational information was jealously guarded, however, by the Commander in Chief, who permitted its dissemination, only to a very limited degree, within the Office of Naval Operations and to the bureaus not at all.

Since bureaus alone possessed adequate information on the status of material programs and received through their operating agencies the requisitions from the field upon which issues and assignment of material were based, the divorce between two essentially related fields of information was almost complete. The Chief of Naval Operation's ignorance of the status of procurement programs could be remedied by a more effective system of progress reporting as suggested in the Booz Report of 1943, the Bureau of the Budget Survey, and the Archer-Wolf Report. The lack of strategic guidance for procuring agencies could only be remedied by the development of a comprehensive logistic plan, based upon the most up-to-date strategic estimates and revised step by step as changes in strategic plans developed.

The development of an Overall Logistic Plan had been assigned to LOPU as a matter of urgency in Admiral King's directive of March. On May 30, therefore, an Overall Logistic Plan Committee was created under the Logistic Plans Division, headed by Captain A. O. Geiselman and including among its other three members Captain Challenger of LOPU. The form and purpose of the Overall Logistic Plan were laid out in detail in a memorandum from the Director of Logistic Plans.

The Overall Logistic Plan, it was intended, should comprehend the requirements for support for the entire naval establishment. Estimates in the plan would state, however, only the major components making up that support, going into detail only in the case of critical items such as spare parts, fuel and ammunition. Requirements would be tabulated by periods of not more than three months so that bureaus would have a guide to their own scheduling. Statements of components already on hand would be set against the total requirement for a given period to indicate a net requirement for delivery during that period.

Information in the plan was to be presented under four major categories. First, the plan would include the strategic and other assumptions upon which all requirements were to be based. These should either be obtained from strategic planners, or, in any case, approved by them. They need not be given as wide a distribution as other information in the plan. The second type of information would indicate the probable deployment by area of all combatant types of ships and aircraft, auxiliary vessels and advance base components. The third type of information would indicate the degree of activity expected in each area, stated in general terms, from which might be deduced the approximate requirements for expendable commodities such as fuel and ammunition. Fourth, the plan would suggest the supply levels to be maintained in various classifications of supplies, although the quantities of material in transit in the "pipelines" necessary to maintain prescribed levels would be estimated by the bureaus.

The first Overall Logistic Plan was completed, after four months study, on September 27, 1944. Its primary purpose was to serve, in conjunction with past experience, as a guide to maintenance and replenishment procurement, and for this it was considered by various officers in the Navy Department to whom it was disclosed to have been admirably conceived and developed. Unfortunately, the plan suffered in two very important ways from the severe restrictions imposed in the interest of security. In the first place, considerable difficulty was experienced even by the members of the committee in securing the strategic information essential to their calculations. Despite its obvious necessity to logistic planning they were required to go "begging on hands and knees" for information, and even then they did not receive enough.

Secondly, even with its limited content of classified strategic information, the plan, once completed, was assigned a "Top-Secret" classification and hence a very limited distribution. The reason for this classification was revealed at a conference of officers in Naval Operations on September 21, at which Admiral Horne appears to have considered that the plan would be used only in the Office of Naval Operations as the basis for breakdown of requirements which would then be passed to the bureaus for procurement.

Unfortunately, no machinery or personnel existed in the Office for that kind of detailed work. End-item planning had necessarily to be performed in the bureaus, and it was there that the guidance offered by the Overall Plan was essential. The classification of "Top-Secret," however, restricted its distribution to the Chiefs and Assistant Chiefs of bureaus and to one or two top planners in each bureau. As a consequence, the plan was little used. Almost all bureaus concurred in the verdict of the Bureau of Ordnance that "Limited distribution within the bureaus is a handicap to its most effective use." Officers in two agencies reported that the Overall Logistic Plan was locked in the Admiral's safe and seen by no one outside his immediate office.

In January, 1945, the publication of a "Secret" version of the plan, minus the strategic assumptions, mitigated somewhat the severity of restrictions on its use. In addition, members of the Overall Logistic Plans Committee as often as possible made specific sections of lower classification available to responsible officers. On the whole, however, this excellent guide to balanced planning and procurement was circumscribed by the complex of security both in the information it could secure and incorporate in the plan itself and in the freedom with which the plan could be employed by those who depended upon it. As a consequence, as one commentator has observed, "planning agencies were forced to continue to rely on their own past experience, slightly salted by active imagination and speculation, while the Overall Logistic Plan, reposing unopened in thrice-locked safes, languished as an expensive repository for the dust of the ages."

Security was an important, but not the sole factor limiting the effective use of the Overall Logistic Plan by the bureaus and other agencies. Maintenance and replenishment plans had necessarily to be worked out with reference to specific commodities and types of equipment and had to be based upon a knowledge of rates of consumption and other usage factors derived from past experience. In some instances, as in the case of LST's, it was impossible to estimate the normal expectancy of such features as hull structures or propulsion equipment because the type itself had not been in employment for a sufficiently long period. In many other cases, where sufficient data did exist, they had never been analyzed, or developed to the point where they were applicable to planning purposes.

The Overall Logistic Plan was not intended to supply such data, but it was obvious that the guidance offered by it in general terms would not be useful for detailed planning and scheduling without some scale of usage factors and consumption rates by which bureaus could govern the rate of flow into and through the "pipelines" themselves. Such a scale could be developed only by the bureaus and went hand in hand with that delegated responsibility for detailed planning and execution upon which the decentralization of naval logistic effort was premised. The difficulties in the way of developing accurate tables of usage were great, particularly the difficulty of securing reliable and comprehensive information from operating forces. Bureaus had for the most part relied, therefore, upon cargo tonnage figures, which indicated previous shipments to the area, but told only indirectly the rates of past consumption of specific items or the current distribution of area stocks. Commodity classifications in cargo tonnage reports were crude and not well standardized; in many instances they were not in accord with the commodity classifications employed in area reports and thus could not be correlated with them to indicate rates of expenditure. In sum, with certain exceptions, the essential data listed by commodity which were necessary for the determination of maintenance requirements on the basis of past performance, were not in existence either in the hands of the bureaus or in the Office of Naval Operations. Without them the usefulness of the Overall Logistic Plan, when it could be employed, was limited.

Progress Review and Inventory Control

THE Overall Logistic Plan provided the first of three essentials for the orderly intake of materials into the logistic support system for distribution. It defined the requirements, albeit in general terms, for substantially all materials required for logistic support with particular emphasis laid upon maintenance and replenishment. Needless to say, however, future requirements indicated in the Overall Logistic Plan would depend not only upon changes in strategic plan or operational schedules, but also upon the status of current procurement programs and upon the unobligated inventories of materials already on hand to meet the requirements defined. The development of the Overall Logistic Plan was accompanied, therefore, by two other measures—the institution of improved methods of progress review and the establishment of a system of inventory control—intended to round out the methods of guidance and control over procurement activity and programming.

The need in the Office of Naval Operations for better methods of progress review had been the subject of comment in every management survey of the naval organization from the Booz Report to the Archer-Wolf Report. The principal problem was the inadequacy of information supplied to CNO by the bureaus by which the former could keep under surveillance their many separate programs and take action in advance to prevent bottlenecks, shortages or unbalanced progress in procurement and delivery of maintenance items.

Basically the dispersion of information was the result of the traditional bureau system and the natural development during a period of highly intensified activity of various separate systems and methods of supply, each answering to the individual needs or situation of a particular bureau or supplying agency. The condition had been aggravated, however, by the tendency of the Office of Naval Operations to avoid coming to grips with the problem of securing adequate

information and to content itself instead with a vaguely
defined "policy control." Late in 1942, for example, shortly
after assuming the new office of Assistant Chief of Naval
Operations for Maintenance, Admiral Farber had issued a
warning to divisions in the Office of Naval Operations not
to interfere "too much with other people's business . . .
it makes for better administration if we [in CNO] stick
purely to policy, detailing only that which is necessary to
stating policy." Thus also when early in 1943 the suggestion
was made that a central information office be set up under
the Chief of Naval Operations, it was turned down on the
objection of the Director of Logistic Plans that since that
division must plan "from the broad viewpoint of general
strategic needs" and "avoid entering too much into details,"
it would have no need for an agency to collect and dis-
semble detailed information and reports. Significantly, several months later when Admiral Badger was conducting his
own survey on the interchange of logistic information, although at least two replies definitely suggested the establishment of a central information office, his reforms were
limited simply to the systematization of existing channels of
information and avoided the suggestion that information
should be routed through the Chief of Naval Operations.

Admittedly the Office of Naval Operations should not
have attempted to burden itself with either detailed information or detailed direction of programs. But it was necessary to recognize, nevertheless, that policy direction, if it was
to have any reference to actuality, must be based upon a
synthesis of information built up systematically out of the
mass of detailed data passing through subordinate echelons.
In its natural desire to delegate responsibility and thus
expedite action, the Office of Naval Operations had leaned
too far in the opposite direction. It had put itself in the
position where continuous review of bureau programs was
impossible for want of synthesized information and where
directives to the bureaus when necessary often took on the

character of arbitrary and uninformed intervention. It was for this reason that Admiral King's directive for the establishment of LOPU had called for "provision for constant review of progress (in bureau programs) and degree of balance throughout."

This task was taken up in July by a subcommittee of LOPU, headed by Captain Mooney, which produced in September a document entitled, "The Navy Logistics Support Program," and intended to provide a mechanism for review and control. The volume was a graphic and statistical summary of the current status of approximately 1,000 items of procurement set up for comparison with scheduled requirements as stipulated in the Overall Logistic Plan. Listing these various items under major headings, such as ships, aircraft, ordnance, supply materials, personnel and advance base components, it covered for the first time in a single summary all of the major items entering into the creation and maintenance of naval operating forces. It demonstrated, in short, that with proper definition of the kind of information desired from the bureaus, it was possible to put together a comprehensive synthesis of essential information. Renamed the "Summary Control Report," this document came to play an important part in the coordination of procurement. In its initial form it suffered from many deficiencies. Its graphics and its statistics were poorly presented and did not indicate as clearly as intended the potential trouble spots in the over-all program. It lacked clear definitions and uniform terminology as a result of the fact that bureau reports themselves, from which its information was derived, followed no standard form of assembly and presentation of data.

Despite these defects, many of which were eliminated in subsequent revisions, the Summary Control Report marked an important advance toward better coordinated programming of procurement activity. In the first place, its scope was more comprehensive than either the planning or review functions as then performed in the Office of Naval Operations. Thus, although as in the Overall Logistic Plan, information had to come from the many separate sources other than in the Office of Naval Operations where planning or review was actually being done, there was gathered in a single document information on all programs of support for the naval establishment. The result was to enhance greatly the ability of the Office of Naval Operations to keep a check upon programs of which it had previously had only the most shadowy cognizance. The Summary Control Report became the basic working text of the Requirements Review Board after its establishment in February 1945. Unfortunately its development into an effective instrument for control as well as a review of progress required time and experimentation. But by the end of the war it had more than demonstrated its usefulness as an essential link between planning and procurement, and must rank therefore as an important landmark in the development of effective logistic administration.

Concurrently with the development of the Summary Control Report, measures were being taken for the improvement of naval inventory procedure. Here, too, the problem was largely one of centralized information, for though substantially accurate information existed in the hands of local agencies on the volume and location of naval stocks, no complete tabulation had been made which might serve as an aid to planners or to agencies responsible for governing the distribution of commodities on more than a local basis. Following the line of almost all other logistic activity during the war, inventory information had been developed and processed through the same decentralized channels that constituted the basic structure of the logistic support system. Initially this produced no deleterious effects. As long as the immediate demand for materials was greater than the supply, materials were drained off fairly rapidly into the hands of consumers. But as the reserves of material were accumulated and stockpiled and the volume of flow began to press more closely against the limit of transport and storage capacity, the likelihood was greatly increased of stocks existing unreported in some backwater of the distribution system against which no requisitions were made by theater agencies, while duplicate orders were placed for procurement. During this period of increasing demand and narrowing margins of availability of raw materials, manpower, and shipping and terminal capacity, no factor bore more closely upon both planning and distribution than did knowledge of the size, character and distribution of existing Navy stocks.

Just where the impetus for reform of inventory procedure originated would be difficult to say. In June 1942 the Office of Procurement and Material had laid down certain specifications for inventory reporting, but compliance was poor. With the adoption of the Controlled Materials Plan in April 1943, improved reporting and controls became essential for materials included under that plan. The Office of Procurement and Material was designated therefore as the responsible agency for maintaining naval inventories, but while it made considerable progress with respect to new materials, little was accomplished in regard to finished commodities. By the beginning of 1944 as shortages developed in storage capacity and dead stock began to obstruct the flow of priority materials, the bureaus themselves were turning attention to problems of inventory procedure and replenishment control within their separate domains. By this time, however, the need for centralization of inventory control was recognizable.

Impetus for action came both from within and without the Navy Department. In reviewing the budget estimates for 1945, for example, the House Appropriations Committee showed an increasing disposition to examine closely into duplicate facilities and naval stocks. In the Senate a resolution requesting the President to initiate investigation into inventories and inventory procedures was introduced by Senator Murray in October 1943, and adopted without amendment on February 7, 1944. In March, the Office of Procurement and Material took up the problem once again and urged coordinated inventory and stock control action throughout the Navy. On March 27, Admiral King's directive to LOPU contained the instruction "to include appropriate inventory control and replenishment of stocks."

The recommendation of the Office of Procurement and Material led to the appointment by the Secretary of three businessmen, Messrs. J. F. Creamer, A. C. Romer, and C. W. Cederberg, from the Sears, Roebuck and Montgomery, Ward companies, to investigate the Navy's inventory and stock control methods. They recommended the establishment of a central inventory control office and on May 23, the Secretary assigned to Rear Admiral J. M. Irish, then in charge of Planning and Statistics in the Office of Procurement and Material, additional duty as Assistant Chief of Naval Operations for Inventory Control.

The report of Creamer, Romer and Cederberg pointed clearly to the need for a closer relation between requirements determination and inventory control. The time for placing maximum orders wherever possible was clearly past. Further accumulation of unbalanced, and in some cases unneeded stocks, would simply add to the congestion in the distribution system and make more difficult the segregation and rapid delivery of critical materials. It suggested that the system of horizontal procurement by model or item be supplanted by functional procurement in order to avoid wasteful and unidentifiable duplication. Like the subsequent report by Archer and Wolf, this report called attention to the need for a better method of parts numbering and identification. Rapid disposal of surplus and obsolete materials was suggested in order to increase storage space and expedite the movement of materials.

The purpose of the Naval Inventory Control Office under

Admiral Irish was not to conduct and maintain inventory itself. That would have to be done by the bureaus, and in particular by the Bureau of Supplies and Accounts. Its function was to define policies and procedures for inventory reporting, supervise the taking of inventory, and prescribe measures for utilization of the overall results. In developing the inventory program stipulated by the Secretary's directive of May, the Navy Inventory Control Office and the Bureau of Supplies and Accounts excluded all plant facilities and production equipment and concentrated upon supply materials for new construction, maintenance and replenishment. In November, however, the Secretary extended the inventory coverage to include all naval materials, whether in naval custody or in the hands of private contractors. At the same time, since inventory reporting was obviously dependent upon standardizing stock nomenclature and cataloguing, he directed that the Bureau of Supplies and Accounts undertake under the direction of the Inventory Control Office the development of a catalog of all naval materials to include the many items not previously covered in the Standard Stock Catalog maintained by that bureau. A third directive assigned to the Naval Inventory Control Office the responsibility for preparation of the Summary Control Report.

The work of the Naval Inventory Control Office was infinitely complex and technical and so centrally situated in the pattern of all logistic activity that its progress can be discussed only in general terms. Initially it had to define the mechanics of securing and processing inventory information, a task which involved unremitting pressure upon bureaus and agencies to submit accurate and comprehensive reports. This effort continued in conjunction with the taking of actual inventory and culminated on June 1, 1945, in the publication of a "Manual of Standards," a bible of inventory control procedure.

The first inventory of naval material, completed on

December 31, 1944, covered approximately 2,000,000 items of supply materials located in more than 800 yards, depots and storehouses and encompassing all types of naval activities within the continental United States. During the following year plans were laid for the extension of this inventory to all naval materials in the United States including plant and industrial equipment and for a system of rotating inventories which would provide a periodic accounting for all activities at least every three months.

The mere taking of inventory and processing of data, essential as a beginning, was not enough, however, to solve the "problem of inventory control" in its relation to the logistic process as a whole. That wider question involved the uses of inventory, particularly its application to planning and procurement on the one hand, and the distribution process on the other. Once inventories had been taken, in other words, it was necessary on the basis of assembled information to establish effective controls over intake into and discharge from the Navy supply system.

One obvious intention of placing the Navy Inventory Control Office partly under the Chief of Naval Operations was to establish a closer relation between inventory control and requirements determination. But unfortunately no close liaison was ever established between the Naval Inventory Control Office and the Logistic Plans Division. The position of the new office in the organizational structure of the Navy Department had been a difficult problem at the time of its creation and remained for some time somewhat anomalous. Admiral Irish had one foot in the Office of the Secretary and the other in the Office of Naval Operations. No one was sure, perhaps not even Admiral Irish himself, just what his responsibilities were in the hyphenated structure of logistic administration within the Navy Department. On the one side his office was closely linked with the civil part of the naval establishment concerned primarily with matters of procurement and therefore with the relation of the Navy to the industrial structure of the nation. It was sponsored and to a certain extent governed by the civilian authority within the Navy. On the other side, as a division director within the Office of Naval Operations he was expected to work closely with that Office in its major task of determining and satisfying requirements which originated in the areas of operations and were governed by the military situation. Functionally and theoretically the process of furnishing material support to the operating forces was a continuous one. But in the pattern of organization within the Navy Department it was divided between the civil and military branches. The Naval Inventory Control Office was situated squarely upon that fissure in the organization of the Navy Department, and significantly the question of its proper location continued from the time of its creation as a subject for debate.

Certain other factors contributed to the failure to establish a close relation between inventory and planning functions. One very understandable reason is that since planning had to be carried on well in advance of the date of delivery, a large portion of the requirements determined by the Logistic Plans Division were already fixed before inventory information was available for use. Secondly, it must be remembered that the Logistic Plans Division was concerned primarily, and almost exclusively, with the determination of requirements and schedules for advance base components, and the initial stock levels required at each base. Inventory information was intended, on the other hand, to serve for replenishment planning, procurement and distribution. Its application was not to the initial establishment of stock levels but rather to the keeping of stocks at required levels. The use of inventory information in determining requirements, therefore, required more than a simple liaison between the Naval Inventory Control Office and the Logistic Plans Division. It required the dissemination of information through all the ramified system to agencies which actually determined requirements.

A third reason is that the failure of the Naval Inventory Control Office to extend its inventory beyond the continental limits of the United States restricted the utility of its information in the Office of Naval Operations. By the Secretary's directive Admiral Irish had received "complete authority over the development and operation of a comprehensive system of inventory control *throughout the Naval Establishment.*" But the inventory undertaken by the Bureau of Supplies and Accounts had been limited to the continental establishment. This limitation is difficult to understand because in May 1944 the Bureau of Supplies and Accounts itself had recommended the creation of an "Area Inventory Distribution Service." Within the Pacific Area itself no steps were taken until June 1945, to set up an over-all inventory procedure for materials already delivered into the theater, and it was just this sort of information, rather than inventory of raw materials and plant facilities, that was of chief concern to the Office of Naval Operations. Its primary concerns were that area stocks be kept at reasonable working levels, and that the flow of materials in response to area requirements be kept within the limits of transport and distribution capacity. To achieve these ends it required a basis of comparison of continental and overseas stocks.

Although belated and limited in its coverage, the work of the Naval Inventory Control Office, like the Summary Control Report and the Overall Logistic Plan, marked an important step forward in the creation of a coherent and comprehensive system of central control. These measures, it is obvious, were intended to clarify and systematize the efforts of agencies within the Navy Department, and by doing so to provide a greater measure of coordination and initial direction to the logistic support system as a whole. It can be pointed out that every effort and recommendation, whether it emanated from civilian "experts" or sources in the naval organization, was only partially successful or complete. Yet placed in their proper perspective against the magnitude and complexity of the task itself and against the inherited incongruities of naval organization, these combined measures represent a considerable achievement in laying down the basic outlines of systematic logistics procedure. Taken together with similar improvements in the continental establishment and area logistics they provided the rudiments of a working system.

CHAPTER VII

DISTRIBUTION

The Nature of the Distribution Task

WRITING shortly after the close of the First World War, Mr. C. E. Fayle, a British historian, summed up British shipping experience succinctly and pointedly: "There is indeed no lesson which stands out more prominently in the economic history of the war than the fundamental unity of the whole complex system of purchase, finance, transport, and distribution which connects the consumer and the producer."

The effort of the Navy to come to grips with that "fundamental unity" is the essence of its logistic experience during 1944. As we have seen in previous chapters dealing with planning and the control of procurement, the Navy had to deal with a vast complex of factors, no one of which could be isolated from another. The process of planning and procurement through which materials were fed into the logistic support system bore also a close relation to the process by which they were distributed and consumed within the system. Finally, distribution itself was a complex of interdependent operations which could be conducted at maximum efficiency only as governed elements within a single, coherent process. The factors of timing, motion, and selection so important in planning and procurement were even more closely the ruling principles of distribution.

This fact can be seen more clearly by examining briefly the nature of the distribution function itself. The first factor to be considered is the capacity of the channels of distribution—railroads, highways, pipelines, storage warehouses, terminals, shipping, and facilities for discharging and receiving at points of destination. Capacity in each of these essential links in the movement chain was determined first by the physical inventory of facilities themselves, i.e. the number of railroad trunk lines and sidings, freight cars, ships, loading berths, stevedore gangs, and square feet of storage. But the capacity of channels of distribution was not a fixed thing.

More than any other factor in the logistic system the capacity of transport and distribution facilities depended upon the efficiency with which all elements were employed and operated, and in particular upon their employment in relation to each other. Thus shipping capacity, for example, could not be reckoned in terms of vessel tonnage alone, but only as the sum of many variable factors such as distance, loading and discharging time, convoy schedules, repair schedules, and loss rates, which made up the sum of operating conditions for shipping itself, and determined the total turnaround time of a ship on a given route. It was possible that a ship of 10,000 tons deadweight capacity, capable of making six trips per year to a base in the Pacific, could be subjected to so many delays that it would make in fact only three trips per year. Instead of lifting 60,000 deadweight tons of cargo during the year, it would lift 30,000 tons, and for all practical purposes would represent, therefore, only half a ship. Multiplied many times by the number of ships required and in service, such possibilities of extended turnaround constituted one of the most important variables in the distribution system.

Shipping capacity itself interacted with other elements in the channels of distribution. Efficient utilization of tonnage depended not only upon the conditions of ship operation, but also upon the availability of cargo properly distributed so as to give the shortest possible haul as well as the maximum employment of loading facilities, railroad cars, line-haul capacity and available stevedore labor. Each of these essential elements might be viewed as the central factor in the channels of distribution, because, in fact, each might become the critical factor and a bottleneck in the total process. Distribution capacity was in sum, therefore, the least common denominator of efficiency of all the elements entering into it.

These variable capacities in the channels of distribution were not, however, the sole factors affecting the distribution process. Transport and distribution of materials was influenced by a number of associated conditions such as the location of sources of procurement or production of various commodities, a factor determined by procuring agencies with reference more often to the exigencies of procurement than of distribution. Thus, for example, when California oil resources were no longer adequate for the support of fleet operations in the Pacific, other resources in the United States and South America had to be utilized, and the problems of distribution were magnified. The character of commodities had also to be taken into account. Lumber, produced in the Northwest, must be shipped to the Pacific from Northwest ports, where a minimum of rail transportation would be involved. Refrigerated cargo, oil, and ammunition all required special transport services and storage facilities. Certain commodities not generally refrigerated had, nevertheless, to be routed through temperate zones lest they deteriorate in transit. Some commodities could be bulk-shipped; others could not. Some were in short supply and required expedited handling from factory to consumer; others were available in ample reserve so that area stocks could be built up and drawn from over a period of time. Thus the conditions attaching to cargo itself were frequently as inflexible as transport capacity was variable. Around them the pattern of distribution had to be woven.

Transport, moreover, was not an end in itself. It was the instrument of supply, which in turn existed only to make possible the conduct of naval operations or the maintenance of naval forces. The whole process of distribution, therefore, was essentially one of articulating and coordinating a series of separate and variable factors in response to military demands so as to raise their common denominator to the highest possible level. This was a task in administration and constituted in fact the essence of military logistics during its mature phase.

By the beginning of 1944 it had become the major problem of all logistics just as procurement and production had been during the previous two years. The fruits of that earlier effort were now available in ever-increasing quantity, in such abundance, in fact, as to put a critical strain upon the system of distribution as it had operated until that time. Operating forces were available and becoming available at a sufficient rate to push the campaign in the Pacific as rapidly as the troops could be transported and the means of supporting fleet forces could be brought up and established. The burden lay, therefore, upon the system of distribution.

West Coast Logistic Organization

By the beginning of 1944 the focal point in the growing problem of distribution was the logistic organization, or more properly the lack of logistic organization, on the West Coast. In a decentralized system such as the Navy employed this condition was, perhaps, inevitable. Materials originated in widely scattered sources and flowed to naval depots, most of which were located at tidewater without any centralized control. At the coast, however, these many separate streams of supply came together by necessity, for though the management of internal traffic was decentralized, the substantial portion of naval overseas traffic had to be carried by ships allocated by the War Shipping Administration on the basis of a single estimate of requirements. The necessity, therefore, of assigning cargo to a single pool of available tonnage (and also of being able to interchange Army and Navy cargo through the medium of the Joint Ship Operations Committee) provided the first instance in the sequential phases of distribution, where naval shipments had to be dealt with as a whole.

Under the decentralized system of internal traffic management the West Coast was also the first place where knowledge existed of what cargo would be made available for shipment during any given period of time. Significantly, the estimates of requirements prepared for the WSA by the Naval Transportation Service were based almost entirely upon the weekly cargo reports of local port directors, stating what cargo had been received and shipped during the week and what remained on hand. Because of the superiority of the port director's information, control of shipping operations had been progressively decentralized from the Naval Transportation Service in Washington to the Port Director in San Francisco, where with cargo and ships actually on hand, he could match both together in the most effective manner. It was, in fact, the central booking office maintained by the San Francisco Port Director that provided the chief mechanism for coordinating the transshipment of naval cargo from the Coast.

The West Coast was also the point to which theater requisitions were first directed, presumably either to the Subordinate Command, Pacific Service Force, or to the Commandant of the Twelfth Naval District. The great majority were filled from stocks in the West Coast depots and yards such as Oakland, San Diego, or Mare Island, and were passed on to sources of supply within the interior only when they could not be satisfied from coastal stocks. Thus the West Coast was the point of principal contact between the available supplies within the United States and the requirements which originated within the theaters.

Finally, despite these important responsibilities, logistic organization on the West Coast was the most poorly coordinated and ill-adapted to effective prosecution of the logistics task of any part of the naval establishment. The Navy Department at Washington was a kind of gothic structure filled with incongruities, but it possessed a nucleus of men who understood its weaknesses and each other and could thus make it work with reasonable success. The theater commands were often distracted from logistic matters by more readily apparent operational problems and had hitherto lacked as well the means of dealing with logistic problems as effectively as desired. These defects were in the process of correction. Of these three major parts of the logistic system, therefore, it was the West Coast establishment that was most critically unrationalized.

Conditions which had prompted the Navy to attempt a wholesale reorganization of the Naval Districts in the proposed General Order of 1943 had been improved not at all by the creation of Assistant Commandants for Logistics. On the contrary, as the Central Pacific campaign gained momentum the seriousness of the situation was intensified. A second, and more forceful, attempt to solve the problem of West Coast organization within the limits imposed by the President was made on February 12, 1944, when an office of Pacific Coast Coordinator of Naval Logistics (Pacornalog) was created. Vice Admiral J. W. Greenslade, who had been Commandant of the Twelfth District until his recent retirement, was appointed Pacornalog.

Although designated as "the representative of the Secretary of the Navy and of the Heads of all offices and bureaus . . . of the Navy Department to effect coordination of procurement, distribution, staging and overseas supply of material and personnel" in all three districts of the Coast, the Coordinator was "not vested with command or administrative authority." His duties were advisory. He worked with a mere handful of assistants, and while he did make several useful surveys of facilities on the West Coast, Pacornalog was never equipped with sufficient authority and staff organization to make real progress against the confusion of logistics agencies and functions on the West Coast. In September, 1944, LOPU reported that "To date, the influence of Pacornalog . . . has been very limited. . . . It must be recognised that as a matter of practical application, it is

probably very difficult for Pacornalog to go beyond this
limited activity without clashing with the Bureaus in
Washington, since the principal administrative control of
the various logistic activities centers in Washington and not
on the Coast."

The major impetus for reform came from the investigation into conditions on the West Coast undertaken by
LOPU shortly after the establishment of Pacornalog. Its
report of September 27, 1944, was an able summary of
activities and administrative and command relationships,
and was to prove one of the most fruitful of its many enter-
prises.

In addition to its comments on the efficiency of Pacornalog, the LOPU investigation demonstrated once again
that District Commandants exercised all too little control
over logistic activities within their districts. The relationship between the Commandant and logistic activities was
"confined largely to military matters," while certain of these
agencies "centered within . . . but operating independently
of the District" had arrogated unto themselves most of the
important logistic responsibilities. Among these agencies
certainly the most important was the Port Director of San
Francisco, who, as Regional Shipping Director, administered
also the activities of all other port directors on the Coast.

"No Navy cargo or personnel moves from the Pacific
Coast, westward, without his knowledge and direction . . .
His office is the focal point to which Navy requests for
shipping space on non-combatant ships . . . are sent and it
is the agency on the West Coast which can make allocations
of shipping in response to such requests."

His operations were not administered by the Commandant and only nominally by the Naval Transportation
Service in Washington. "The Port Director, San Francisco," said the report, "to all practical purposes operates
as an independent agency."

What was true of the Port Director was true also in some

measure of other agencies such as the Subordinate Command, which took its direction from the Fleet and had "increased tremendously"; Naval Supply Depot, Oakland, administered by the Bureau of Supplies and Accounts; Naval Supply Depot, Clearfield, Utah, "controlled insofar as the inflow and outgo of material is concerned" by three other depots and three separate bureaus; the Advance Base Office, Pacific, which was "primarily a policing agency for CNO in the flow of initial movements"; and District Property Transportation Offices, established in 1943 by the Bureau of Supplies and Accounts to control railroad traffic into the ports. All told, some dozen major agencies and a host of minor agencies operated logistic services on the West Coast, governed largely by the necessities of the separate systems or services to which they belonged.

The report concluded: "There is no overall coordinated supervision of the operation of logistic activities on the Pacific Coast. The logistic support of the Pacific Areas is being conducted on the West Coast by an organization which has evolved as the result of a series of developments to meet the changing and increasing demands of the Fleet as the war progressed. Coordination is sporadic and extracurricular, and is the result largely of the informal understandings which have grown up from time to time. This organization would not have been able to perform the necessary task, had it not been for certain individuals of outstanding ability, located in key positions, who cut across organizational lines in order to meet the requirements and emergencies as they arose."

Noting also that "At the present time there is no individual or agency in the CNO organization who is solely responsible for the operation of the logistic agencies supporting the Fleets in the Pacific," LOPU recommended two steps: first, centralized "control" of logistic activities on the Coast, and second, the designation of the Assistant CNO for Material to develop "coordination" of logistic activities in the Navy Department between the bureaus and the divisions of CNO. Under two such agencies, properly established and linked by close liaison, it believed the logistic organization problem would be satisfactorily solved.

The report of LOPU was not the only recommendation for reform of logistic reorganization on the West Coast. During April the Base Maintenance Division in CNO suggested an elaborate plan of reorganization which had more merit in its procedural suggestions than in its plan of organization, and will be referred to later. The Bureau of Supplies and Accounts suggested in May the creation of a "Commander Logistics Pacific," a plan which contained considerable merit but would have achieved regional centralization on the West Coast at the expense of greater decentralization within the Navy Department. This plan was discussed in July at a conference in the Navy Department, but a feeling that it had not fully covered the ground, plus an inherent reluctance to impair the integrity of the district organization militated against it. It remained, therefore, for the fully documented survey of LOPU to prompt the Navy to attempt once more that centralization which it had sought in 1943.

On November 8, 1944, Admiral R. E. Ingersoll, formerly Commander in Chief Atlantic Fleet, was assigned to duty as Commander Western Sea Frontier, with the duties and authority of that command greatly expanded. Hitherto simply an operational command, Commander Western Sea Frontier, was now assigned "the control and coordination of all Naval activities and functions on the Pacific Coast, including the 11th, 12th, and 13th Naval Districts." Under his immediate command exercised as Deputy Commander in Chief, Deputy CNO, were placed District Commandants and "all agencies of the Navy Department . . . located and operated within . . . but not assigned to the districts."

Close comparison of the orders issued to Admiral Ingersoll and the proposed General Order of 1943 indicates that in effect the Navy had achieved in the former the same purposes it had sought to realize in the reorganization of the Districts. Just why, then, was it possible to achieve a reorganization in 1944 which had been impossible in 1943? The full explanation cannot be made at this time, but two factors may be suggested which certainly contributed. First, the situation and critical importance of logistic organization on the West Coast was certainly more apparent in 1944 than in the previous year. With the war in Europe coming to a close, the Pacific Coast was obviously destined to become shortly the platform for a mighty concentration of forces and material support for the final offensive against Japan. The possibility of a breakdown in logistic support was simply too much to risk. Secondly, it may be observed that while in substance Admiral Ingersoll's orders achieved the same purpose as the proposed General Order, they did not formally impair the integrity of district organization. Admiral Ingersoll himself was careful to make clear that he intended to carry out his instructions without violating the basic structure of district organization, and once he had assumed his duties, he proceeded very cautiously in this respect.

In setting up his headquarters in San Francisco, Admiral Ingersoll took with him from the Navy Department, Captain Pihl and several of the able junior officers of LOPU who had assisted in the survey of West Coast logistics organization. Since LOPU had been engaged not only in the study of organization for logistics, but had been for some time at the center of discussion of logistics problems in general, the inclusion on his staff of certain of its members was a great asset for the new Commander Western Sea Frontier. Time was required before the various projects undertaken by these officers could bear fruit. But during the following year in the successful development of information and control mechanisms the wisdom of this action was borne out.

One final point must be made regarding the authority

vested in the Commander Western Sea Frontier as compared with that given to the Assistant Chief of Naval Operations for Material. The recommendations of LOPU had envisioned these two offices as parallel agencies working closely together, but each in its proper sphere, for the coordination of logistic activity. Under such an arrangement it might be anticipated that the Navy Department agency, being the more centrally located, would assume a natural primacy in direction. But as a Deputy Cominch-Deputy CNO, the Commander Western Sea Frontier stood several echelons higher in the naval organization than did the Assistant CNO for Material. A similar difference was reflected in the wordings of their respective directives. The Commander Western Sea Frontier was to exercise "control and coordination" over "all" naval activities in his area. The Assistant CNO was to provide only "coordination" among the Navy Department agencies interested in distribution. Given the existing condition of decentralization of logistic activity, these factors contributed to the subsequent tendency toward too great a concentration of control in the regional agency and too little in the central agency in the Navy Department.

Continental Distribution

FOR the sake of clarity, it has seemed advisable to pursue the study of West Coast logistic organization up to the point of the reorganization of the Western Sea Frontier Command without close reference to the actual conduct of logistic activity during 1944. Under existing conditions of departmental organization the successful solution of the distribution problem obviously required such a regional authority as a first requisite. Meanwhile, however, early in 1944 the problems of distribution broke in full force upon the existing system of support, and it is necessary to consider, therefore, just how the task was accomplished within that existing framework. Pending the necessary reform on the Coast, the furnishing of support had to be carried out within the system already operating. In effect this meant the bureau system, the personal system of Admiral Horne, the assistance rendered by Admiral Greenslade as Pacornalog and by committee procedure and informal liaison. Within this perhaps bewildering and ill-defined "system" of logistic administration the tremendous task emerging in 1944 was dealt with.

Just what that task was to consist of in its more serious form is perhaps most succinctly described in the text of a dispatch which was prepared and circulated in the Navy Department in April 1944, but not sent:

"Dry cargo for shipment to Pacific is reaching West Coast faster than total available shipping can remove it. Ports, warehouses and sidings as far east as Salt Lake City are full. Material which it is already known will be ready now exceeds available dry cargo lift by 50 sailings per month. Increasing congestion will soon curtail further shipments to coast by immobilizing rolling stock and will effectively block later urgent shipments.

"This situation coupled with the fact that Operating forces are not complaining of shortages or delays indicates that excessive orders have been placed or that excessive stocks have been built up in the Operating Areas, or both. In any case immediate steps must be taken to relieve present congestion, and adjust the timing of future orders for our material to our total available cargo lift."

The situation in April referred to in this draft dispatch was the direct result of the great increase in shipments preparatory to the launching of the Marianas operation. That operation was the largest attempted to date and required therefore an unprecedented build-up of forces, concentrated within a relatively brief period of time. But although the congestion in April was the most serious thus far, it was not the first time that such a crisis had developed during the period prior to a major operation. In October and November, as shipments were increased in anticipation of the Kwajalein landings, a similar congestion had developed in the San Francisco Bay Area. It was clear, therefore, that if the tempo of operations scheduled for 1944 was to be maintained, some method must be found of preventing the stoppage foreseen in the dispatch.

Many of the remedies proposed and attempted were concrete and specific, aiming at the improvement of one phase of this complex of operations either by the expansion of facilities or by the better utilization of facilities already existing. Some expansion of facilities was always possible, but by the beginning of 1944 we were already approaching the limits of elasticity of basic facilities. The solution must come, therefore, largely through improved utilization and management of existing facilities, by better timing and selection.

One of the approaches to the problem of West Coast congestion was an attempt to secure a better distribution of port load, not only upon the West Coast itself, but also as between the West Coast ports and the East and Gulf Coasts. It is indicative of the faulty control of port loads, for example, that early in 1944, when serious signs of congestion were appearing in San Francisco, the port of Seattle was complaining of a sharp falling off in the level of its activity. Suggestions had been made that Seattle assume part of the responsibility for shipments to the Central Pacific to compensate for the declining shipments to Alaska. But although such a step would ultimately be necessary, it was viewed unsympathetically by the Regional Shipping Director in San Francisco, who believed that congestion in the Bay Area was only temporary and preferred to utilize presently established channels to their maximum capacity. In this he was backed up by the Bureau of Supplies and Accounts, which contended that "It is not a simple problem to divert a specified tonnage of cargo from existing channels to another transshipment port." Ultimately, means were found to utilize facilities in Seattle, but temporarily it remained one of the examples on the West Coast of maldistribution of port load.

As an alternative to the utilization of Seattle, the Bureau of Supplies and Accounts recommended that measures be taken from a long-range point of view to provide for greater shipments from the East and Gulf Coasts. To this end it suggested the establishment of a Naval Overseas Freight Terminal in New Orleans to supplement the terminals in San Francisco, which since the beginning of the war had borne the brunt of naval cargo shipments. At the same time it recommended that certain commodities susceptible of bulk shipment be stocked at Norfolk for shipment to Pearl Harbor. The Office of Naval Operations concurred in the suggestion of a terminal at New Orleans, and the Naval Transportation Service reported that vessels could be made available to lift shipments. Unfortunately the one condition essential to draining off any large portion of shipments through the Delta Area was not fulfilled. Lacking adequate control over the flow of requisitions for supplies, the Navy was unable to divert them to sources of supply in the lower Mississippi region from which materials normally moved to New Orleans for transshipment. The result was that no great volume of cargo was diverted from the West Coast for shipment through New Orleans.

In May, Pacornalog completed a survey of West Coast port facilities in which he recommended that routine maintenance shipments be shifted to East Coast ports as vessels became available. He also found that a greater dispersion of activity among the West Coast ports was feasible. In July the whole matter of the West Coast ports was brought for review before the Joint Military Transportation Committee of the Joint Chiefs of Staff when the War Shipping Administration, seconded by the Army, sought the establishment of a Port Utilization Committee, which would have as its main objective the allocation of shipments to various ports in accordance with their current capacities, ship availability, and repair facilities. Captain Davis, the Navy's regional Shipping Director, appeared at these meetings and explained the West Coast situation as he saw it. Although there existed at that time no central allocating agency for the Coast as a whole, he believed that the work was done in effect through the Navy's central booking office and through the workings of the Joint Army, Navy, WSA Ship Operations Committee which had been established early in 1943.

The key to the problem, however, was indicated by Commander Toal, the Bureau of Supplies and Accounts transportation officer. As he explained it, "part of the inflexibility of the Navy was due to the fact that supply installations are seaboard." Moreover, having no central control of the flow of requisitions and therefore of the flow-back of requisitioned material, the Navy, he said, "is not prepared to divert traffic in as large a block as is required." What Commander Toal had in mind was the diversion or rerouting of naval cargo on short notice, which was indeed impossible since the Navy did not maintain centralized control or accounting on goods while in transit, and since a large portion of naval shipments passed not through interior depots, from which they could be rerouted as occasion required, but "directly . . . in carload lots from contractor's plant to vessel at transshipment activity." As Commander Toal had pointed out earlier in the case of Seattle, "There are important considerations other than transportation. Loadings in any appreciable volume to the Central Pacific and supplying and filling requisitions for such an area involve as well substantial problems of procurement, stock and storage."

In short, the problem of better utilization of port capacity could not be limited to the ports themselves, but extended rather into such related matters as the flow of requisitions, the assignment of missions to major supply depots, the establishment of appropriate stock levels, and the total management of distribution within the continental limits of the United States. Lacking an elaborate layout of physical facilities for distribution through which goods could be routed in various alternate ways subject to central traffic management control, the Navy must approach such problems as the diversion of shipments from West Coast to East Coast or from one port to another on a long term basis beginning with a redefinition of depot missions and the development of stock levels at various depots capable of supporting the new mission assigned.

In undertaking such a major redistribution of stocks, however, the Navy was compelled to proceed cautiously. Because of the need for conserving shipping it was essential to maintain West Coast shipments at a maximum, despite occasional periods when congestion occurred, and for this reason it hesitated to undertake any radical redistribution until the need for it was obvious. By October, however, this need could no longer be denied, and in a dispatch of October 14 to theater commanders the Chief of Naval Operations directed that requisitions for maintenance materials, certain categories excepted, be forwarded to eastern sources. The procedure entailed by this directive was cumbersome and the process itself was slowed down somewhat by a qualifying condition that West Coast transshipment activity would continue to be maintained at the "maximum practicable" level. Some such major distribution of shipping load was essential, however. With the end of the war in Europe then viewed as imminent and with a far greater concentration of forces in the Pacific obviously impending, it was essential to give some relief to the hard-pressed rail and terminal facilities on the West Coast. Even though the war in Europe did not end as rapidly as had been expected, the action was taken none too soon.

A second method of dealing with the congestion crisis was the institution of closer control over the movement of railroad freight cars. Up until the beginning of 1944 the Bureau of Supplies and Accounts Transportation Division had kept cursory watch over freight car movements through the medium of its District Property Transportation Officers, but for the most part had practiced a decentralization of control which left to individual bureaus and their inspectors the authority to release shipments of material under their cognizance. The most critical factor in the San Francisco congestion of April, however, was the rising rate of demurrage of freight cars at terminals and the danger of such a critical dislocation of rail traffic as might require months to readjust. Under a threat from the Office of Defense Transportation to withdraw the Navy's block permits for the release of shipments the Bureau decided in April 1944 to establish a more centralized control. Henceforth on the basis of daily reports submitted by its District Property Transportation Officers it kept close watch over banks of railroad cars at all points where congestion might arise. Such a method, it should be pointed out, was limited to the control of freight car movements, and did not refer to the materials within railroad cars. Its applicability to the control of material flow was therefore limited. The system established did, however, prevent further critical congestion of freight cars and enabled depots to keep as a rule the reasonable working level of not more than three days' bank of railroad cars.

A third problem, in many respects the most critical factor in the Navy's distribution system, was the inadequacy and frequently the misuse of naval storage space. Between the outbreak of war and the beginning of 1944, for example, while naval shipments via commercial transportation facilities in the United States had increased nine-fold, the Navy's covered storage space at principal yards and depots had scarcely more than doubled. The greater portion of naval storage space, moreover, was located at tidewater points, approximately 42 per cent within the limits of the West Coast Naval Districts and the remainder distributed along the East and Gulf Coasts. This concentration of storage facilities in the coastal areas had served the purpose of combining in a single activity the storage of materials and issues of supplies to vessels at a time when most naval vessels were based on and supported by continental facilities. As the war progressed, however, and vessels returned less and less frequently to continental bases, the need for storing materials for direct issue to operating forces became less. At the same time as tidewater points were more and more involved in transshipping functions, storage facilities became more an integral part of the system of transport and distribution through which materials flowed. In this relation their location at tidewater served simply to introduce an element of inflexibility into the continental system of distribution.

Early in the war the Bureau of Supplies and Accounts had developed a plan for four inland supply depots at Clearfield, Utah; Spokane, Washington; Barstow, California, and Scotia, New York, in addition to a depot at Mechanicsburg begun in 1941. These depots were intended originally to back up coastal facilities and to provide that flexibility in the distribution of stocks which could not be had from storage located directly on the Coast. The concept itself was sound. Unfortunately the projects were conceived somewhat belatedly and on too small a scale.

Part of the explanation for the Navy's inadequate storage space can be found also in too rigid adherence to the idea that efficient employment of storage required that it be utilized 100 per cent. In peacetime or under ordinary conditions when mobility is not essential, such a policy might have some justification. In wartime, however, when storage has become but one element in the channels of distribution, it is impossible to utilize storage effectively unless there is a sufficient margin of unemployed space to allow some mobility of materials within the depot.

Even more responsible for the inadequacies of the storage program was the fact that the Bureau of Supplies and Accounts, which was charged with responsibility for storage of naval materials, did not in fact control much of the storage space the Navy possessed. At the inland depots in particular allotments of space were made to individual bureaus, which utilized it as their particular needs dictated. Supplies and Accounts, moreover, had no means of checking upon the volume and schedules of procurement by other bureaus and thus of estimating accurately their prospective requirements for storage space. The result was not only a shortage of facilities, but also a lack of concerted policy on their utilization which contributed in no small measure to the difficulties of distribution.

In July 1944 efforts were made to improve the Navy's storage position, first, by securing and constructing additional facilities in the most critical areas, and second, by centralizing policy control over the utilization of existing space. A Navy Storage Control Committee was created with representatives from each of the bureaus and offices of CNO, under the chairmanship of an officer of CNO. The Bureau of Supplies and Accounts was made in effect the administrative agent of the committee and of CNO for the execution of a central storage policy. Through it programs for new facilities, for the improvement of records, for the removal of dead stock, and for improved distribution of stock to meet storage requirements were to be developed. These measures were a step in the right direction and did something to improve conditions in the storage situation. By 1945, however, it was found that the committee procedure was too unwieldy, and in May control of storage was centralized even more in the hands of the Bureau of Supplies and Accounts with the understanding that it would be exercised under policy direction by the Assistant Chief of Naval Operations for Material.

The Navy's experience with storage facilities is an excellent illustration of the dangers inherent in too great decentralization. Ideally storage policy control should have resided in the Office of Naval Operations from the beginning. It was too much to expect that with procurement and scheduling of material programs decentralized to the various bureaus, still another bureau could keep abreast of their various requirements for storage and could control their utilization of the space assigned. The tremendous expansion in the flow of material support beginning at the end of 1943 demonstrated only too clearly the necessity for a higher authority which would bring the essential phases of the distribution process together into a coherent operation. In this case the Bureau of Supplies and Accounts must be held responsible for clinging too tenaciously to a responsibility which it had neither the means nor the initiative to discharge.

A fourth problem affecting the distribution of materials was the difficulty of controlling the flow of requisitions to supply sources so that stocks could be effectively planned and utilized. The establishment of a central requisition clearance agency had been recommended by LOPU and by the Bureau of Supplies and Accounts, and was to become one of the major projects of the Commander Western Sea Frontier during 1945. Meanwhile, however, another approach was possible which might reduce the excessive amount of detail work involved in the system of individual requisitions. Late in 1943 the Bureau of Supplies and Accounts developed the idea of a Basic Boxed Base (BBB) Load of replenishment and maintenance supplies for the use of advance base units. This BBB load (or AKS load in the case of a stores ship,) was an assembly of a single unit of maintenance materials and supplies including clothing, small stores, and other consumables required to support 10,000 men for a period of sixty days. It represented an attempt to reduce into wholesale terms many of the calculable items of supply which had hitherto had to be dealt with on the basis of individual requisitions.

Beginning late in 1943 the Bureau of Supplies and Accounts began to build up stocks in the Naval Supply Depot, Spokane for assembly into BBB and AKS loads. By the middle of 1944 this action was serving a dual purpose. It permitted the shipment of an increasing percentage of maintenance materials to the Central Pacific on a wholesale, and therefore a simpler, basis; and it provided an excellent method of utilizing available terminal facilities in the Puget Sound Area. BBB loads could not be expected to fit exactly the needs of all base units in all areas. Experience with this kind of shipment dictated certain changes in the composition of the load. But while stocks shipped by BBB load tended at times to get out of balance at individual bases, the saving in time and detailed effort afforded by the system more than justified these minor disadvantages.

Shipping Control

OF all the many interdependent elements in the system of distribution, shipping was unquestionably the most important single factor. Physically it furnished the bridge between available supply within the United States and consumption within the theaters of operation. Once production programs were successfully under way, there would never be enough shipping. No matter how much tonnage space was available, the only constant in the shipping situation was the need for more. Yet at the same time shipping capacity itself was the most variable of the elements of the channels of distribution, the most dependent upon the proper functioning of all the other phases of the process, the most susceptible to waste. Shipping availability was thus frequently the most critical link in the chain of distribution.

In an amphibious war such as that of the Pacific the relation of shipping to the actual conduct of operations was naturally close and immediate. The conduct of operations and the buildup of logistic support in the theaters depended directly upon the current availability of shipping. But though shipping availability was thus tied directly to local operations it was also in a sense the circulatory system of the total war effort—for war production, Lend-Lease, civilian economies, and relief and rehabilitation as well as for the export of men and material for our naval and military forces. Allocations of shipping to any single claimant or command had to be made in relation to all the requirements for tonnage; and conversely the efficiency of employment of shipping within any single command or for any single purpose determined the amount of tonnage available for all.

One other general point deserves to be brought out in connection with the administration of shipping. As an instrument or servant of supply, shipping employment was determined primarily by the demands for material. Ships moved in response to the need for material movement, and effective shipping control was therefore dependent to a large extent upon effective material control. This relation between shipping control and material control was to become increasingly important as the campaign in the Pacific was extended and intensified.

The problem of shipping control strictly speaking, i.e. control of the movements of vessels, including loading, discharge and return to the mainland, was one of the thorniest and most vexing issues of 1944. During that year shipping shortages became so acute that they threatened either to imperil the success of operations already under way or to force the postponement of operations which had been approved and were impending. With all due consideration given to the tempo, magnitude, and uncertainty of operations, much of the responsibility for acute shortages in shipping must be ascribed to the lack of effective shipping control in the areas.

The problem of shipping control had many facets, of which perhaps the most important was the primitive and poorly managed condition of the ports in the forward areas, a matter which had given serious concern to the Naval Transportation Service in Washington ever since congestion developed in the harbor of Noumea in the autumn of 1942. Faced with the necessity of justifying to the WSA the statements of vessel requirements submitted by Area Commanders, when large numbers of vessels were immobilized in the areas awaiting discharge, it felt keenly its inability to exercise an effective control or even to secure adequate information on the movements of vessels and the condition of discharge points. Another factor which aggravated area port congestion and therefore contributed to deficits in available tonnage, was the tendency of Area Commanders to submit requirements for shipping without sufficient reference to the possibility of discharging material once it arrived at advanced bases.

For their part, Area Commanders were constantly hampered by the lack of sufficient shipping for local employment between bases and between staging areas and forward points. In 1942 a program had been laid out for the construction of small cargo vessels of about 5,000 deadweight tons capacity (C1-MAV-1), similar to the Baltic Coaster type, which were intended to be assigned to Theater Commanders for these purposes. This construction program had lagged persistently, however, with the result that Theater Commanders had been compelled to retain larger and faster vessels for use in area shuttle services. The lack of smaller vessels had also resulted in more complicated itineraries for ships sailing from the United States, which added to the time of turnaround.

Still another factor contributing to the lack of shipping control was the fact that allocations of shipping by the Joint Military Transportation Committee were made to too many different accounts within a given area. In the Pacific Ocean Area, for example, without counting the South Pacific Area, allocations of shipping were made by the committee to six different services or commands. While the worst effects of such a fragmentary system of allocation were mitigated by the work of the Joint Ship Operations Committee in San Francisco, which arranged for the exchange of vessels and cargo between services, and by joint logistic planning and control under CincPoa, the system of separate accounts made difficult the fixing of responsibility for misuse of vessels once they had moved forward or the establishment of any overall system of reporting on vessel movements.

The effects of these various conditions were best illustrated in the rising figures for ship retentions in the areas during the early months of 1944. By June, 18 per cent of the total tonnage controlled by the War Shipping Administration was tied up in retentions, leaving only 72 per cent available as a sailing fleet after a reduction for vessels under repair. During April, 3,423,700 tons of WSA shipping were tied up in retentions. In May this amount increased to 4,247,800 tons—more than offsetting the gain from new construction.

In April 1944, as the congestion crisis on the West Coast developed, deficits in the available tonnage necessary to lift materials off the Coast were also increasing. The Joint Military Transportation Committee indicated in April that unless stated requirements were scaled down or pending operations were deferred, deficits for the Pacific would be approximately 56 ships in May, 85 ships in June, and 35 ships in July. Since the deficits for May and June represented about one-third of the total shipping requirement, they must clearly be classed as "unmanageable."

This alarming forecast indicated the necessity of immediate and drastic action if operational schedules were to be maintained. Accordingly, the Joint Chiefs of Staff determined to convene a conference of all theater shipping representatives with the Joint Military Transportation Committee at which the shipping situation might be reviewed in detail. The conference met in Washington from April 18 to April 25.

Three principal accomplishments emerged from the general shipping conference in April. Although theater representatives were unable to scale down their requirements to any appreciable degree, the impending deficits were reduced to manageable proportions by the transfer of certain vessels from the Atlantic pool to the Pacific. Thus the immediate crisis was tided over. From the long-range point of view it was necessary, however, to find a means to prevent further congestion and greater deficits in the future. For this purpose agreement was reached upon a method under which Area Commanders would henceforth report the number of vessels required for retention in the area and would be accountable for any retentions in excess of the number reported by the Area Commander and approved by the Joint Chiefs of Staff. This system, it was hoped, would not only give a more direct indication of the nature of the requirement for which ships were retained; it should also discourage Area Commanders from calling forward vessels in excess of area capacity to discharge them within a given period. At the same time, it recognized the obvious need of Area Commanders to retain a certain amount of shipping for local employment at their own discretion, and thus put the practice of retention upon a formal and official basis.

It was also agreed to institute a system of priorities for maintenance shipments overseas based upon a three-fold classification of shipments as: (a) indispensable, (b) necessary, and (c) desirable cargoes. Within the limits of shipping allocated to them by the Joint Military Transportation Committee, Theater Commanders would indicate on this basis the priority of movement of maintenance material available for shipment. Determination of the priority, it was stressed, would be the responsibility of the Theater Commander; application of the priority to specific cargo and ships would be carried out by continental shipping agencies.

The system adopted at the April conference was, however, not a great deal more than a gesture in the direction of priority control of maintenance shipments. The categories themselves were so loosely defined as to be susceptible of almost any interpretation in application. No procedure was defined under which the definitions could be applied to actual shipments, even less indicate with reference to specific ships or sailings the schedules on which materials would move.

Finally, the priorities would regulate movements only from the Coast into the theater and not from inland sources to the Coast. Such halfway measures could hardly be expected to solve a problem which had its origin in the chaotic and unregulated flow of materials within the country.

This indivisibility of priority control was recognized in a plan for the "Control of Shipments to the Pacific" first put forward in April by the Base Maintenance Division in CNO and revised in June. Pointing out that no genuine system of priority control had ever been developed for maintenance shipments, the plan suggested a system under which the relative priority of shipments would be indicated on requisitions for material submitted by Theater Commanders instead of indicating only the date when materials would be required, as heretofore done. Thus, for example, as between a shipment of beer and a shipment of electronic spare parts, both requested for July, the former would have the lower priority number and would be deferred in case of a shipping deficit during that month. Under the existing system the continental Port Director, not the Area Commander, made the choice in such a case. The system would have carried priorities all the way through the process of continental distribution to sources of supply, or as the plan described it would "in effect serve as a guide to all procuring, storing, assembling, and shipping activities in the United States as to the relative urgency of the requirement."

The significant thing about the priorities plan was that it was a plan primarily for materials control in which shipping control would come as a natural by-product. Its effect would have been to extend the system developed in the Joint Personnel Priority List of 1943 for initial movements of organized units to all material shipments overseas. The plan was discussed in San Francisco in May at a meeting of area representatives, West Coast shipping officers, and officers of the Navy Department, at which it appeared to have had the approval of all parties concerned, and in particular of officers from the theater. Meanwhile, however, objections were being raised within the Navy Department. The Naval Transportation Service had drawn up an alternative plan premised upon maintaining existing organization and procedures without attempting to apply priorities except to ocean shipments. The Bureau of Supplies and Accounts, which was responsible for traffic management within the United States, believed the priorities plan unworkable. Pointing to the decentralized requisition system and the fact that many materials moved as automatic supply rather than on requisition, it said, "Neither requisitions nor automatic supply are assembled for movement as whole units. Ship shortages, varying times necessary for procurement, varying sources of supply, all contribute to a pattern of supply, which, possibly simple in theory, becomes exceedingly intricate in operation. The task of applying and integrating such priorities with actual shipments becoming available daily at hundreds of different points makes under present methods of supply a very complicated operation." In this the Bureau of Supplies and Accounts was on firm ground. Given the existing decentralization of procurement and continental distribution detailed priorities control was probably impracticable. To have established priorities control for naval shipments from point of origin into the theater would have required wholesale reorganization of the Navy's method of logistic operation.

Meanwhile area representatives had returned to the Pacific under the assumption that some such priorities plan as had been suggested would be put into effect. On June 3 CincPoa signified by dispatch his acceptance of the plan as developed at the San Francisco conference. On June 9 the Chief of Naval Operations replied that "Implementation of the Op-30 (Base Maintenance Division) plan by U.S. supply and procurement agencies contains complications requiring further detailed study." At a meeting of July 19 in the Navy Department at which Admiral Greenslade, the Pacific Coast Coordinator, and Captain Davis, the Regional Shipping Director, were present, the plan to establish an over-all and integrated system of material movement control was finally abandoned. Opinion appears to have been almost unanimous against an attempt to institute detailed priority control. The Chief of the Bureau of Supplies and Accounts contended that priorities were impracticable. Commander Toal of the Bureau's Transportation Division stated that there was no prospective rail shortage. Rear Admiral Smith, Director of the Naval Transportation Service, considered the shipping situation to be "in pretty good shape." Members of LOPU, who had themselves been working on a plan for priorities control, had by now swung to the idea of establishing major overseas depots to which "bulk" shipments might be made, and considered this wholesale method preferable to a cargo priorities system for retail shipments. Captain Davis preferred to continue with the system of a Central Booking Office such as he was already operating, and believed with the Bureau of Supplies and Accounts that freight priorities would be impossible to control. Rear Admiral McCormick, Director of the Logistic Plans Division, believed that cargo priorities were unnecessary, a view in which Admiral Horne concurred.

The plan thus set aside was in many respects the most comprehensive suggestion for integrating naval distribution procedure that had been made. In focusing attention first upon the control of material it went to the heart of the problem of distribution. It offered as well in its system of project or priority numbers a single guiding index for each sequential phase in procurement and distribution. Yet, despite these obvious virtues, it had limitations. It was premised upon the assumption that the Navy would continue to ship materials from the continent on a retail basis, an assumption which did not take account of the possibilities offered by the establishment of major overseas depots or of bulk maintenance shipments such as the BBB load. Even more important, however, was the question of practicability. The judgment of the Bureau of Supplies and Accounts that under existing conditions priorities control was unworkable was probably correct. To have attempted to institute such a system at this critical juncture would have jeopardized perhaps all programs of distribution and possibly even led to a complete breakdown.

The plan for priorities control offered by the Base Maintenance Division did not pass entirely without result, however, for though the Navy Department was unwilling to attempt detailed priority control of all materials both in continental and overseas distribution, it could have no objection to new procedures governing the movement of materials within and into forward areas. The upshot, therefore, was the institution in the Pacific Ocean Areas Command of a system known as the Garrison Shipping Procedure, a method of governing the shipment of materials and supporting forces to newly-won bases during the assault and garrison phases.

The Garrison Shipping Procedure was basically a development of procedure already operating within the Central Pacific for the conduct of landing operations and base development. It appears also to have borrowed certain features from the Base Development Plan for priorities control. It contained certain features not present in either which were worked out by officers from the theater and from the Naval Transportation Service early in 1944.

The basic idea of echeloning movements, upon which the Garrison procedure rested, was not new. Echeloning exists in any planned military operation during the combat or assault phases at least. It had been applied to logistic movements since the establishment of bases in the South Pacific early in 1942 as a simple expedient to avoid unnecessary congestion in undeveloped harbors and as a means to the orderly construction of bases. Late in 1943 the procedures which were to apply in the campaign in the Central Pacific began to receive definition by the Joint Staff under CincPoa. On November 3 a directive of CincPoa, "Planning and Preparation in connection with the establishment of facilities at Advance Bases, Central Pacific Area," outlined the substructure of planning and assembly procedures under which type commanders would operate with the Joint Logistic Staff in the preparation of advance base movements. On November 15 a supplementary directive marked out a period of sixty days after the beginning of assault operations during which "automatic supply" would govern the movement of materials, and defined the methods for planning and echeloning shipments. The directive stated, however, that supplies would move forward as "shipping is available" and provided, therefore, no close link between planning ship employment and planning the movement of materials.

On December 19, 1943, a procedure was defined for determining equipment to accompany landing forces and garrison troops and for the loading of ships. Responsibility for ship loading was divided between the Commander of Amphibious Forces for ships expected to arrive at the target within D plus 5, and, for subsequent shipments, the Joint Shipping Control Office (JOSCO), a forwarding agency which had been established in October along the lines of the central booking office in San Francisco. Significantly, however, the procedure defined made "no change in the existing procedure and arrangement for the transportation of personnel and cargo to and from the mainland," and was based therefore on the assumption that the agencies and commands dealing with JOSCO would be located on Oahu and that materials to be shipped would be those already available in the theater.

Early in April 1944 CincPoa took one further step toward the Garrison procedure by organizing garrison troops into task groups under the prospective island commander. Garrison elements were to be organized into a single group sixty days in advance of their departure from the mounting area in order to provide for their final training, staging and loading under a single administrative command. Thus the garrison force received a more precise identity sufficiently far in advance to allow for suitable preparation for movement. It should be noted, however, that this measure did not affect the ultimate responsibility for loading and for assigning shipping to the particular garrison task force, which remained as before the joint responsibility of the Amphibious Commander and JOSCO.

Garrison schedules could be made sufficiently inclusive to provide direction for mainland as well as theater agencies in the movement forward of garrison or base development forces and materials. Thus in larger operations such as the Marianas, where staging was carried on not only in Pearl Harbor but also in the South Pacific and the continental United States, movements of garrison forces from all directions could be coordinated with each other and with the availability of shipping in a single advance schedule of movement. Most important of all, garrison echeloning was based on and governed by conditions in the forward areas. Thus it not only reduced the possibility of wasteful harbor congestion at advanced bases, it also ensured that during the critical phases of an operation, when our forces and shipping were most susceptible to enemy attack, ships would spend the least possible time in dangerous waters.

The Marianas operation was the first in which this elaborated procedure was employed. It was experimental in its beginning, yet it is noteworthy that for the three islands of Saipan, Tinian, and Guam the garrison period continued for approximately one year through 32 different movement echelons before it gave way completely to the less closely regulated procedure for maintenance shipments. In all, of the 5,000,000 tons of materials shipped to the Marianas between June 15, 1944, and the termination of the war, approximately 2,831,000, or 57 per cent, were shipped under the Garrison procedure.

In raising detailed ship movement scheduling to the level of a planned operation the Garrison shipping procedure added much to the work of the theater planning staff. Unless echeloning was transmitted in advance to continental agencies, the process of assembly and continental distribution was hampered by lack of information as to the schedules it must meet. Frequent changes in operational plans, or unforeseen developments in the forward areas necessitated frequent revisions of the Garrison schedules. Echeloning of movements in the Okinawa operation, for example, was in a constant state of flux. Yet with all its attendant difficulties, the Garrison shipping procedure was a notable achievement in the control of movements into and within the forward areas. It assured in principle, and to a large degree in practice, that shipping would not move forward into advanced harbors until need existed for the materials and until the vessels could be discharged. For a not inconsiderable portion of naval overseas shipments to forward areas it thus provided a mechanism for planned shipping and material control.

While the Garrison procedure provided an efficient system for meeting operational requirements, it did not apply to the great bulk of maintenance shipments into the Pacific Ocean Areas, which by the close of 1944, it may be recalled, comprised 80 per cent of all shipments to the Pacific. The major portion of maintenance shipments were directed to rear area bases. Yet there existed an intermediate zone both in time and location in which both garrison and maintenance shipments were directed to a single base. As a base passed from operational to non-operational status it began to receive in addition to the closely regulated garrison shipments the relatively unregulated maintenance shipments. The effect of the latter, of course, was to defeat much of the purpose of the former.

The basic difference between garrison and maintenance shipments was the fact that the former were simply the transport phase of a system of controlled material flow, while the latter were not. Shipping control in the former case was the natural corollary of material control. In the case of maintenance shipments, however, shipping control must be applied independently of and frequently in opposition to the considerations governing supply policy. Isolated from its natural relation with the logistic process as a whole, shipping control had necessarily to be approached as a shipping problem alone. Vessel employment must be regulated and subjected to overall control irrespective of the forces determining the movement of material.

Under these conditions there were three basic requisites to effective shipping control. The first of these was an adequate Port Director system, projected into the theaters and responsible to the Theater Commander, but at the same time sufficiently "tied in" with central shipping agencies such as the Naval Transportation Service and the Joint Military Transportation Committee to ensure adherence to central policy. The second was timely information as to the movement and positions of all vessels operating within the theaters. The third requisite was accurate information regarding the discharging capacity, current and prospective, of the harbors to which shipping was directed.

Efforts of the Naval Transportation Service, begun in 1942 and continued through 1943, to extend and improve the Port Director system, had borne some fruit, but they had never succeeded in providing a system through which central shipping control could be exercised from Washington. To accomplish this the Naval Transportation Service believed it necessary to extend its own authority and identity into the theaters, creating an organization distinct from the remainder of the theater logistic organization, which would have as its primary concern the efficient employment of shipping.

In August 1944 this view was expounded by the Naval Transportation Service Planning officer, Commander T. H.

Ross: "In order to operate effectively in shipping control consideration should be given to a plan whereby the Naval Transportation Service could install as a part of CincPoa's staff (not as a part of the Logistics Division of CincPoa) an organization . . . with authority and responsibility . . . to be designed much along the same plan as the Pacific Regional Shipping Director's Office under Com. 12. This Naval Transportation Service organization should have under its supervision not only the entire Pacific Ocean Port Directors Organization, but should be CincPoa's shipping agency to handle inter and intra-area shipping problems which come under his jurisdiction."

On September 2, 1944, these general views were formulated into a plan and suggested to CincPoa by the Chief of Naval Operations. The proposal was discussed briefly between Admirals King and Nimitz at a conference in San Francisco during September and again a few weeks later by their respective Chiefs of Staff, Admirals McMorris and Cooke. On both these occasions CincPoa was agreeable to the designation of an officer with special duties for shipping control and agreed as well that closer coordination of shipping in the Pacific Ocean Areas was necessary. He did not agree, however, to the establishment of a separate office or shipping control agency distinct from the Logistic Division, J-4. In this position CincPoa showed the natural resistance of any theater commander to vertical lines of authority extending into the theater, over which we would not have full control. Such a tendency would certainly result from the projection of the Naval Transportation Service organization into the theaters. In insisting upon placing the shipping control agency within the Logistics Division, CincPoa stood upon solid ground. In Washington shipping officers were frequently prone to regard shipping as a specialty distinct from "logistics," with the result that the lack of coherence in distribution had been accentuated. CincPoa's insistence upon placing shipping control under the Logistics Division indicated a clear conception of that fundamental unity in the logistic process.

On October 20 CincPoa submitted his own plan for the reorganization of shipping control in the Pacific Ocean Areas. The key to the plan was the reduction in the number of allocation accounts made to the area and their consolidation into one allocation made by the Joint Chiefs of Staff to the Area Commander, from which he would reallocate tonnage as the needs of his various type and area commanders dictated. With certain other modifications the CincPoa plan became the basis for reorganization of shipping and allocation control within the Pacific Ocean Areas. Approved on December 20 as J.C.S. 762/10 ("Procedures Relating to the Allocation and Control of Cargo Shipping in the Pacific Ocean Areas") it became the cornerstone of shipping policy and procedure. The procedures for allocation defined by the Joint Chiefs of Staff provided that in addition to operational shipping, which was already under unified control, "to provide flexibility, all the non-operational dry cargo ships made available on the Pacific Coast for the support of all forces in the Central and South Pacific Areas will be considered as one non-operational group of ships. CincPoa is authorized to assign vessels from this group for single outward voyages to best meet the non-operational requirements listed. . . ." The effect of the Joint Chiefs of Staff directive was thus to concentrate control over the employment of all assigned tonnage in the hands of CincPoa.

Meanwhile, however, the actual shipping situation had gone from bad to worse. On November 6 the deteriorating position of Pacific shipping was reviewed at length by the Naval Transportation Service planning officer. So far as the Navy was concerned, said Commander Ross, the Pacific situation was "unmanageable" because of lack of vessels to sail.

An excessive amount of tonnage was banked on the European continent, waiting to be unloaded or otherwise out

of ocean service. Mediterranean requirements, which had
been expected to drop as the year progressed, had in fact
risen sharply as civilian relief programs claimed political attention and priority. High retentions in the Southwest Pacific particularly, and in the Pacific areas generally, had so
reduced the number of "returners" that deficits had risen
sharply and might be expected to continue rising. Since May
the Retention Fleet had risen from approximately 4,000,000
deadweight tons to over 7,000,000. The percentage of ships
retained had risen from 18 per cent to almost 30 per cent of
all available tonnage.

In addition to authorized retentions a vast amount of
tonnage was lying idle, waiting to be unloaded in Pacific
ports. Surveys throughout the Pacific showed that there was
no real lack of tonnage within the theaters themselves;
rather the fact of a surplus of shipping in relation to capacity
to employ it seemed to be demonstrated by the chronic congestion of the ports. Despite these facts, requirements stated
by Area Commanders continued to reflect the most optimistic estimates of capacity to ship from the mainland. There
was obvious need of drastic measures which would call the
attention of Area Commanders to the dependency of continental shipping agencies upon vessels returning from the
theaters, some way of relating allocations to theaters to their
actual capacity to receive, and some more systematic system
of reporting on vessels and their use.

On November 14, the matter was brought before the
Joint Military Transportation Committee on the motion of
the War Shipping Administration to institute a more effective system of reporting and control of vessel movements.
Pointing out in a well documented report that "The present
critical shortage of ships is wholly due to the retention of
large numbers of vessels in the four major theaters of war and
the inability of theaters to discharge and release ships
promptly," it recommended that "specific steps" be taken
by the Army, Navy, and WSA in Washington which would

enable "some degree of supervision to be exercised from Washington over the use of vessels . . . and a reduction in sailings from the U.S. to any theater which is failing to turn vessels around promptly."

On November 18 acting on a proposal by General Somervell, the Joint Chiefs of Staff approved and sent to the President a memorandum recommending steps to be taken to meet the current critical shipping shortage. Specifically it recommended reductions in vessels allocations to the United Kingdom Import Program, British Lend-Lease, Russian Protocol, civilian relief programs, and other non-military programs in order that more vessels might be available to meet military requirements. Even with this drastic curtailment in non-military and Allied shipments, the JCS averred, United States military sailings to the Pacific would show serious deficits.

The President replied with alacrity. Noting that as of the middle of November 300 ships were awaiting discharge berths in the several war theaters and that 400 others were retained for local operational use, he said: "With due allowance for the delays inevitable in wartime, it nevertheless seems to me that the most urgent representation should be made by the Chiefs of Staff to the theater commanders to improve this situation. Obviously the number of sailings from the U.S. into any operational area should be carefully geared to reception capacity." The President approved the reduction in allocations to the United Kingdom Import Program, but indicated that no other reductions in allocations would be approved until he was "convinced that we have done everything on our part to meet the needs of the shipping situation."

The firm stand taken by the President turned the problem directly back to the military shipping agencies. The growing requirements for civilian relief, justified on grounds of political necessity, could not be ignored, and if more tonnage was to be available for military programs, some at least must come from correction of abuses in the military administration of shipping. Both services, it must be stated, had been aware of abuses and had pressed for their correction. On November 9 the Chief of Naval Operations had pointed out to CincPoa the growing acuteness of the shipping situation, and he in turn had instructed subordinate commanders "to insure that all possible measures are taken to eliminate delaying shipping." Whenever port capacities were exceeded deferment of further shipping was to be requested. The War Department, too, had issued repeated warnings to the Southwest Pacific, but seemingly to little avail.

On December 9, therefore, the Joint Chiefs of Staff approved a memorandum of policy defining specific abuses which must be stopped and directing that the policy be followed by all United States commanders of areas under executive direction of the Joint Chiefs of Staff. Henceforth the use of ocean shipping for storage purposes, a common practice where storage or unloading facilities were inadequate, would be prohibited. Estimates of shipping requirements must be based upon a realistic appraisal of discharge capacities, and supply levels would be scaled down until they were consistent with the imperatives of shipping economy. Selective discharging of ships, resulting in the partial unloading of a number of vessels, would be discontinued save in the early stages of amphibious or other urgent operations. The use of large ocean vessels for local, small deliveries would also be discontinued.

These prohibitory directives were followed by two positive measures designed to provide the information essential for the exercise of a greater measure of shipping control from Washington. Carrying out a provision in the J.C.S. Policy Memorandum the Joint Military Transportation Committee approved on December 16 a system of detailed reporting of ship movements and positions by Area Commanders. By dispatch that day CNO directed that a weekly activities report (Actrep) indicating the daily position of all vessels in all harbors be submitted for the use of the War Department, the Navy Department, and the War Shipping Administration. The purpose behind the report was to provide a uniform system of information which would disclose flagrant cases of vessel idleness, would provide planners with more reliable indications of availability, would keep before Area Commanders the continuing problem of turnaround, and would, finally, provide the JMTC with sufficent information to compel adherence to the remedial measures directed in the Memorandum of Policy of December 9.

In order to round out this system of reporting and to provide a background of port information against which ship activity reports could be analyzed the JMTC recommended on January 6, 1945 the submission of an additional weekly report on port activity (Pacrep). Indicating the number of tons loaded and discharged each day and the estimated capacity of the port for the ensuing thirty days, Pacrep provided a basis on which shipping control agencies could regulate the movement of ships into and within an area with some reference to the possibilities of discharge and turnaround.

Taken together these various measures dealing with the organization and management of shipping control provided a vastly improved system of shipping administration. In their development they were not wholly related to each other, nor were they necessarily conceived and developed in close relation to other measures taken in the field of distribution. The entire approach to logistic problems during 1944 had been essentially one of trial and error, of patching, and of taking those steps which conditions indicated were absolutely essential. In sum the various measures added up to a considerable development in logistic organization and administrative machinery, but they were, for the most part, parochially inspired and were directed toward the improvement of particular conditions in separate segments of the logistic process.

Summary

IN keeping abreast of the expanding logistic task Navy management authorities had perforce to grapple with a multitude of disparate and frequently untractable elements in the logistic process. Even the cursory survey made thus far of the many related or sequent operations involved in planning, procuring, and distributing material support should indicate how far beyond the problems of ordinary business management the problems of logistic administration extended. Surveys made by business management experts and officials of the Bureau of the Budget had all pointed to the need for greater application of business techniques and principles in logistic administration, and it is certain that the Navy's logistic system stood to gain much from improved business methods. But for all the many parallels between business and logistic administration, it is equally clear that methods employed successfully in business could not embrace all the factors involved in logistics.

Naval logistic support in 1944 involved not only an operation carried out on a scale hitherto unprecedented either in peace or war, over vast distances and amidst great uncertainty. It involved also constant operation under great urgency within an economic structure already saturated by demand. It has been estimated that 25 per cent of the nation's economic output was being devoted during 1944 to the support of the United States naval forces. Perhaps another third of our industrial output was being devoted to the support of Army and Air Forces. Still more goods were being allocated through Lend-Lease and civilian relief programs to the large scale conduct of the war. What is most important about this vast effort in support of the war is that by 1944 it was no longer simply a production effort; it was by now an export effort, placing a tremendous strain upon the distributing facilities at our disposal both in this country and overseas.

Progress made in 1944 in the development of the Navy's system of logistic administration and operation had been considerable. Its direction had been toward integration of the many separate operations making up the process as a whole, toward what in business would be called rationalization. No general reorganization had been possible; indeed it may fairly be said that, while by this time many officers perceived the integral character of the logistics function, few of them would have agreed that the Navy required a wholesale reorganization of its logistic machinery to bring it into coincidence with the lines of the logistic task. Reforms and improvements had, therefore, been directed at specific defects in the system, such as storage, requisitions, rail and water transportation. These measures were taken with a growing understanding of their interdependence, prompted by the accumulating evidence that the process itself was one and inseparable. But, either because it was believed unnecessary or because it was believed impossible, no effort had been made at an organic and wholesale revision of the Navy's logistic system. Judging from observable results the guiding policy had been one of moderation and gradualism, characterized by a high degree of practicality and caution.

Perhaps the most outstanding achievement of 1944 had been the improvement of procedures of logistic control and operation within the theaters. The Garrison plan begun in the spring of 1944 marked certainly the farthest advance in administrative technique in any theater toward bringing the flow of logistic support into operational areas under orderly and managed control. It may best be described as an extension backwards, into later operational phases, of the detailed planning and control mechanisms employed in assault and landing operations themselves. In logistic operating techniques the system of mobile base support offered in Service Squadron 10 and the even more mobile combat logistic support supplied by Service Squadron 6 was equally significant development. Thus the development of amphibious assault tactics, which marked such a tremendous advance in naval warfare, was accompanied by equally important, if less spectacular, progress in methods of logistic support. Together they made possible the strategy of our advance across the Pacific.

The most important, and certainly the most continually vexatious, problem of logistic support in 1944 was the management and control of that great bulk of shipments and services coming under the head of "maintenance." It was these which made up the great percentage of shipments of material, which absorbed the carrying capacity of ships and rail carriers, which clogged storage facilities and loading terminals and were responsible for the great bulk of paper work in administration. It was maintenance requirements which were so little susceptible of accurate estimate, and maintenance materials once procured that posed the most serious problems of material distribution control.

The crux of the Navy's problem in distribution was the fact that the character of logistic support required was passing through a profound change. Not until the basing of the fleet at Pearl Harbor in 1940, and more properly not until the war in the Pacific was well under way, had the Navy ever been compelled to furnish continued support for the fleet outside the continental limits of the United States. War Plans developed between 1920 and 1940 had toyed with the idea of mobile base support and of advance base development as a means of projecting fleet support over great distances in the Pacific, and there had been implied in these plans the assumption that naval forces would cut loose, at least temporarily, from their continental base of support. But any student of naval war planning during these two decades of peace must be impressed not only with the lack of realism in the War Plans, but also with the lack of follow-through in setting up the means by which ideas in the plans could be implemented. Whether resulting from lack of congressional support or from the traditional inanition which infects a military organization in times of peace, the result had been the same. In all those detailed working procedures which extend down through its interstices and constitute its living tissue the Navy's logistic system had remained substantially a system of continental support.

As a consequence the Navy's organization for distribution was premised upon the assumption that supplies and services would be delivered to its forces at the major tidewater depots and yards which had been built up over many years. To ensure flexibility in delivering support at tidewater the Navy had practiced a decentralized and retail system of distribution within the continental limits. When this premise was abandoned, the Navy was able as the result of an outstanding production effort to provide the physical facilities in the form of advance base materials, floating dry docks, stores ships and tankers, and the great mass of specialized paraphernalia of support, which were shipped out and set up in the theaters. But it continued to employ an administrative system geared to the needs of continental support.

The fact of transition from continental to overseas logistic support without any basic change in the substructure of logistics administration does much to explain the piecemeal and patchwork character of logistic developments during the war. Men charged with such awesome responsibilities as were placed upon the military leaders of the war may be forgiven for leaning in the direction of cautious pragmatism. There was, in fact, no royal road to logistic organization and administration which could safely be embarked upon. Progress had to be achieved through the many by-ways of reform, invention, and development, and in sum those many particulars of progress added up to a considerable achievement.

CHAPTER VIII

THE CONCLUSION OF THE WAR

Setting the Stage

THE Battle of the Bulge, which culminated at the end of December in a temporary setback to American progress on the Western Front, threw its dark shadow briefly over the whole conduct of the war. It brought about a thorough reappraisal of our global strategic position, a more sober estimate of the capacity of German resistance, and consequently a shift in the basic assumptions upon which strategic and logistic plans were being formulated. Yet the tide of pessimism which momentarily engulfed the public mind late in December was not as severe in the minds of military planners. It was apparent that the assumption of a speedy conclusion of the war in Europe must be modified. But a thorough review of the German strategic position indicated that, while the Germans might still be able to concentrate forces effectively for limited aims and while they were still capable of an intensified U-boat campaign against Atlantic shipping lanes, their long-range capacity to resist had been seriously impaired. For planning purposes it was possible with some assurance to fix the estimated date of German surrender or defeat at July 1, 1945.

One reason for the difference between the public and military reactions to the German counter-offensive was that it was possible for the military to measure more quickly the true proportions of the German success and its ultimate cost to the Germans themselves. But a more important factor in the military calculations was the fact that long before the German forces burst out of their ring of encirclement in the Ardennes certain of the assumptions of military planning had begun to disintegrate, particularly the assumption made for strategic and logistic planning purposes that German resistance would end in September or October of 1944. How that assumption was arrived at cannot be determined here, but it should be apparent that as the autumn progressed without the defeat of the Germans, the logistic consequences of this strategic miscalculation were being felt long before the Battle of the Bulge. The spectacular German action provided a dramatic occasion for a recalculation which was already necessary.

The effects of the continuance of the war in Europe on a large scale were indicated most quickly in the increasing stringency of our shipping position, for upon the expanding programs in the Pacific there were now superimposed much larger European requirements than had been anticipated. Other factors added to the unfavorable shipping prospect. Requirements for civilian relief and rehabilitation, which had already risen sharply at the end of 1944 with the emergence of Italian and French programs, would certainly rise even more sharply with the liberation of the continent as a whole. Nor was there any appreciable cushion in shipping allocated to the United Kingdom Import Program from which benefit to military programs might be derived.

The outlook was, in fact, so unpromising that early in December the British Chiefs of Staff recommended a thorough over-all review of the cargo shipping position. About mid-December they sent a mission under Mr. Richard Law to the United States for this purpose and also to discuss the possibility of admitting vessels to French ports for the French rehabilitation program. The over-all review, undertaken by the Combined Chiefs of Staff in collaboration with the Combined Shipping Adjustment Board, extended through the month of December and into the Malta conference of January. With respect to cargo shipping the report concluded that, whereas there might be slight improvement during the first quarter of 1945, deficits in the second quarter, particularly in the Pacific, would approach "unmanageable" proportions.

The prospective shipping shortage provided one of the principal logistic issues at the Malta ("Argonaut") conference in January. The United States Chiefs of Staff finally secured the adoption of the principle that approved military programs should take priority over all other claims upon shipping resources. Supplies to liberated countries, it was agreed, should be considered in the allocation of shipping only insofar as they contributed to the over-all war-making capacity of the United Nations. "In the event of a deficit in shipping resources, first priority should be given to the basic undertakings in support of over-all strategic concepts as agreed in Argonaut. So long as these first priority requirements are not adequately covered, shipping for other requirements will not be allocated without prior consultation with the appropriate Chiefs of Staff." In principle, therefore, military requirements would be met in full, and deficits applied to all other programs. In practice, however, it was clearly understood that there were certain minima below which allocations to the United Kingdom Import Program, Lend-Lease, and relief programs could not go. The principle adopted at Malta would not in practice constitute an over-riding priority. This fact was borne out by the stipulation in the Malta paper that the Chiefs of Staff should give careful consideration to the shipping implications of proposed undertakings lest "urgent operational requirements" get out of hand, and that they should "require rigid compliance of Theater Commanders with their orders relative to the control of shipping." This latter point obviously referred to the instructions for the correction of abuses in shipping control issued by the Joint and Combined Chiefs of Staff in December. It pointed up the fact that the adequacy of tonnage to meet military requirements would depend largely upon the ability of the military services themselves to employ allocated shipping efficiently.

With the exception of the shipping situation, however, the continuation of the war in Europe did not seriously or directly affect the Navy's own logistic or supply programs. The delay in transferring LST's and other self-discharging craft from the Atlantic to the Pacific was felt, and indirectly the tying up of Army Service and Engineer troops in the European theater aggravated the shortage of naval construction personnel required for base development in the Pacific. The Navy was involved in the immense task of redeploying troops from the European to the Pacific theater and had therefore to take into account the intensification of redeployment schedules which followed as a consequence of delayed victory in Europe. But by far the greater portion of naval material shipments and naval forces were for the Pacific, and it was there that the Navy's logistic problems had their roots.

The Pacific campaign itself continued to be a compound of uncertainties. The sudden decision to attack Leyte and Samar in the Central Philippines had entailed many readjustments in schedules of logistic support. It was followed by a period of uncertainty in which the issue of whether to launch the next offensive against Luzon or Formosa was debated at length. This in turn had to be considered against the background of the wider issue whether the Pacific campaign might be carried directly to the home islands of Japan or whether it would be necessary to establish a firm foothold in China and there first come to grips with a major Japanese land force. Once the Okinawa operation had been determined upon, it was followed by great uncertainty as to what other offensives in the Ryukyus and on the coast of China might be necessary in order to establish a firm platform for further assaults.

Meanwhile, as our position in the Philippines was being extended and consolidated and as the fleet extended its operations deeper into the China Sea and the home waters of Japan, the requirements for fleet support and maintenance in the forward areas continued to mount. As soon as the decision had been taken to attack the Central Philippines, the Commander Seventh Fleet had laid plans for base facilities at Leyte. On November 18, he requested facilities to support one-third of the Pacific Fleet at some major point in the Philippines. But the question whether the major Philippines base should be established on Luzon, at Leyte-Samar, or elsewhere continued undetermined, and as late as December 23, no firm plan for a naval base in the Philippines had been submitted to the Chief of Naval Operations. When the decision was finally taken to develop facilities at Leyte-Samar, it was made in the face of adverse weather prospects at that site and largely because of the need to reach some decision without further delay. During the early months of 1945, however, plans were gradually forming for the two climactic operations of the Pacific War—Olympic and Coronet—to begin in November, and these slowly emerged as the nodes of all strategic and logistic planning.

If uncertainty continued to be the chief characteristic of strategic planning there were, however, certain obvious certainties in the general outlines of the impending logistic task. The volume of shipments of both material and personnel would continue to rise sharply. Operational requirements for Okinawa, for the Kyushu and Honshu operations. and for the continued operations of fleet striking forces would be considerably higher than for preceding operations and would be concentrated within a briefer period of time. Army shipments to the Pacific would show even greater percentage increases than those of the Navy and would utilize an increasing proportion of Pacific shipping allocations, continental transshipping facilities and area discharging capacity. The requirements of both services together, whatever might be the schedules of operations or the detailed composition of forces, would exceed the capacity of all facilities for distribution hitherto employed. The administrative problems posed by this impending logistic task were thus an intensification of those problems which had been building up during the preceding year. There was obviously necessary a fuller and more efficient use of all continental transshipping facilities—of loading berths, long-term and in-transit storage, stevedore labor and railroad line-haul capacity. To achieve this objective the Navy must first redistribute its work load along the West Coast itself, concentrating a smaller percentage upon the San Francisco Bay area, and secondly provide for the shipment of a much larger portion of its Pacific materials from the East and Gulf Coasts.

Shipping must be more effectively controlled and must be made to serve more exactly the true requirements of supply programs. At the same time if shipping was not to be wasted, there must be an intensive development of area receiving and discharging capacities and a closer correlation in shipping schedules between unloading operations at advance bases and programs of assembly and loading on the mainland.

Still another necessity was an improved inventory of Pacific area stocks upon the basis of which Area Commanders might avail themselves of usable materials within the area. Various programs for the roll-up of rear bases had been sketched out during 1944, but up to the close of that year little had been accomplished. Area Commanders had continued to rely largely upon shipments from the United States and had drawn only slightly upon rear base components, equipment and material stocks which were much nearer at hand. With most materials available in ample quantities in the United States even to the point of clogging established "pipelines" there had been little disposition to depart from existing channels of supply.

Finally, there was need for continued effort along the lines laid down in the Overall Logistic Plan and the Summary Control Report to develop systematic information and techniques for keeping procurement programs in balance with each other and for assuring that delivery schedules did not feed more material into the logistic support system from industrial sources than could be consumed, stored or delivered.

In summary, these various factors in the logistic task could be considered as two general problems. In the first case, where the issues were of purely naval concern, they resolved into that problem, so persistent in the Navy's decentralized logistic system, of developing the mechanism of control and coordination of logistic operations on an overall basis. It was necessary, in short, to draw all these separate but interrelated factors together into a single, manageable process.

In those matters which were of common concern with the Army, where two logistic systems by no means similar had to operate harmoniously within a single theater, utilizing the same pool of economic resources and aiming toward a common operation against the enemy, the problem was perhaps even more complex and difficult. Much of the mechanism for joint effort and cooperation had already been developed under the Joint Chiefs of Staff and their various subcommittees and in the arrangements made under unified theater commands. These were supplemented by a vast array of standing and ad hoc joint committees, whose mere catalogue might fill a volume. But just as there was within the Navy itself no single authority or controlling agency comprehending all the elements in the logistic process, so between the two services the means of logistic cooperation and coordination at the highest level were at best imperfect.

The major logistic achievement of 1945 was that as plans were developed for operations Olympic and Coronet, both these needs were at least partially met. Toward this end the two major landmarks of administrative history in the field of logistics during the concluding phases of the war were the Material Distribution Committee and the Joint Army-Navy Shipping and Supply Conference during the spring of 1945.

The Material Distribution Committee

THE Material Distribution Committee of April 1945 was the last, and in many respects the most successful, of the Navy's efforts during the war to coordinate the various elements of transport and supply involved in distribution. For the first time during the war all the factors entering into both requirements and capacities were reviewed together by a single body composed of all the major agencies participating in the Navy's logistic task.

It had its origin ostensibly in the necessity to prepare a naval agenda for the Army-Navy Shipping and Supply Conference convened on May 1. But there is evidence to suggest that even had no such conference with the Army been impending, the Navy itself was coming to the point where some such thorough and over-all review of its logistic position would have been made. The organization of the committee grew, in fact, out of discussions initiated by Rear Admiral Flanigan, Director of the Naval Transportation Service, to secure more naval cargo for loading on the East and Gulf Coasts.

The problem with which the Naval Transportation Service was faced was two-fold. In the first place, the strain upon West Coast facilities, which since early 1944 had been steadily increasing, was now coming to the breaking point. By January, for example, there was a backlog of advance base component and maintenance materials awaiting shipment at Port Hueneme of over 1,000,000 tons. Similar conditions existed in other West Coast ports. During the last week in January, moreover, the situation was further aggravated by a sharp cut-back in the number of ships allotted by General MacArthur for movement into the Southwest Pacific. The original allotment of 31 vessels, most of which were already loaded or loading, was cut suddenly to 12.

The situation thus developed by the lack of receiving capacity in the forward areas was felt all the way back through the "pipeline." Suggestions were made that some of the backlog materials be pulled back from tidewater to inland depots like the Naval Supply Depot at Clearfield, Utah, but this was in fact impracticable. Inland depots were already jammed themselves, and were having difficulty in keeping abreast of the continual flow of east-to-west shipments for later assemblies.

The second factor was the difficulty in making vessels available on the West Coast to meet the constantly rising shipping requirements of CincPoa. In February, for example, CincPoa's March shipping requirement was suddenly increased by twenty-five vessels. But no additional shipping was available on the West Coast to meet this requirement. On the East Coast, where the War Shipping Administration could make vessels available from the Atlantic pool, the Navy was unable on such short notice to provide sufficient cargo of the type desired. It was necessary therefore, to send the vessels in ballast through the Canal to the West Coast, a procedure to which both the Army and the War Shipping Administration vigorously objected.

The incident of the March requirement, although a forceful illustration, was not an isolated case. In the opinion of Admiral Flanigan the only source from which mounting Pacific requirements could be met in the future would be the Atlantic shipping pool. But regardless of what over-all monthly allocations might be made by the Joint Military Transportation Committee and the War Shipping Administration, unless the Navy could make cargo available on the East Coast, vessels would not actually be assigned to meet the allocations. Instead they would go to whatever other claimants, military or otherwise, could provide cargo, and in all likelihood would remain in service in the Atlantic.

This realistic appraisal was undoubtedly correct. Yet the first efforts to secure greater diversions of cargo to the East Coast by consultation with representatives of the bureaus produced only meager results. The necessity for concerted action by bureaus responsible for internal routing of cargo was being increasingly recognized, but it was not until a meeting of March 15, in the Bureau of Supplies and Accounts, at which a decision was reached to form the Material Distribution Committee, that the basis was laid for a wholesale redistribution of the transshipment work load.

The Material Distribution Committee held its first meeting on March 24. Under the chairmanship of Rear Admiral Purnell, the Assistant CNO for Material, it included as regular members representatives of all the bureaus, the Marine Corps, Coast Guard, the Office of Procurement and Material and most of the divisions in the Office of Naval Operations. Before the committee had completed its work representatives of CincPoa, the Commander Western Sea Frontier, and the Joint Logistic Plans Committee had also participated and lent assistance.

The agenda of the committee was broken down into four major items which were intended to serve as the basis for a fifth item, the agenda for the Army-Navy Shipping and Supply Conference. The first matter to be determined was the total estimated quarterly requirement in personnel and material for shipment to the Pacific from July 1, 1945, to July 1, 1946. This period would include base development at Okinawa subsequent to the completion of that operation, whatever other operations in the Ryukyus or China might follow Okinawa, the assault upon Kyushu scheduled for November 1, 1945, and most of the assault phases of the Honshu operation scheduled for the early months of 1946. In addition to other base development projects in the Central Pacific and the Philippines the estimate must also include the much larger percentage of shipments required for maintenance.

Secondly, the committee proposed to determine the maximum transshipment capacity of Navy West Coast facilities, taking into consideration Army, Marine Corps, and civilian requirements. Thirdly, by a comparison of figures in the first two items the committee would determine what volume of shipments would be required from the East and Gulf Coasts and what arrangements would be necessary to deliver at tidewater and load the cargo required. Lastly, the committee would look into the supply and requisitioning procedures of the Navy in order to determine what changes would be necessary in order to facilitate the control of logistic movements and to assure closer coordination between area and continent shipping and supply programs.

The major problems of a general nature which had affected the Navy's task of distribution were those already described: lack of ships at the time and place needed, lack of Pacific discharging capacity, overloaded rail and port facilities, the difficulty of integrating shiploading on the various coasts into CincPoa's shipping procedure, the absence of a central requisition control and the unbalanced distribution of stocks within the United States. The mere listing of these various problems should indicate that even in its broadest aspects the task was fraught with complexity. But no sooner had the committee begun its deliberations than it became apparent that each of these problems was in itself a matter of almost infinite ramifications.

In the determination of requirements the committee was compelled to consider finally three different sets of figures, determined respectively by the Joint Logistic Plans Committee, the Logistic Controls Section of the Western Sea Frontier, and by the individual bureaus of the Navy Department and the Marine Corps Headquarters. Between the highest and lowest of these estimates there was a difference of almost 800,000 tons per quarter, nearly one-sixth of the total of the lowest estimate. Ultimately the committee fixed upon an average figure of 1,815,000 tons per month, which was actually only a little below the highest estimate, submitted by the Joint Logistic Plans Committee.

In determining the capacity of West Coast transshipping

facilities the committee had to proceed upon a broader and more realistic basis than had ever been done before. Since 1943, the Bureau of Supplies and Accounts had carried on a periodic port capacity survey known as the "Navy Traffic Flow Study," but the assumptions upon which it had been based were curiously unrealistic. Two major assumptions, for example, which underlay its report of January 2, 1945, were that "adequate labor [would be] available at the port for unloading cars and loading vessels" and that "sufficient ships [would be] always available to lift cargo." More recently the Commander Western Sea Frontier had undertaken a survey of Pacific Coast facilities in which the factor of stevedore labor was included, and this survey was rushed to completion for the use of the committee.

The final report, based upon the combined studies of the Bureau and the Commander Western Sea Frontier, reflected the limiting factor of stevedore labor. Available loading berths were not taken into account, since it was soon discovered that under any circumstances berth capacity would exceed both railroad line-haul capacity and available stevedore labor. Of the latter two, although rail capacity was fast approaching a critical state, labor was still considered to be the more serious. Even with this careful calculation, however, it was still necessary to assume "not only the availability of ships to meet the maximum requirements, but also the availability of a reserve of shipping in excess of requirements to meet the exigencies of the operations and permit a steady and even flow of cargo through the various facilities."

The estimate submitted by the subcommittee set a maximum figure for the Navy's West Coast facilities of 4,000,000 measurement tons per quarter or one and one-third million tons per month. But in setting the estimate as high as this the sub-committee felt constrained to issue a warning:

"This subcommittee wishes to reiterate the statement in its interim report that even the best port capacity estimates should be accepted with full understanding of their limitations and imperfections; that a shift or change in one of many variable factors controlling port capacity may alter such capacity considerably; that the Navy should as a matter of safety assume a relatively low capacity and seek to find means to adjust and modify its supply and requisition procedure so as to achieve a degree of flexibility which will permit rapid shifts in the transshipment load to take advantage of unused capacity or avoid congested port facilities as the case may be."

The remainder of the work of the committee, the determination of required shifts in loadings, stock levels, internal routing and the categories of materials to be shifted, was, if anything, more difficult than the question of port capacity. Starting with two basic principles set forth by CincPoa—that "inventories at major distribution centers in the forward area are to be kept at a reasonably low working level" and that "The continental United States sources of supply for these bases in the forward area should be as close to that area as possible"—the committee was compelled to take into account a host of other limiting conditions before it could arrive at a final plan.

It began by analyzing the probable requirements of major bases and areas during the period under consideration. Thus, for example, since the initial construction phase at Manus had been completed and its stocks already brought to the required level, it was assumed that its volume of shipments would remain relatively constant. Shipments to Pearl Harbor would also remain on a level. Guam was in an advanced stage of construction, but material required for the build-up of stocks and the augmentating of facilities would more than compensate for the decline in construction components. Okinawa, Leyte, Samar and other Philippine bases were still in their initial construction phases and would therefore absorb the greater portion of the increase in Navy shipments.

In deciding what redistribution could be made in the loading task as between East and West Coasts it was necessary also to recognize certain categories of shipments which must move from the West Coast. First, material produced on the West Coast, such as lumber and canned fruits, should obviously not be shipped across the country to be loaded in the East. Other materials which were in short supply must also be routed to the loading points nearest the theater. In a third group of cases special loading, assembly and storage facilities were largely concentrated on the West Coast, and no substitutes could be developed on the East Coast. Other special considerations such as the shortage of refrigerated shipping space and the necessity of having available an adequate amount of filler and deck cargo had also to be taken into account. Nor was it possible to overlook entirely the basic doctrine promulgated and reiterated throughout the war by West Coast shipping authorities that in order to hold stevedore labor at the ports West Coast facilities should be employed to the maximum before any redistribution of port load was considered.

The final report of the committee indicated that of the average 1,815,000 measurement tons per month expected to be shipped a minimum of 1,167,000 tons would have to move from the West Coast. Since this represented a division between the two coasts of 68 per cent to 32 per cent which was already assumed to prevail, the committee's recommendations were not revolutionary. But since that ratio had in fact never prevailed, despite the directive of the previous October which sought to establish it, the careful examination into the means and conditions of accomplishing it may be said to have served a useful purpose.

This detailed review of the deliberations of the Material Distribution Committee has been intended to serve two purposes. In the first place, it should indicate something of the nature and scope of distribution problems at this critical phase of the war. And secondly, it should indicate just what the Material Distribution Committee was and what it was not. The committee may be distinguished clearly from other projects or groups such as LOPU and the Archer-Wolf Group in that it dealt with substantive problems of logistics rather than with matters of organization and procedure. This point is illustrated by the fact that subcommittee No. 4, which had intended to review the Navy's requisitioning and supply procedures in order to secure greater flexibility in continental distribution dropped that subject completely and devoted itself instead to the analysis of probable trends in shipments by areas and bases.

In essence, the committee came into being and operated as an ad hoc organization. It was able to perform its work successfully partly by virtue of the urgency of the problem and partly because, since this was the concluding phase of the war, the logistic task could be brought within limits and defined in substantive terms. For a given period and for definite and scheduled operations it was possible to calculate and reduce into manageable terms the many elements involved.

The Material Distribution Committee should not, therefore, be regarded as the first step in the institution of a new and continuing procedure applicable to any set of circumstances. It might ultimately have become so had the turn of circumstances been otherwise. Certainly there were many who recognized a new departure in the novel circumstance of all logistic agencies working in close concert under a single coordinating control. There were many, too, who hoped that the committee itself might evolve into a continuing agency for over-all logistics coordination and control. In fact, however, it remained an ad hoc agency preparing what might be called a large-scale and general logistic operating plan. In most minds it was considered essentially as a preface to the Army-Navy Shipping and Supply Conference which was to follow. Yet as the first successful attempt to bring all logistic agencies and all logistic factors together under a single, coherent direction, however briefly, it was a landmark in the Navy's logistic history during this war.

The Joint Army-Navy Shipping and Supply Conference

THE Army and Navy Shipping and Supply Conference of May 1945 was an attempt by both services to draw together the many threads of logistic support for the Pacific campaign and in particular to relate to the strategic plan and the logistic capacities of the area the many programs of movement and support which would converge in the Pacific from many directions. Its problem as stated in the final report of the conference was:

"Review the forecasted logistic support required to conduct the Pacific War as related to:

(a) Continental U.S. supply and transshipping capabilities;

(b) Area capabilities;

(c) Ship availability and allocations; and

(d) Integration between requisitioning and shipping procedures necessary to achieve the most effective utilization of the capabilities as developed through (a), (b), and (c) above."

The conference was supplied amply with representation from all commands and agencies which would participate in the final phases of the Pacific war. For the Navy, the delegation headed by Admiral Ingersoll, Commander Western Sea Frontier, who acted as chairman of the conference, included full representation from the Navy Department, more or less identical with the membership of the Material Distribution Committee. The head of the Army delegation was Lieutenant General Styer, representing the Army Service Forces, who was about to assume the post of Commander Army Service Forces Pacific, under General MacArthur.

With him were representatives of the War Department and various area commands paralleling those of the Navy.

The accomplishments of the conference were many, and with one notable exception it may be said that both services emerged from the conference with a clearer conception of the problems involved in future Pacific support and in complete accord upon the methods to be pursued in meeting them. Beginning with total requirements for both services it was estimated that total shipments would increase from 11,944,000 measurement tons in the third quarter of 1945, to 15,416,000 tons in the last quarter of 1946. Against this it was necessary to set an absolute ceiling of 11,000,000 measurement tons per quarter upon the transshipment capacity of the West Coast ports. Both services agreed to redistribute stock and storage activities in order to keep the shipments of each within the ceiling of West Coast facilities currently allotted to them and to divert any overflow to ports on the East Coast. For the Navy this meant a diversion to the East Coast of 700,000 measurement tons in addition to shipments already being made from that area. Implied, though not stated in the report, was the certainty that if the Navy was to accomplish its Pacific Coast loading program it would have to make a fuller use of potential West Coast facilities available to it outside the San Francisco Bay Area.

As far as joint use of continental transport, terminal, and storage facilities was concerned, the conference concluded that present arrangements were entirely satisfactory. The Navy would continue to enjoy the use of Army Holding and Reconsignment Points with the strict understanding, however, that their use would be limited to in-transit cargo and not extended to dead storage or to slow-moving materials.

In the all-important issue of whether area receiving capacities would be adequate to deal with required shipments as projected by the planning agencies the combined reports of theater representatives were encouraging. Although the conference reported that, "No current estimate for adequacy of Pacific overseas port capacities can be stipulated," the over-all estimate of Pacific port capacity within active zones of operation was put at 17,000,000 measurement tons per quarter. Of this three-quarters, or 12,750,000 tons of capacity, could be utilized for discharging, the remainder being reserved for staging and outloading operations. The latter figure on capacity available for discharge fell several million tons below the estimated requirements at their highest point, but "giving consideration to the additional discharge capacity that it is assumed will be available during 1946, for discharge over beaches, ship-to-ship and through ports not covered [in the port estimate] . . ." the conference concluded that "the present and planned over-all receiving capacity in the Pacific appears adequate to handle the projected requirements." But as the report pointed out, no estimate of port capacity in the abstract could be entirely satisfactory. The factor of "demand requirement by destination" would itself depend upon a variety of factors such as the distribution of Army and Navy stocks within the area and the progress of the campaign.

The major Army distribution points, it was planned, would be located in the Philippines with air depots at Guam, Manila and ultimately on Okinawa. Only the assault and initial movement phases of Army operations would be staged and supported from Pacific bases, however. All other support would be shipped direct from the Zone of the Interior in the United States. The Navy for its part would rely principally upon Guam, Samar, Okinawa and Pearl Harbor with a little less than half of its support being rendered directly from bases and a little more than half from floating support units such as Service Squadrons 6 and 10. Both services planned to integrate the roll-up of materials from the South and Southwest Pacific areas into the programs of support from the mainland in order to make use of nearby resources and to diminish as far as possible the pressures upon extended lines of supply.

The development of this structure of support as outlined

would place various special demands upon shipping resources. Both services were in need of additional shipping for intra-area services in order to attain and maintain a better balanced distribution of their stocks within the area. The Navy would require an increase in mobile or floating storage, particularly in view of the prospect that planned facilities at Okinawa would be delayed in their construction. Accomplishment of the Army's roll-up from the Southwest Pacific to the Philippines, where discharge facilities were very inadequate, would also require the assistance of additional LST's, AKA's and other craft suitable for lightering. These the Navy agreed should be made available subject to the condition that crew training operations of assault craft would not be sacrificed and with the understanding that a number of these craft would be transferred from the European theater to the Pacific.

The requirement during the peak of our military operations in the Pacific was estimated at 26,300,000 deadweight tons of shipping. Comparing this figure with the remaining 7,000,000 deadweight tons then allocated for non-military purposes, one can see clearly that the operations planned in the Pacific were to demand the maximum of the nation's logistic resources. Since the requirements as tabulated by this conference were only a little above those for which Justice Byrnes and Judge Vinson had guaranteed that shipping would be available, the conference felt justified, however, in the assumption that shipping requirements would be met.

The report of the conference represented a considerable measure of clarification and accord on the problems of logistic support of the Pacific campaign. On one important point, however, the organization of shipping control and its integration into Army and Navy systems of supply and requisitioning, the conference was unable to reach an agreement.

During the major part of the war in the Pacific, it will be recalled, operations had been carried on under two separate and distinct theater commands. General MacArthur in the Southwest Pacific Area and Admiral Nimitz in the Pacific Ocean Area had each exercised a unified command over all services within their areas for which they had been responsible directly to the Joint Chiefs of Staff. In each of these commands, needless to say, administrative and logistic procedures had been developed during the course of the war which in each case had been tailored to the peculiar exigencies of the campaign and to the composition of forces within the theater. The result had been a system in the Southwest Pacific under which each service was primarily responsible for its own support subject to joint control during the initial phases of combat operations and at the top level. In the Pacific Ocean Areas, on the other hand, there had been a progressive integration of logistic and supply services, until in almost every phase of logistic operations CincPoa was a unified command. Through a joint staff, whose logistic section was, in fact, headed by an Army officer, CincPoa exercised a close coordinating control over every aspect of logistic operations for all services.

The capture and investiture of the Philippines by General MacArthur's forces and the seizure of Okinawa by those of Admiral Nimitz brought our campaign to the limit of the areas originally comprised in the separate theaters of command. Subsequent operations against the Japanese homeland would necessitate a merging of all forces in the Pacific in a single effort and in an area not originally within the purview of either of the theater commanders. Some new provision for command was therefore necessary.

On April 6, 1945, the Joint Chiefs of Staff issued a directive to all commanders concerned redefining the command relationship which was to obtain for the concluding phases of the war. The directive, however, lent confusion rather than clarity to the command picture in the Pacific. Without definitely abrogating the existing geographical division of command between General MacArthur and Admiral Nimitz, it provided that, "The Supreme Commander, Southwest Pacific Area, is hereby also designated Commander in Chief, U.S. Army Forces, Pacific (CincAFPac) and . . . all United States Army resources in the Pacific Theater . . . are placed under his command." Similarly, Admiral Nimitz, while remaining as Commander Pacific Ocean Areas, was designated as commander of all naval forces in the Pacific. Each was charged respectively as "responsible for the provision of [Army or Navy] resources to meet the requirements for operations in the Pacific directed by the Joint Chiefs of Staff."

Single command of all forces would be established for specific operations so that presumably either General MacArthur or Admiral Nimitz would assume over-all command, depending upon whether the operation was predominantly a naval or land campaign. But it was not contemplated that such a single command would seriously affect command arrangements in the original areas since these would be primarily in a non-operational status.

Meanwhile, the directive apparently envisaged not an immediate but a gradual rearrangement of logistic responsibilities and procedures in the Pacific.

"Until passed to other command by mutual agreement or by direction of the Joint Chiefs of Staff, the localities under command of CincSWPa and the Naval forces allocated to him will remain under his command and similarly, the areas under command of CincPoa and the Army forces allocated to him will remain under his command. Changes in command of forces or localities and changes made in existing Joint logistical procedures will be effected by progressive rearrangements made by mutual agreement, or as may be directed by the Joint Chiefs of Staff."

The results of this démarche were several. Clearly, with command relations now organized both on horizontal and vertical lines, by geographical area and by respective service cognizance, a large measure of confusion was to be expected before the progressive rearrangements contemplated had been successfully effected and lines of responsibility had settled once again into a clear and intelligible pattern. In respect to logistic procedures and responsibilities the effect of the directive was even more cataclysmic. If each service was to be separately responsible for the provision of its own resources, the result could only be to wipe the slate clean of almost every progressive step made during the war toward joint logistic services and to revert essentially to the condition which existed in March 1943, before the Basic Logistical Plan for the Pacific was promulgated. Certainly no such radical intention was in the mind of the Joint Chiefs of Staff, but by the wording of the directive the way was opened for either service to seek such new arrangements or procedures as might be more congenial to its own particular interest.

The most serious effect of the directive was that it left the structure of Pacific logistics suspended in uncertainty. Some changes were certain, but they were dependent upon future "mutual agreement" of the Theater Commanders or upon subsequent directives of the Joint Chiefs of Staff. Forced thus to plan in a vacuum, the conference did well to reach agreement upon as many points as it did.

The sole point of disagreement in the conference concerned the issue of Pacific shipping control, which was reopened as a result of the new command directive. The Army, contending that "supply and the control of its flow is a function of command," desired to separate the shipping control procedures so that each service might regulate the distribution of its resources independently of the other and in direct line with command responsibility. "Separate Army and Navy commands having been set up," it said, "separate Army and Navy controls follow." The Navy, concerned primarily with the preservation of the carefully integrated CincPoa shipping procedure, took the position that "The procedures now in effect covering allocation and control of shipping in the Pacific Ocean Areas should be continued unless otherwise directed by the Joint Chiefs of Staff."

In justice to the position of the Army it must be said that the system as practiced in the Pacific Ocean Areas was in many respects not compatible with its general system of supply and requisition and with its continental distribution procedures. Quite naturally, and perhaps justifiably, it believed that its own system of distribution was a more satisfactory one than that of the Navy. In any case, it was better adapted to the nature of Army logistic problems. It had accepted the CincPoa system and had adapted its own methods to it because the Pacific Ocean Area command was naval, and it had recognized a preponderant naval interest in that area. Believing now, however, that the Pacific war would become increasingly a land campaign, and given the new vertical command relationship, it desired to rewed its supply control procedure to the command function wherever Army command was exercised.

This view did not, however, assume a complete split between the Army and Navy shipping systems throughout the entire Pacific. The Army believed that there was a "solid core of command functions embracing supply functions in the Pacific Theater almost wholly a matter of Army concern" and another solid core almost wholly a matter of Navy concern. But it also acknowledged that "inherent in the Pacific situation there are and will be localities and operations where Army and Navy interests are so closely interwoven that reconciliation by joint or unified control is and will be required by mutual agreement between the commanders concerned or by direction of the J.C.S."

On the Navy's side it appears incontestable that the shipping procedure worked out so painstakingly under CincPoa was the most efficient and most productive of economy in shipping space of any of the shipping control systems practiced in various theaters of command during the war. It was the result of steady evolution and improvement, aiming always at the development of a closely integrated system of joint operations. Certainly by comparison with either the European theater or the Southwest Pacific it cannot be denied that turnarounds in the Pacific Ocean Area were rapid and unauthorized retentions at a minimum. The Navy, moreover, did not argue for the extension of this system into the new areas not already under the command of CincPoa. It desired simply to maintain a unified and integrated control of shipping within the Pacific Ocean Area. Wherever the supply system of one service was perfectly distinct from the other it recognized that each service would desire to control its own shipping. It recognized also that at the assault objective the Army interest would be paramount, and that it should therefore control all unloading operations.

In the discussions held upon this issue it became obvious that the problem was one of the extent to which each service would be dealing in a separate sphere as opposed to those situations and times when joint operations would be in force and joint control would be required. On such a hypothetical issue, however, it was impossible to reach any firm conclusion. The Navy pointed out that although geographically it might be possible to demarcate separate spheres of interest, and although for purposes of joint operations a joint system might be established temporarily under one command or the other, it would be impossible in practice to distinguish between these two conditions. Operational shipping must pass through areas which were devoted entirely to maintenance. In other cases shipments to an operational area would originate in non-operational areas. The use of shipping for one purpose impinged on its use for another purpose. In short, shipping control was a seamless garment; the problem must be dealt with as a whole.

In summary, then, the desire of the Navy was twofold. First it desired to maintain intact the system of shipping control already in force within the geographical limits then defined as the Pacific Ocean Areas. Within the new area of operations it desired that shipping be controlled and regulated by a joint agency representing both the Army and Navy commands, with the condition that by virtue of paramount interest unloading at the assault objective would be controlled by CincAFPac.

The Army insisted, however, that it could no longer go along with a system under which its supply procedure was thrown out of gear with the exercise of the command function. Were there to be a single command, it said, it would subscribe to a single system of shipping control. With separate command it insisted that the relation between the command and supply functions must be the governing factor. Thus, in the end the two services were compelled to submit separate reports and relegate the issue for decision to the theater commanders, or failing their agreement to the Joint Chiefs of Staff.

The lack of decision on the form of shipping control was a serious deficiency in the achievements of the conference. Because of the chronic shipping shortage and its key position in relation to all other factors of supply, shipping was the keystone in the logistic arch of the Pacific. Failure to employ tonnage effectively or to coordinate properly the shipping activities of the two services could under certain circumstances spell the difference between the success or failure of the great operations impending. Certainly the record of past experience would seem to indicate only too clearly the necessity of the closest coordination in shipping matters between Army and Navy in the Pacific.

Fortunately, although the factor of shipping control was closely related in fact to the other matters discussed at the conference, it was possible in the discussions to isolate it and to reach a firm agreement upon the other matters. In drawing together the best informed estimate of Pacific requirements and in reviewing these in relation to continental supply and transshipment capacities, area capacities and ship availability the conference performed a notable preparatory service for the concluding campaigns in the Pacific. Both services emerged from the conference with a clearer notion not only of the other's plans, but also of their own. They had canvassed existing procedures for logistic support in all its phases and were in agreement either on the continuation of existing methods and agencies or else on what modifications were necessary. The issue of shipping control was the sole exception to the general rule.

The Requirements Review Board

JUST how successful the arrangements worked out during the early months of 1945 would have been during the concluding phases of the war is difficult to determine. All the measures of planning and implementation taken during this period were directed toward a single end—the invasion and conquest of Japan beginning on the first of November, 1945. Fortunately that invasion was never necessary. The surrender of the Japanese Empire in mid-August brought to a rapid conclusion the various logistic programs directed toward operations Olympic and Coronet before they were fairly on the way to implementation and set up new programs aiming at quite different objectives. We are unable therefore— happily—to apply the customary pragmatic yardstick in assessing the feasibility of the plans, methods and organization conceived during these months.

Despite this truncated quality in the Navy's wartime logistic history, it is possible to observe certain significant trends in logistic development through August 1945 which are attributable in part to the efforts of the Material Distribution Committee and the Joint Army-Navy Conference. It is important also to observe developments in naval logistic organization and technique emanating from other sources which served to round out the naval logistic system as it developed during the war. These developments were not confined to any part of the logistic organization. Steady progress in the creation of more systematic procedure and organization may be observed in the Navy Department, in the continental shore establishment and finally within the Pacific theater itself. All contributed in some measure to the successful prosecution of the ever-growing task.

In the field of planning the outstanding event was the establishment of the Requirements Review Board. It was created on February 9, 1945, by direction of the Secretary to maintain balance "within and between Navy material and personnel procurement programs and to keep procurement levels consistent with actual needs." The Requirements Review Board was thus intended to follow along lines first laid down by the Summary Control Report, which it took as its working text. But, whereas the Summary Control Report in itself had been simply a repository of certain systematized information which could be either utilized or ignored, the membership of the new board now provided the channels for executive action through which problems raised by the report could be met. It was intended to bridge the gap between the stated military requirements of the Commander in Chief and Chief of Naval Operations and the sum of detailed planning and procurement activity which made up the civil function of the Navy Department.

The membership of the board indicates fairly clearly the purpose it was intended to achieve. Assistant Secretary Hensel, its chairman, represented the ultimate civilian authority in the Navy Department over all civil or material affairs, Admiral Horne represented in turn the concern of the Chief of Naval Operations in the military aspects of material programs. Rear Admiral DeLany was the direct representative of the Commander in Chief, while Admiral Robinson, the Director of the Office of Procurement and Material, spoke for the office most directly concerned with the coordination of procurement activity itself. It may be added that together they represented the sum of authority in the Navy Department which was exercised over the bureaus.

In seeking to maintain balance "within and between" procurement programs the Requirements Review Board achieved some success. Yet it was hampered constantly by doubts as to just how far it could extend the "requirements review" function, and specifically whether it could or should attempt to question the requirements set forth by the Commander in Chief. In its first meetings it was agreed that the board should not question the validity of stated requirements, but should seek simply to determine whether current procurement programs would achieve the goals set forth. In short, the board would not review requirements, but would review instead the procurement programs intended to fulfill requirements. As its work progressed, however, as the inventory program began to uncover accumulated reserves of unobligated materials, as impetus developed behind the roll-up of rear bases, as a review of shipping indicated that only a part of the materials being procured and assembled could be shipped and a study of the ammunition "pipeline" suggested more economical means of achieving the same delivery rates, there was an increasing disposition on the part of the board to guard not only against shortages and "lack of balance," but also against excessive or duplicate procurement which would clog the channels of distribution and ultimately leave the Navy with surpluses of unused and unusable stocks. In summary, although the Requirements Review Board began its work after most of the program goals were already fixed and procurement was well under way, it provided a much needed focus for over-all review and control within the hyphenated and atomistic structure of Navy Department organization.

Distribution Control

In the field of distribution significant changes were also taking place. The need for distribution control had been recognized in the assignment of this function in the Navy Department to the Assistant CNO for Material and in the reorganization of the Western Sea Frontier command. By a directive of November 14, 1944, the Assistant CNO had been charged with "authority and responsibility for the coordination of activities of existing Navy transportation agencies with those of agencies charged with the procurement, storage, assembly and distribution of material. . . ." The job of putting this coordination into effect fell largely to a small section headed by a Supply Corps officer, Commander C. Stein, acting under the direction of Captain W. A. Corn, the head of the Progress Section in CNO.

It will be recalled that when this directive had been issued in November as the result of the recommendations of LOPU, the authority granted to the Commander Western Sea Frontier had been considerably broader than that given to the Assistant CNO for Material. To the former was given power to "control" logistic agencies, while the latter was only authorized to "coordinate." This limitation of authority played an important part, in the character of the work undertaken by Commander Stein and Captain Corn. They conceived their role as primarily that of a staff agency for the Chief of Naval Operations, collecting and disseminating information and seeking through the time-honoured method of persuasion to achieve a better integrated effort.

The development of synthesized information was begun early in 1945 as the "Material Distribution and Analysis Program." It sought to cover three fundamental points in the flow of Navy material: (1) "Distribution of storage and levels of supply within the Continental United States," (2) "Tidewater transshipment activities in the Continental United States," and (3) "Overseas bases receiving activities and distribution of levels of supply." Its objective was defined as "not only to gauge the efficiency of material flow but also to forecast the points of possible disruption and to supply the facts upon which the remedial action may be quickly taken." It thus paralleled in the field of distribution the work being attempted by the Requirements Review Board in planning and procurement.

Beginning in January, a "Weekly Progress Report" was published which attempted to give a birdseye view of all major distribution programs, but unfortunately it was discovered that only in the second field of study, tidewater transshipment activity, was the basic data sufficiently accurate, complete and susceptible to synthesis. In seeking to define the Navy's continental stock position, for example, the program was hampered first by the lack of a uniform system among the bureaus of cataloguing and classifying materials and second, by the impossibility of determining what portion of the Navy's continental stocks were available for export and what portion were obligated for continental use. In analyzing overseas distribution the problem was equally difficult. Until June 1945, when the Commander Service Forces Pacific, instituted a "Uniform Method of Monthly Stock replenishment and Stock Status Reporting," adequate inventories of area stocks were not available. Monthly logistic reports from the areas to CNO were found to be incomplete both in their geographical coverage and in the scope of their commodity classification. In many cases such as ammunition, where shipments were recorded in tons when they left the United States and in numbers of rounds when they arrived in the area, bureau data were found to offer no basis for analysis.

Even with these limitations, however, the "Weekly Progress Reports" on distribution provided a vastly improved instrument for forecasting trouble spots and for achieving better coordination. They more than justified the premise of the analysis program that the key to the problem of more efficient logistic administration was information.

In many other respects this section under the Assistant CNO for Material played an important role. Once the decision had been made to form the Material Distribution Committee, it was Captain Corn and his junior officers who laid out its program, gathered much of the data, and painstakingly guided its deliberations. As the analysis program was developed, moreover, it was instrumental in securing the improvement of many of the basic reports which had previously been deficient. It served also as an important point of liaison between the Office of Naval Operations and the Commander Western Sea Frontier, and finally it became gradually an important source of information and advice on matters of distribution for the Vice Chief of Naval Operations and for the Navy Department as a whole.

Despite the very real measure of progress made in the Navy Department during these months, it was overshadowed by the reforms undertaken by the new Commander Western Sea Frontier. The West Coast was not only the major transshipment area for support of the Pacific; it was also strategically located with respect both to the flow of information from the theater and to the flow of cargo from various sources within the United States. With so great a preponderance of support being delivered through the Pacific Coast region it was inevitable that the regional authority should enjoy a controlling position in many ways paramount to that of the central command in the Office of Naval Operations. This tendency was fortified by the terms of authority and the seniority of rank of Admiral Ingersoll.

At a meeting in the Navy Department in November, just before he assumed his new duties, Admiral Ingersoll had summed up his mission as one of expediting the flow of support through the West Coast to the Pacific. He viewed the coastal activity as primarily a transshipment or export task, but called attention also to the need for controlling the inflow of requisitions if control of the flow-back of material was to be achieved. His organization was mainly concerned, therefore, with the collection of information on actual and possible levels of activity, with coordination of activity, and with the establishment of such over-all controls as had hitherto been lacking.

During the early months of 1945, after his initial surveys had been completed, Admiral Ingersoll's original concept was elaborated into a three-point logistic program. His first task was to formulate as accurate and detailed a picture of export requirements as possible in the form of a program of "Planned Employment of West Coast Ports." Secondly, he must govern the activities of supply depots and other logistic agencies backing up the ports so that they would in fact support the planned export activity of each port. Lastly, he must control the receipt of requisitions from various areas and fleet commands and forward them to the depot best suited to fill them in accordance with the planned employment program.

The planned employment was worked out largely on the basis of the survey of West Coast port capacity which had been furnished to the Material Distribution Committee. Its objective was two-fold; first, to raise the capacity of each individual port to its highest possible level, and second, to increase the capacity of the Coast as a whole by a better distribution of work load among the various ports. In particular, it was necessary to direct a greater portion of the flow of cargo to ports other than those in the San Francisco Bay Area.

Gearing the various supply and other back-up activities to the planned employment of ports proved to be a more complex and difficult job, for not only were the elements more numerous and diverse; the problem also involved cooperation with the bureaus and offices in the Navy Department as well as the coordination of the field agencies themselves. The task involved also a multitude of separate projects all carried forward within a single general framework. A survey of housing facilities was undertaken as the basis for a better distribution and utilization of available West Coast labor. Increased storage facilities were secured either from commercial sources or by the construction of large new naval facilities such as the Rough and Ready Island project in

California. The increased flow of construction or functional component materials was handled through a new advance base depot at Tacoma and by diversion of shipments to Los Angeles from the older advance base depot at Port Hueneme. New facilities for stocking and shipping refrigerated provisions were pressed into service in Seattle; general stores were shipped increasingly in the wholesale BBB lots from Astoria. In June, the Commander Western Sea Frontier took over from the Bureau of Supplies and Accounts the routing and control of all railroad traffic into and within the Western Sea Frontier. This step was protested vigorously by both the bureau and the Naval Transportation Service, but was upheld by Admiral Ingersoll on the grounds that it was essential to his planned employment program.

The Requisition Control Unit was slower to go into operation, partly because of doubt as to just how it should operate and partly because of the increasing stringency of personnel. By July 1, however, it had begun operation and by the first of August it was processing requisitions for general supply, ships spares, ordnance and medical materials. Its operations came too late to have any great effect upon the conduct of the war, but it was, nevertheless, an important step in the development of the Navy's logistic procedure.

The success of the Western Sea Frontier logistic program may be seen in the increased levels of activity on the Coast up to the conclusion of the war. Total overseas shipments, excluding aircraft, rose from an average of 960,000 measurements tons per month, from October 1944 to April 1945, to an average of 1,230,000 tons per month during the period of May through July—a 25 per cent over-all increase. This rate was only 10 per cent below the maximum planned employment of West Coast facilities expected to be reached during the last quarter of 1945 and the first quarter of 1946. San Francisco and Port Hueneme continued to bear the brunt of naval material shipments, but as over-all coastal shipments expanded, most of the increase was taken up by other ports. The San Francisco percentage of total shipments dropped from 65 per cent during the first quarter of 1945 to approximately 45 per cent during the second quarter.

The movement of personnel kept pace with the movement of material. During the second quarter of 1945 an average of 60,000 naval personnel per month were shipped to the Pacific, an increase of 10,000 per month over the period from October through April. During this same period an average of 44,000 persons per month returned to West Coast ports, 15 per cent of whom were casualties. Throughout the period from November 1944 to the end of the war the Western Sea Frontier contained some 15 per cent of the entire naval population, more than two-thirds of whom were in a transient status.

On the whole, the success with which the West Coast handled its increased workload up until the end of the war would appear to justify the assumption that it would have continued to bear the load planned for it by the Material Distribution Committee and the Army-Navy Conference. It is noteworthy, however, that during this period the ratio between West Coast and East Coast shipments did not reach that of 68-32 prescribed by the Material Distribution Committee. From October 1944 through July 1945, 75 per cent of naval material shipments to the Pacific went from the West Coast. Until the West Coast ceiling was reached, it might be expected that increased shipments would be made from there. The "Weekly Progress Reports" of CNO indicate, moreover, that during this period adequate banks of cargo were being maintained at East and Gulf Coast ports to meet the availability of vessels. But it is impossible to say on the basis of present evidence that when the time came the necessary diversions to the East Coast would have been achieved as successfully as was the planned capacity of the West Coast.

The continued emphasis upon utilizing West Coast facilities was the result of more than the obvious logic of shipping from the point nearest the theater. Since the beginning of the war the tendency toward regional dominance over the central command had been noticeable. It had tended to perpetuate itself by the skillful manner in which delegated or assumed authority was exercised, first by such officers as the Regional Shipping Director, Captain Davis, and later on a much broader basis by Admiral Ingersoll. His assumption from the Bureau of Supplies and Accounts of control of railroad traffic, a function which more than any other might appear to require undivided and centralized administration, is illustrative of the ever-present tendency toward geographical decentralization in the Navy's logistic organization.

Shipping in the Pacific Theater

WITHIN the Pacific theater problems of logistics were closely interwoven with the changes in command relationships announced in April. In particular, the vital issue of shipping control, which had been left in abeyance by the Army-Navy Conference, was affected by the new arrangement.

On June 5, Admiral King submitted a memorandum to the Joint Chiefs of Staff in which he recommended the creation of a joint agency for the coordination of shipping within the Pacific. A proposed draft of a message to the Theater Commanders accompanied his memorandum, but no action was ever taken by the Joint Chiefs of Staff upon this recommendation.

Meanwhile, in the Pacific theater itself, staff conferences were being held at Guam from June 1-3, 1945, between representatives of General MacArthur and Admiral Nimitz, which culminated in an agreement on the "Preparation, Initiation and Coordination of Operation Olympic." The arrangements were broad in scope, covering a variety of matters of command responsibility, communications and logistics. From the point of view of logistics the most significant part of the agreement was the attempt to resolve the issue of shipping control which had thus far failed of solution either by the Army-Navy Conference or by the Joint Chiefs of Staff.

While the agreement reached at Guam was limited to the control of shipping for Olympic, and while it contained no specific provisions abrogating the CincPoa system within the Pacific Ocean Areas, it did reflect substantially the Army views on Pacific shipping control. Each commander would be responsible for the procurement and operation of logistic support shipping for the forces under his control wherever the ports of destination were to be operated exclusively by one service or another. In common ports in the operational areas port operations and the movement of ships forward to the ports would be under varying degrees of control by the Army. Shipping movements would be regulated through the medium of two regulating stations, at Ulithi and Okinawa, from which vessels would be called forward as conditions within the ports permitted.

The system of regulating stations, if properly administered, would provide insurance against congestion of ships in forward area harbors. It offered no guarantee, however, that the regulating station would not itself become congested and thus a point at which tonnage was wasted. Nor did it offer that close correlation between shipping movements and other factors such as supply levels, base construction programs and garrison movements which had been developed under the CincPoa Garrison shipping system. The system, in other words, resembled more the loosely constructed procedure which had operated in the Southwest Pacific Command than the closely integrated system which had been worked out under CincPoa. The great virtue of the Garrison shipping procedure, however difficult it may have been to work, was that in a single schedule it supplied controls for both supply and shipping. That desirable feature appears to have been lost in this arrangement.

No final judgment should be passed upon this system, however, without a careful and detailed analysis of its relation to the Army system of supply and logistic control. Such an analysis is impossible here. It must also be kept in mind that Army shipments to the Pacific projected in the report of the Army-Navy Conference were in an approximate ratio of 3-2 to projected Navy shipments. A large portion of naval shipments was destined for Guam, moreover, and would not be seriously affected by the system of regulating stations and unified control. While the plan may not have been entirely congenial to Navy procedures, and while it did contain certain provisions which were potential sources of confusion, there can be no question but that the Army's interest in this issue, if not overriding, was at least paramount.

Perhaps the most difficult problem experienced during this period was that of maintaining area receiving capacity at a level commensurate with the outloading capacity of established United States ports and with shipping and supply schedules. The most serious trouble spots during the concluding months of the war were the Philippines, Guam, and Okinawa. In the Philippines, Manila presented the greatest problem, largely because of the over-optimistic estimates of how soon the harbor might be cleared and piers restored, and also because of the impossibility of meeting all General MacArthur's requirements for self-discharging craft with which to roll up materials from the South and Southwest Pacific. The condition at Guam was inherited from the later months of 1944. Early in May, however, some improvement could be noted. Although shipments to Guam in April were 150,000 long tons as compared with a monthly average of 81,000 during the previous three months, discharging capacity jumped sharply from 50,000 to 70,000 long tons per week, and the situation began gradually to come under control. At no time until the end of the war was the congestion in Guam completely abated, but it was gradually whittled down to more manageable proportions.

Okinawa suffered from many of the difficulties which had characterized port congestion in the Pacific. The hope of employing even the meager port facilities at Naha was not immediately realized, and it was necessary to use points to the north, where coral heads seriously hampered port operations. The decision to develop air facilities on Okinawa far beyond anything anticipated meant much heavier shipments of base construction units and other functional components. Garrison schedules were in a constant state of flux. Naval storage facilities on the island were slow in development, with the result that stock levels had to be kept lower and echelon intervals shortened in order to maintain the required rate of delivery. Correlation between United States shipments to Okinawa and movements from within the theater was difficult to achieve, particularly after April, when the command status of the Ryukyus became uncertain. During June, for example, shipments from the United States under approved garrison schedules monopolized 93 per cent of Okinawa's discharging capacity, leaving only a few thousand tons per day for material originating within the theater.

Roll-Up

THE monopolizing of harbor capacity by United States shipments was one of the principal difficulties encountered in attempting to roll up base facilities from rear to forward areas. Both services had developed elaborate base facilities in the South and Southwest Pacific which were gradually falling into disuse as the combat area was pushed closer and closer toward Japan. Until the beginning of 1945 the uncertainty of strategic plans had retarded the development of roll-up plans, for logistic planners could not be certain of just how much support would be required for the operating forces from established bases like Espiritu Santo. As strategic plans became firmer during the early months of 1945, the necessity for rolling up rear bases became acute, particularly since the presence of base equipment in the rear areas tied down much needed personnel required to maintain it.

In February, the Sub Chief of Naval Operations, Rear

Admiral Farber, made an extended tour of Pacific bases in order to survey the possibilities of speeding up the roll-up program. He found that extensive roll-up had already been carried out from the South Pacific, comprising one hundred and forty components or organized units and including some 56,000 personnel and 1,750,000 measurement tons of material. He found about 35,000 personnel and 2,000,000 measurement tons of material which he believed might profitably be moved forward or returned to the United States for further disposal. Despite the obvious savings in shipping space to be gained by shipping to the Central Pacific from this nearer point, there was considerable opposition both in the Navy Department and in the theater to a wholesale and unselective roll-up. Area Commanders were sceptical of the quality of rolled-up components and equipment and preferred as a rule to allot scarce port capacity to new shipments from the United States. Officers concerned with problems of continental distribution were more interested in maintaining a constant flow of goods through normal "pipelines." The Naval Transportation Service favored the roll-up of materials but opposed any return of goods to the United States on the grounds that unloading on the West Coast would hamper the export operations of its ports. Ultimately most of the personnel and about one-quarter of the materials earmarked by Admiral Farber were rolled forward and a smaller portion was returned to the United States. The problem of the South Pacific roll-up illustrates very clearly, however, the nature of the logistic job in the Pacific. The logic of rolling forward rear bases was impeccable. In the case of personnel its urgency could not be denied. But to set up a cross current against the normal flow of supply and support proved to be extremely difficult, if not impracticable. Much of the usable material was in fact moved forward. The rest remained in the South Pacific to be locally disposed of or to stand as a monument to the unsparing waste of war and the greater importance of time over cost.

CHAPTER IX

LOGISTIC LESSONS OF THE WAR

THE concluding months of the war saw deployment in the Pacific of the greatest naval force and the most extensive system of logistic support in the history of warfare. By mid-August 1945, ninety per cent of the United States naval forces of submarine size or larger were concentrated in the Pacific, totalling 1,137 combat vessels, 14,847 combat aircraft, 2,783 large landing craft and many thousands of smaller landing craft. To support this tremendous force over 400 advance bases, large and small, had been established. At advance bases and anchorages 152 floating dry docks of varying dimensions were in operation. Hundreds of vessels of the Pacific Fleet Service Squadrons plied between the United States and advance bases and between bases and ships providing direct support to the fleet. Supplementing these vessels nearly a million deadweight tons of WSA-controlled shipping was allocated to the Navy to carry forward the necessary supplies and materials. Through all the "pipelines" of supply 600,000 long tons per month were being shipped from the United States for the support of naval operating forces and for the preparation of coming operations.

The magnitude of this operation bears witness to the remarkable expansion and development of the Navy's logistic system. Physically this vast structure of support was as spectacular and impressive as the naval striking forces which it so tirelessly maintained. Throughout the vast reaches of the Pacific, American forces had carried on unremitting warfare on jungle island and coral atoll against distance, disease, time and the primitive emptiness of an ocean waste. The success of their labors was now manifest in the teeming activity, ashore and afloat, and in the din of industry that rose above the islands of the Pacific. Within the circle of the bay lay auxiliary vessels of a hundred descriptions from the lowly "honeybarge" to the mighty dry dock, floating unconcernedly with a battleship in its lap. Along the shores there sprawled the new cities of the Pacific. Long lines of trucks pounded the coral roads between pier and warehouse. Machine shops hummed. Bulldozers beat back the tangled growth, plowed out revetments for aircraft, levelled the roads and landing fields. Above all, the Navy's skilled craftsmen, trained in every essential trade, brought to these outposts the remarkable ingenuity and mechanical talent of America. Across thousands of miles there had been transported these tools and working populations; across the same distances there continued to flow the supplies, spare parts and replacements required to maintain them.

How many turns of the screw, how many strokes of the hammer, how many weary hours of separation from home this all entailed is not the business of this history to record. This product of sweat and toil, without which victory in the Pacific would have been impossible, was the result of the individual efforts of men, and there will be, we may hope, a literature to preserve and recall it. This study of naval administration, however, is the biography of a system. It seeks to explain how the separate actions of many men and the products of their toil were given direction toward the achievement of certain defined ends. For behind this vast structure of support, giving it form and direction, there was necessarily planning and purpose.

Plans and systems are also the product of the separate actions of individual men, and in the last analysis it is the personalities and talents of men which determine the success or failure of any system. But an undertaking on such a scale as this transcends the bounds of any single mind; it must perforce be the product of many minds acting together and forming a kind of composite, directing intelligence. And it is in the manner in which that composite intelligence responds to the problems at hand that the system is defined.

The Navy's logistic system was a kind of palimpsest—the product of gradual, almost reluctant, accommodation to the most urgent dictates of the war. Anyone who observed its evolution during the war, comparing the things that needed ·to be done and the things that were done, must often have been discouraged by the perdurable nature of faulty administrative practices. He must have wondered from day to day how any system of administration, apparently so deficient, could claim responsibility for the extraordinary accomplishment which unfolded before his eyes. In retrospect, however, he is compelled to acknowledge that progress in the administration of logistics during the war was considerable.

The problem of administration with which we have been concerned was that of providing military direction to the variegated economic activity essential to the conduct of modern war. As we have seen, logistics may be divided into three principal parts—planning or the definition of requirements, procurement, and distribution—each of which impinges closely upon the others.

In theory it is the plan which provides the beginning and the pattern for all other activity, but in fact as the war demonstrated, there could be no fixed pattern of logistic activity. The plan itself was often the product of the circumstances to which it was intended to apply.

Logistic requirements must be determined in the light of strategic aims, and for that purpose logistic planners must have firm guidance and accurate information as to strategic plans. Yet for almost half the war logistic planners lacked the information essential to their task. Not until late in 1943, for example, was the Director of the Logistic Plans Division in CNO given access to the "Top-Secret" dispatch board of the Commander in Chief. The Overall Logistic Plan first promulgated in the autumn of 1944 provided a partial remedy for this condition, but it, too, was circumscribed by the complex of security.

Another persistent weakness of the logistic planning performed under the Chief of Naval Operations was its lack of comprehensiveness. The Navy entered the war with no clear understanding of the function of logistic planning and with even less organization to perform it. Strategic and logistic planning were for some time mixed together to the detriment of both. Much of the high-level planning passed by default to the bureaus, the implementing agencies whose programs, set in motion without adequate reference to each other, were ultimately to determine the character of the Navy's logistic effort. With the organization of a Logistic Plans Division in December 1942, the function of logistic planning received a certain identity of its own. But at no time during the war did the Logistic Plans Division assume responsibility for planning all major logistic programs. Without a comprehensive plan including all the major elements entering into logistic support it was impossible for the Chief of Naval Operations to provide the pattern for balanced programs of procurement and distribution.

During the latter half of the war logistic planning was concerned primarily with the definition of requirements for replenishment or maintenance. Maintenance requirements are dependent upon a host of factors such as the material already on hand and in the "pipelines," the rates of consumption, the necessary margin of reserve and the distribution of stocks. For this kind of planning the central agency was dependent upon information which could be secured only from the bureaus and field agencies. Its efforts were directed, therefore, toward securing the necessary synthesis of information by which it could keep under review the bureau programs of procurement and distribution and deduct from its estimated requirements the inventories already on hand. Toward this end the Summary Control Report, the Inventory Control Program, and finally the Requirements Review Board contributed. But logistic planning was only to a certain extent the controlling factor over material programs. Throughout the war it had to remain flexible enough not only to absorb the shock of changes in strategic plan, but also to adapt itself to the imperatives of the material programs themselves. Apart from the advance base program, which from the beginning was the special responsibility of the Chief of Naval Operations, the most that could be accomplished in logistic planning during the war was general guidance by the Chief of Naval Operations over the programs of the bureaus and a kind of crystal-gazing guesswork as to the prospective outline of the strategic situation. Given our surplus of resources and the remarkable productivity of our industrial system, this much planning proved to be adequate for the needs of the war.

Even without comprehensive planning, procurement programs could be set in motion. Bureaus had the necessary authority and funds to procure, and only in occasional cases could they be accused of setting their sights too low. When the logistic problem shifted, however, from one of procurement to one of distribution, the Navy's lack of centralized logistic control became a matter of greater importance.

The problem of distribution may be summarized briefly. From the close of 1943 the volume of goods flowing to the Pacific tended to exceed the capacity of the established channels of transport and distribution. With the exception, however, of shipping and discharging capacity at the ports of destination there was unused capacity which could have been utilized had the Navy possessed greater flexibility in its continental system of distribution. The reorganization of the Western Sea Frontier Command late in 1944 paved the way for a fuller utilization of West Coast export capacity, but the larger problem of distributing the work load more efficiently throughout the United States as a whole persisted without a true solution.

Early in 1945 the Material Distribution Committee provided a stopgap, ad hoc solution. For the first time during the war all the agencies responsible for naval distribution were gathered together and all the elements involved in the task were reviewed as a single problem. The committee made no changes in the basic procedures of distribution. Its work was substantive rather than procedural. But because the end of the war was now in sight and the remaining logistic task could be brought within limits and defined in substantive terms, the committee was able to draw up for the remainder of the war a general logistic operating plan based upon the approved strategic plan.

Under the revised pattern of continental distribution the Commander Western Sea Frontier was able during the remaining months to deal successfully with the planned increases in the West Coast's export load. Whether or not the Navy Department, lacking adequate central control and information, could have successfully diverted the remaining increment to other continental outlets can be only a matter of conjecture. It is quite possible that once the final operations had got under way the West Coast would have been swamped once again by a flow of goods above its planned capacity which the Navy Department was powerless to control.

The administration of shipping was one of the major logistic tasks of the war. During the first year the principal problem was the development of a system of over-all allocation and control which would satisfy military requirements and at the same time take into account the larger issues raised by non-military and Allied demands for tonnage. The working balance of authority which ultimately developed between the Joint Chiefs of Staff and the War Shipping Administration was a cumbersome compromise, but it did result on the whole in a fair and proper distribution of tonnage to meet all the essential demands of the war.

Within this general system the principal difficulty in the military administration of shipping was that of maintaining control over the movements of vessels in order to secure expeditious turnaround and avoid idle and wasted tonnage. This, too, involved the question of central control. Since ships moved in response to the demands for material and supplies, the root of the problem lay in the need for material control. As we have seen, the Garrison shipping procedure developed under CincPoa established the necessary correlation between supply schedules and shipping schedules for initial movements into the Forward Areas. But in the larger volume of maintenance shipments the Navy had to rely upon techniques of shipping control which had too little reference to material control and, therefore, could be only partly satisfactory.

Throughout the Navy's logistic system decentralization was the keynote. During the early stages of the war it allowed greater exercise of initiative, direct action and in some respects a higher degree of flexibility in the support of naval forces. After two years of war, however, decentralization had proceeded too far. The increased scale of the logistic effort in relation to the capacity of distribution facilities made it necessary to deal with the problem as a whole. The aims of timing, motion and selection, which were essential to an orderly flow of support, could be achieved only through an integrated operation. Detailed implementation of the many related programs must be made to correspond to a single policy defined at the center.

Too frequently centralized control by the Chief of Naval Operations was assumed to imply centralized execution of policies or at least centralized approval of detailed execution. But in reality there was no necessity for the Navy Department to hobble the initiative of local commanders in order to achieve the degree of centralization required. Armed with adequate information—not the massive, detailed data of local agencies, but an up-to-date synthesis of all relevant information—the Navy Department would have been able to formulate realistic policy and to assure its execution. But an organization traditionally disinclined toward administrative matters, disposed to place a higher premium on deck jobs than on desk jobs, was understandably slow to perceive the necessity of a well-trained, well-staffed administrative organization. Throughout the Navy's logistic system during the war there existed situations in which a few dozen desk workers, analyzing, synthesizing and organizing for high-level purposes the mass of available data, might have saved the labors of many times their number of deck workers. They would have provided the means for coherent and informed management control which were all too frequently lacking. With better information Navy Department policy could have been more often the mold of circumstance, rather than the victim, as it frequently was.

The Navy's logistic system underwent during the war a number of important changes which on the whole kept it abreast of the task with which it was confronted. Certain phases of logistic support—notably the system of advance base development and the work of the "mobile base" Service Squadrons—represented outstanding achievements. The simple, amazingly versatile steel pontoon, the concept of the functional component and the remarkable organization of Sea Bees are examples of fertile imagination and organizing skill. Service Squadron 6, which provided the final link between the operating force and the shore establishment, was similarly a product of bold imagination and enterprise. Many of these outstanding achievements were originally conceived in peacetime and carried forward during the war when funds and the impetus to action were provided.

But in the basic lines of its logistic administration the inheritance from peacetime practice and organization was a hindrance rather than a help to naval logistics. A system of supply and support geared to the maintenance of the fleet at the continental seaboard could not easily be tranformed into an organization for export through which the facilities for logistic support could be projected five thousand miles beyond the continental limits. A departmental organization traditionally dependent upon the cooperation of the bureaus could not at once be subjected to centralized military direction. Bureau "sovereignty" was too deeply entrenched, while CNO, the central agency, lacked the habit of authority and the organization required to exercise it. Nor could the rank and file of regular naval officers, traditionally disposed by training and temperament to avoid logistic and other administrative assignments, be expected to perceive at once the importance and nature of logistics. Logistics played a relatively small part in the operation and command of the peacetime Navy, and logistic assignments were quite naturally regarded as the "kiss of death," the prelude to being passed over. Being human, the average naval officer, who stood ready to sacrifice his life for his country, was not willing to sacrifice his career.

The problem of developing logisticians within the ranks of the regular Navy is part of the broader problem of all specialists within the naval organization, whether it be the engineer, the supply officer, the research scientist or the administrator. In this day of specialization the notion must be abandoned that every naval officer can be all things successfully. No simple solution exists for the problem of the specialist, but it must be obvious that a naval officer who is more than superficially acquainted with the problems of ocean transport, planning, railroad management or production engineering is an asset to the naval organization, and should be offered suitable inducements to pursue his specialty. It will not suffice merely to make a specialist of the logistician, for logistics is part of the exercise of command. Within the present pattern of naval warfare at least the record of the Second World War suggests that the naval commander must be indoctrinated in the problems of providing as well as of making use of the means of warfare.

Since the conclusion of the war many steps have already been taken to capitalize on the logistic lessons of the war. The Office of the Chief of Naval Operations has been extensively revamped by executive order so as to give it in effect the character of a general staff. The new organization requires only permanent statutory authority. A new naval supply system built around major overseas supply depots, which seeks to resolve the problems of overseas distribution, is in the process of development. Cleaner lines of functional organization should expedite the flow of essential information throughout the naval establishment. Logistics has also been included in the curriculum at various levels of naval officer training from the Naval Academy at Annapolis to the War College, and for academic purposes there is now a wealth of precept and experience. What is needed to make the lessons permanent is the most difficult thing to achieve in any peacetime military establishment—to realize by a constant exercise of the imagination that the logistic lessons of the last war will not suffice for the next.

BIBLIOGRAPHY

THIS study of naval logistics has been based almost entirely upon manuscript sources in the Navy Department, many of which were classified at the time they were used. Since much of this material will probably not be available to the general student for some time, footnote references have been omitted in this printed volume. A manuscript copy of this study containing complete documentation is deposited, however, in Widener Library, Cambridge, Mass.

BIBLIOGRAPHIES:

No published bibliography on naval logistics exists at the present time. *Expansion of the United States Navy 1931-1939*, Washington, 1939, a selected list of references compiled by Grace H. Fuller, Library of Congress, provides a good index to Congressional Hearings and reports and other government documents on the Navy. During the war the Logistics Section of the Naval War College compiled a list of logistic references. The Naval Supply Officers Training Center at Bayonne, N.J., has developed a large library of logistic documents of the recent war. Appendix C to the *Report of the Committee to Study Post War Logistic Training*, CNO, December 1945, also contains a useful list of logistic reference data.

WAR HISTORIES:

During the war "first draft" histories were prepared under the direction of the Director of Naval History for all the principal commands and activities of the Navy. From May 1944 to May 1946 I was a member of the historical staff of the Office of the Chief of Naval Operations and have made considerable use of the histories prepared in that office. The principal wartime historical studies of CNO were: *Origins of the Office of Naval Operations*, by E. E. Morison; *Aspects of Logistic Planning*, by M. P. Gilmore and J. Blum; *The Logistics of Advance Bases*, by J. Gleason; *The Logistics of Fleet Maintenance*, by W. Askew; *The Control of Naval Logistics*, by R. W. Paul; *Aviation in the Office* of *Naval Operations,* by L. Sorenson; and my own study of *Shipping in Naval Logistics.* These various studies deal with aspects of logistic administration as carried on under the Chief of Naval Operations and correspond to the principal divisions or "Op's" in that Office which had cognizance of logistic matters. They are based largely on the files of the divisions, on interviews and on personal observation by the respective authors.

During the course of its work the CNO historical staff prepared for its own use a file of documents relating to logistics which is now deposited with the Office of Naval Records and Library (CNO). Other "first draft" histories prepared for the Director of Naval History which have been of assistance are: *History of Commander, Service Forces, U.S. Pacific Fleet* and *History of Commander, Western Sea Frontier.*

DEPARTMENTAL FILES AND CLASSIFIED SOURCES:

The major source of materials for this study has been the files of the Navy Department and in particular those of the Office of the Chief of Naval Operations. These files include all the formal correspondence originated or received by CNO and in addition operational and logistic plans, studies of organization, unserialized memoranda and correspondence, minutes of meetings, conference reports, records of telephone conversations, dispatches, directives, routing slips, preliminary drafts and statistical data. Some use has also been made of the files of the Bureau of Yards and Docks, the Bureau of Supplies and Accounts (Transportation Division), the General Board, the Headquarters of the Commander in Chief and the Joint Army-Navy Board, the precursor of the Joint Chiefs of Staff. CNO files often contain copies of Fleet or Area Command and War Department plans and communications not formally routed to CNO.

Another important source of information has been the

files of the Joint and Combined Chiefs of Staff and of their various sub-committees. In addition to certain of the JCS and CCS papers themselves, use has been made of the papers of the Joint Military Transportation Committee (JMTC), the Joint Logistics Committee (JLC) and the strategic studies of the Joint Staff Planners (JSP). The most important source of statistical data on shipping is the *Monthly Shipping Summary* published by the War Shipping Administration. Some of the material on the origins of the War Shipping Administration was taken from the files of the Bureau of the Budget. For the first chapter the CNO files and the general files of the Secretary of the Navy in the National Archives and the Archives of the Naval War College, Newport, R.I., have been useful.

As a general rule Navy Department files are retired periodically to the National Archives. Frequently, however, many important documents remain in the Navy Department in the working "desk" files of the various sections and divisions.

PERSONAL OBSERVATION:

As a member of the CNO historical staff I have had access not only to the department files but also to important meetings and to officers in the Navy Department. Material in the files has, therefore, been supplemented by personal interviews and direct observation. The historical section was attached to the immediate office of the Vice Chief of Naval Operations, where it performed various special, non-historical duties which gave to its members a better insight into the problems of CNO.

PUBLISHED SOURCES:

Published and unclassified materials dealing with naval logistics are relatively few. The subject of logistics is referred to sparsely in most of the historical literature on the Navy and then generally under such headings as "administration," "material," "bases," or "the shore establishment." Under the general heading of naval administration and organization the following have been consulted and are particularly useful: *Selected Documents on Navy Department Organization 1915-1940*, with prefaces by E. E. Morison, printed for the Navy Department, 1945. C. O. Paullin's series of articles on naval administration, printed in *U.S. Naval Institute Proceedings* (1906-1914) is an invaluable source of information on naval administration and the shore establishment and deserves to be reprinted as a single volume. A. T. Mahan's two essays, "The Principles of Naval Administration" and "The United States Navy Department," reprinted in *Naval Administration and Warfare*, Boston, 1908, are still pertinent. E. E. Morison, *Admiral Sims and the Modern American Navy*, Boston, 1942, deals at length with the history of the Moody-Mahan Commission of 1908. B. A. Fiske, *From Midshipman to Rear Admiral*, New York, 1919, and Josephus Daniels, *The Wilson Era*, Vol. I, Chapel Hill, 1944, give the pro's and con's on the issue of a general staff.

On the general background of naval logistics in addition to the archival material mentioned above, the Annual Reports of the Secretary of the Navy have been consulted. Reports of the years 1883, 1901, 1909, 1917-1919, 1923 and 1940 are particularly useful. Hearings before the Congressional Committees on Naval Affairs, Appropriations and occasionally Merchant Marine contain material on logistics. The hearings before the Senate Committee on Naval Affairs on the Hepburn Board Report of 1938, for example, deal with our need for advance bases. The testimony of Admirals Stark and Richardson before the special Pearl Harbor Investigating Committee throws light on the basing of the fleet at Pearl Harbor prior to the war. The Theodore Roosevelt Collection and the Allen Collection of periodical literature on the Navy, both in Widener Library, Cambridge, Mass., contain useful material on the early period. *The U.S. Naval Institute Proceedings* provide a good index to service opinion.

Among other books consulted on the background of

naval logistics the following have been found most useful:
A. T. Mahan, *The Influence of Sea Power upon History*,
Boston, 1890; G. A. Ballard, *Rulers of the Indian Ocean*,
London, 1927; Harold and Margaret Sprout, *The Rise of
American Naval Power 1776-1918*, rev. ed. Princeton, 1942
and *Toward a New Order of Sea Power*, Princeton, 1943;
G. T. Davis, *A Navy Second to None*, New York, 1940;
Bernard Brodie, *Sea Power in the Machine Age*, Princeton,
1940; G. V. Fox, *Confidential Correspondence*, ed. by
R. M. Thompson and R. Wainwright, New York, 1918-
1919; F. M. Bennett, *The Steam Navy of the United States*,
Pittsburgh, 1896; H. W. Wilson, *The Downfall of Spain*,
London, 1900; F. T. Jane, *Heresies of Sea Power*, London,
1906; C. C. Gill, *Naval Power in the War*, New York, 1918;
H. B. Wilson, *An Account of the Operations of the Ameri-
can Navy in France during the War with Germany*, 1919;
W. D. Hines, *War History of American Railroads*, New
York, 1928; Sir Arthur Salter, *Allied Shipping Control*,
London: New York, 1921; C. E. Fayle, *The War and the
Shipping Industry*, London, 1927, and *Seaborne Trade*,
London, 1920-1924; Josephus Daniels, *Our Navy at War*,
New York, 1922; *The American Naval Planning Section*;
London, Navy Department, Washington, 1923; Dudley
Knox, *The Eclipse of American Sea Power*, 1922; H. C.
Bywater, *Navies and Nations*, London, 1927, and *Sea Power
in the Pacific*, London, 1934; S. Denlinger and C. B. Gary,
War in the Pacific, New York, 1936.

For the period of the Second World War two invaluable
sources of information have been *U.S. Navy at War 1941-
1945*, Official Reports to the Secretary of the Navy by Fleet
Admiral Ernest J. King, U.S.N., Navy Department, Washington, 1946, and the report by Mr. Ferdinand Eberstadt to
the Secretary of the Navy on unification of the services, 25
September 1945, Senate Naval Affairs Committee Print,
79th Congress, 1st Session. The Report of the Secretary
(1945) contains an excellent statistical summary of logistic
programs during the war.

INDEX

Acorn, development of, 58, 102-3, 111-13, 171, 174.
Admiralty Islands, invasion of, 171, 174.
Advance Base Assembly Depot, Canal Zone, 63; Davisville, 64, 76, 124; Port Hueneme, 124, 145.
Aeronautics, Bureau of, 62, 115.
Archer, T. P., 185.
Archer-Wolf Report, naval organization, 185-8, 190, 194, 199, 262.
Army, 22, 24, 66-70, 112, 119, 122, 124; distribution system in Pacific, 265; holding and reconsignment points, 264; increased Pacific shipments, 252; Services of Supply, 125-7; Transport Service, 76, 79. See also Joint Army-Navy Logistics.
Arthur Middleton, S.S., 69.
Atlantic Theater, strategic outlook, 44-5.
Automatic Supply, 174.
Auxiliary Vessels Board, 139, 178.

Badger, O. C., Rear Admiral, 110, 125-6, 136, 141-3, 147, 149, 181, 183, 195.
Bakenhus, R. E., Captain, 30-1.
Base Aircraft Service Unit (BASU), 114.
Base Force, 78, 80, 95-7, 99; Subordinate Command, 96-7. See also Service Forces.
Bases, advance, 11-12, 35, 42-4, 57-9, 60-76, 102-3, 110-16, 161-2, 265, 287; Admiralty Islands, 171; Alaska, 26, 42, 61, 162; Atlantic, 44-5; Auckland, N.Z.,

71, 73-4, 98; Bora-Bora, 66-71, 75; British and French in India, 9-10; Canal Zone, 28, 42; Canton, 40, 153; Cavite, 16, 18, 39; Civil War, 11; comments of Mahan, 11; development, 174-5; Efate, 71-3, 75, 153; equipment, 64-5; Espiritu Santo, 111, 133, 153, 162; Fiji Islands, 71, 75; functional component, 113-16; Guam, 19, 27, 29, 38-9, 60; Guantanamo, 14; Johnston, 40, 42, 61; Key West, 14; Leyte-Samar, 252, 260; Manila, 284; Manus, 167, 260; Marianas Islands, 260, 284; Midway, 27, 40, 42, 61, 153; mobile, 16, 33, see also Service Forces; Noumea, 71, 73-4, 112, 118, 123, 133, 152, 162; Okinawa, 260, 284-5, as shipping regulating station, 283; Olangapo, 16, 19, 39; Pacific, 19, 26-8, 40-4, 60-2, 66-76; Palmyra, 40, 42, 61, 153; Pearl Harbor, 16, 18-20, 26, 28, 36-7, 39, 42, 61, 97, 133-4, 152, 156, 162, 260; plans and programs, 57-8; Samoa, 12, 27, 40, 42, 71-3, 75; San Juan, P.R., 16, 61; South Pacific, 110-16; Tongatabu, 71-3, 75; Tulagi, 153; Ulithi, as shipping regulating station, 283; Wake, 27, 38, 61; World War I, 21, 23-4.
Basic Boxed Base (BBB) Load, 224-5, 232, 280.
Basic Logistical Plan, 128-31, 134, 151-2, 154, 157-8, 269; for Central and South Pacific, 154.